LAMBS DANCING WITH WOLVES

PUBLISHING

OMF International works in most East Asian countries, and among East Asian peoples around the world. It was founded by James Hudson Taylor in 1865 as the China Inland Mission. Our overall purpose is to glorify God through the urgent evangelisation of East Asia's billions, and this is reflected in our publishing.

Through our books, booklets, website and quarterly magazine, *East Asia's Billions*, OMF Publishing aims to motivate Christians for world mission, and to equip them for playing a part in it. Publications include:

- contemporary mission issues
- the biblical basis of mission
- the life of faith
- stories and biographies related to God's work in East Asia
- accounts of the growth and development of the church in Asia
- studies of Asian culture and religion relating to the spiritual needs of her peoples

Visit our website at *www.omf.org*

Addresses for OMF English-speaking centres can be found at the back of this book.

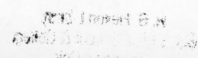

Lambs Dancing with Wolves

A Manual for Christian Workers Overseas

Michael Griffiths

Monarch
BOOKS

First published by Monarch Books in the UK in 2001,
Concorde House, Grenville Place,
Mill Hill, London, NW7 3SA.

ISBN 1 85424 505 8

British Library Cataloguing Data
A catalogue record for this book is available
from the British Library.

Designed and produced for the publishers by
Bookprint Creative Services
P.O. Box 827, BN21 3YJ, England.
Printed in Great Britain.

'Go! I am sending you out like lambs among wolves.'
(Luke 10:3)

CONTENTS

INTRODUCTION

This book is a manual for Christian workers and missionaries, arriving or about to arrive in a new country for the first time. It owes its conception, in part, to a comment by Rhena Taylor in a review of my earlier book *Tinker, Tailor, Missionary?* (IVP 1992), that I had said nothing about relating with national Christians. As that book focused on decisions to be made before leaving the home country, it became clear that I needed to write something about what happened after arriving in the receiving country.

Many of us enjoy sci-fi adventures where space travellers encounter, and try to understand, alien life forms in other imaginary worlds in different time warps from our own. There is a comparable, real-life adventure in entering different communities of human beings living in our own time scale in this present real world. We can enjoy the privilege of crossing cultural boundaries, and meeting real fellow human beings, whose culture, ways of thinking and language are entirely different from our own. I have tried to express the excitement of that 'venture into the unknown' and the enrichment it brings. To remain monocultural in today's global village is to impoverish oneself, and to leave vast areas of our potential memory banks as cold, draughty, empty vaults. The creator has provided every one of us with the capacity for cross-cultural communication, and to neglect this might be seen as a malfunctioning of our God-given human capability.

While tourists traverse other cultures from the safe distance of glass-bottomed boats, and a few may have the courage to snorkel for two or three weeks, they aren't touching on the real adventure. The real adventure is to risk learning to live and breathe in a new cultural environment. The creator is a God who communicates, and has blessed us his creatures by giving us the capacity to communicate. Indeed, his command that we love all our neighbours as ourselves means we must learn to communicate. And more than that – to enjoy the privilege of building relationships across cultural fences, so that we bond with other human beings of different tribes, tongues and nations. This can be a foretaste of heaven to come.

My somewhat enigmatic title is based upon the command of Jesus to the seventy (or seventy-two): 'I am sending you out like lambs among wolves.'[1] I have combined this with an oblique reference to Michael Blake's novel *Dances with Wolves*[2] (subsequently introduced to a wider audience through Kevin Costner's film using the same name). Blake's story provides a fascinating paradigm of the way a lone expatriate comes to terms with what he first sees as a hostile culture and an alien language. Eventually he reaches the point of coming to love and appreciate, and indeed to bond with those who belong to it.

Some interesting background to the words of Jesus in Luke 10:3 are found in a rabbinic conversation dated cAD 90 where a certain Hadrian says to Rabbi Jehoshua, 'There is something great about the sheep (Israel) that can persist among seventy wolves (the Gentile nations, that is).'[3] Though this conversation is half a century later than Jesus, it may reflect a proverb already current during his ministry. It seems that Luke means us to read the sending of the seventy as prefiguring the subsequent mission to the Gentiles in which he had been involved with Paul for some years at the time when he was writing Luke-Acts. Seventy Gentile nations are listed in the Hebrew text of Genesis 10 though the Greek text (Septuagint) makes it seventy-two, explaining the apparent discrepancy between English translations. That the Romans themselves claimed that Romulus and Remus had been brought up by wolves lends further force to the Jewish experience of these particularly 'wolfish' Gentiles. While his lambs may experience hostility from Jews and Gentiles, Christ does not send his lambs out to live among wolves to destroy the wolf pack, but to bond with them and win them over.

On first arriving in a foreign country, Christian workers sent out by Christ's church may well feel like lambs in the midst of wolves. But what was initially alien becomes familiar, accepted, appreciated and finally loved. You might say that the lambs have to get inside the skin of the wolves and become lambs in wolves' clothing! Like the child Mowgli, they have to learn the customs and the language of a particular wolf pack.

I would like to express appreciation to those who gave me the opportunity to develop this theme. First, to my former colleague Dr R.T. France, who invited me to give the Chavasse Lectures 1995 at Wycliffe College, Oxford: something I counted a special privilege, as I had already given the 'Shaking the Sleeping Beauty' series back in 1978. The opening chapters of the book of that title[4] are based on material prepared for those lectures. Second, to those who invited me to give a public lecture with this title at Regent College, Vancouver Summer School 1995. Third, to my OMF colleague Cecil McSparron, who asked me to give an enlarged version at London Bible College in January 1996. The additional chapters are rewritten versions of lectures on cross-cultural communication given while teaching mission at Regent College, Vancouver from 1990–1993. I would like to express appreciation also to Professor Mary Tay and Dr Grace Pettigrew (the linguistic and medical consultants of OMF International) who both offered helpful advice. In consequence I omitted a draft chapter on health altogether, because even a whole book on medical matters would still have to generalise so much that it might not be sufficiently detailed to assist in localised areas about specific regional hazards. Finally I would also like to express my great appreciation to Julia Cameron and Eleanor Trotter for their encouragement and help, and also to Ms. Noriko Inagaki for her help in producing the table of Japanese characters. Special thanks to my wife Valerie for the references to women missionaries in China, and for her encouragement throughout.

A difficulty faced by any missionary writing such a book is the inevitably limited experience any one person has of the whole worldwide scene. My East Asian bias will be obvious to any reader. My responsibilities in OMF did enable me to travel in parts of four continents, and more recently, as a minister at large with IFES, I have been privileged to travel more widely still. I have tried to draw my illustrations from as wide an area as possible, but apologise for these inevitable limitations, even though it is forty years since my wife and I first left our home country to 'dance among wolves'.

It is my hope that this book might serve as useful background reading, and as a source book, for giving cross-cultural orientation to missionaries in training, including those in short-term or self-supporting roles.

MICHAEL GRIFFITHS
Guildford, Surrey

Notes

1. Luke 10:3.
2. Michael Blake, *Dances with Wolves* (London: Penguin Books, 1991).
3. Howard Marshall, *The Gospel of Luke* (Exeter: Paternoster, 1978), p.417.
4. Michael Griffiths, *Shaking the Sleeping Beauty* (Leicester: IVP, 1980).

CHAPTER ONE

LAMBS LEARN THE LANGUAGE OF THE WOLF–PACK

This book is about the need to bond and to identify with others. You cannot do that effectively without speaking a common language. Unless English is the language of trade or education, as it was in British India and Anglophone Africa, missionaries will have to learn one or more other languages to communicate effectively. Language study is number one priority for the first one or two years of most missionaries' service, and should remain a significant element happily ever after. The attitudes outlined in the next couple of chapters are basic, and need to be formed before we start language learning in earnest. Until the missionary lamb learns to communicate with friendly wolves, it will be virtually impossible to achieve rapport, empathy and meaningful friendship.

The frustrating inability to communicate

Blake's book *Dances with Wolves* tells of a lone American cavalry officer's encounter with Comanche Indians (Costner converts them into Sioux). At first John Dunbar knows nothing about them, and waits for them to come to him –

which they do, to steal his horse! He is bathing naked when his first visitor, Kicking Bird, arrives, and they scare each other silly: his nakedness vividly portrays just how vulnerable the new arrival can feel.

In the second encounter, Wind in His Hair leads a party to steal the white man's horse, and the two men confront each other, apparently unafraid. The Indian shouts out, 'I am Wind in His Hair. Do you see I am not afraid of you? Do you see?' and then hurtles off. The words are clearly some kind of declaration or threat, but incomprehensible to Dunbar, who passes out from shock. The mutual fear and failure to communicate is apparent. Both sides have a communication problem.

Dunbar decides his approach has been too passive, and resolves to visit the Indians. Putting on all his military finery, he rides over carrying the American flag, unaware that dressing up for battle might prove to be a suicidal approach. Providentially (or to fit with the author's plot), on the way he meets the woman Stands with a Fist attempting suicide following the death of her husband. He binds up her wounds with strips of the American flag and his shirt, and now somewhat dishevelled, rides over to the Indian encampment to deliver the unconscious woman.

In a beautiful scene he sees for the first time thirty to forty conical houses, bathed in the afternoon sun, a warm and peaceful human settlement. It is utterly different from anything he has met in his life before, yet at the same time has so much in common with all other communities of fellow humans. He can hear the laughter of women and children down by the stream. But when they see this stranger approaching, they flee in panic and the whole band gathers at the village entrance: 'It was a dream of wild people, clothed in skins and coloured fabric, a *whole separate race of humans* watching him breathlessly not a hundred yards away' (my italics).[1] He passes the woman to Wind in His Hair, who tells him to clear off. The words are incomprehensible, but the gestures are unmistakable. In a moving paragraph, Blake describes Dunbar's culture shock:

> The lieutenant stood motionless in front of his horse . . . and he felt the spirit run out of him. These were not his people. He would never know them. He might as well have been a thousand miles away. He wanted to be small, small enough to crawl into the smallest darkest hole. What had he expected of these people? He must have thought they would run out and throw their arms around him, have him to supper, share his jokes . . . how lonely he must be. How pitiful he was to entertain any expectations at all. . . . [Riding home] he let his heart bleed free, sobbing as piteously as an inconsolable child.[2]

In fact, unknown to himself, he had made a most useful first approach, as we see from the Indian reaction: 'The white soldier had showed extreme bravery in coming alone to their camp. And he had obviously come with a single intention, not to steal, or cheat, or fight, but to return something he had found, something that belonged to them.'[3]

It is interesting to compare this with Archibald Fleming's reactions in Baffin Island: 'My excitement mounted when I saw the cluster of igloos, a whole village of them, and realised I was about to become a member of that community. In my exhilaration I felt it a glory to become one with the people and to "sit where they sat".'[4]

The Indians then decide to make friendly overtures to Dunbar and send over eight warriors to see him. Kicking Bird and Wind in His Hair approach and engage in very limited conversation: Dunbar mimes the word buffalo to general puzzlement and amusement. On the second visit he invites them to have coffee liberally flavoured with sugar. Dunbar is thrilled to be with people after all this time, and anxious for his guests to stay awhile. They go off with sugar and coffee, and tin cups. As they assess their visit, Kicking Bird realises that he likes the white man and that in spite of language barriers, this feeling is reciprocated. Rapport is gradually being established. Even the bloodthirsty Wind in His Hair feels the man has shown courage; he was friendly, and funny too, not least in miming the buffalo.

Later they come back bearing a gift of buffalo hide. Gifts like this can express friendship and desire for friendship. One of my most treasured possessions is a pen tray, carved out of a vegetable chopping board, embossed with a map of the Japanese islands. That a busy Japanese Christian leader, Ohtawa Koichi, would take time to make this as a gift to me means a great deal: I have known him since he was a student, and he is now Associate General Secretary of IFES.

Starting to learn language

But what about language? How will Dunbar communicate? The Indians cannot speak Dunbar's language: so he must learn to use theirs. There can be no real growth in their relationship until he does. Even the most expressive mimes and gestures will not overcome the huge barrier of mutually incomprehensible sounds. There were certainly no text books, let alone cassettes, for Dunbar to learn Comanche. Most conveniently for the plot, the woman called Stands with a Fist turns out to be the kidnapped daughter of murdered white settlers, who had been brought up from childhood as a Comanche. And she remembers sufficient English to become his language teacher.

His ability to relate to others steadily deepens, in parallel with his progress in language learning. Though culturally he is an infant, Dunbar makes friends, and becomes accepted by the tribe. He alerts the tribe to the nearness of a buffalo herd, and joins the hunt that follows. He saves Smiles a Lot from being killed by a wounded buffalo bull. Wind in His Hair initiates him into eating raw buffalo liver, and exchanges Dunbar's uniform tunic for a Comanche breastplate. Dunbar is given an Indian name 'Dances with Wolves', and slowly identifies with the tribe, and so bonds with its members. The process is finalised when he becomes misunderstood and rejected by his own western culture, which remains alienated, fearful and hostile to Indians. From their standpoint he has 'gone native' and become a traitor to his own people.

It seems tragic that 'going native' should be despised, when it is a great compliment, certainly for the missionary. This was the fate of many of the best missionaries in the colonial era. Twenty years ago, visiting a museum in Johannesburg I found an exhibit criticising an early missionary as being a 'noted negrophilist', that is a lover of black people. They could have paid him no greater compliment! Hopefully in today's more modern world it is possible to identify and bond with a new culture, without necessarily having to be rejected by one's own. Some missionaries identify so closely that they become so biased in favour of their new culture that they take on board the hostilities of their hosts. This happened with some missionaries to China in the thirties and forties who bonded so closely with the Chinese that they became anti-Japanese. And in the same way, missionaries in Laos accepted Lao antipathy to the Thai to such an extent that after the closure of Laos, they were mostly unable to transfer to work in Thailand, even though the languages were closely related.

Even if you have decided, after consulting with your teacher and Lord (or even perhaps without doing so), that you will never attempt to learn any foreign language, you at least need to understand the joys and frustrations of those your church sends out to serve cross-culturally. They will have to learn language: you will need to pray intelligently for them, so lend me your ears.

Appreciating your God-given software

We can seriously undervalue the capacity for language built into the human brain, and fail to praise and thank our maker for it. All of us carry round with us an incredible database loaded with gigabytes – all packed away inside our heads. It is possible to be born, mature, live and die using only a small proportion of our astonishing brain capacity. Entering a new culture means opening hundreds of new directories and files: we will be astonished to find that our minds have been 'fearfully and wonderfully' programmed (Psalm 139:14) so that the ability to assimilate language is already there. Many of us look back with disappointment to our failure to learn French in the classroom. That has very little to do with 'the Baptist method' of language learning – ie by total immersion in another culture!

When we find ourselves surrounded by others speaking an unknown language, our immediate response is to try to find patterns and the relation between certain words and actions or situations. The human brain is programmed to understand these patterns and then to imitate and reproduce them. Every one of us has the potential to mimic others – even better than a Rory Bremner. That is how we first learned our own language. As adults we can learn a second or a third language much more quickly.

Language is a significant part of culture; indeed, we cannot usually understand a culture as a whole without some kind of grasp of the language. Learning one of the more difficult oriental languages today – Cantonese, Korean or Japanese – often means at least two years of full-time study, followed by continuing part-time study. Learning to speak colloquial and read classical Arabic together, probably takes even longer. Some other languages like Malay or Indonesian are much simpler, and people studying them are able to understand much that they hear after six months, and may even start preaching after eight or nine months. Most missions take language study seriously today: though there have been black spots. First termers in Sheikh Othman, near Aden, with one denominational agency were not given time off to study Arabic until they came back for a second term! And workers in the Arctic even today seem to be given minimal time to study Inuktituk (Eskimo) dialects.

Dances with Wolves beautifully illustrates the mutual frustration of the solitary American and the curious Comanche, who have decided to try to talk to one another rather than to kill each other. The story wonderfully conveys a sense of being on the edge of an enormous human adventure: but both parties are limited and frustrated to start with until communication begins to be established.[5] Like Mowgli in Kipling's *Jungle Book,* the missionary 'lamb' must learn to speak the language of the wolf-pack. 'Stands with a Fist' had learned Comanche as a small child, in the way that we all learn the language of our parents and the community in which we are brought up. The ability to learn language seems to be innate, written into the genetic make-up of human beings.

All the evidence suggests that children are not born with a predisposition to learn one language rather than any other. So we may assume all children, regardless of race and parentage, are born with the same ability for learning languages. It does seem that all babies make the same noises of protest and hunger irrespective of race, nationality or gender. In fact, there does seem to be a genetically-transmitted language faculty, once referred to as the LAD or 'language acquisition device' which enables children's acquisition of their native language.[6]

It takes a few years the first time, and our vocabulary continues to grow right through the period of our education. Some reach a minimum level of communication and stick there: those privileged to belong to a literate, reading and conversing community keep on extending their vocabulary and their powers of communication.

The naivety of early Protestants

On 24 September 1795 following morning service at the Surrey Chapel, the Rev. Thomas Haweis argued the advantages of a mission to Otaheite (Tahiti) on various grounds including the allegedly easier language. 'On the coast of Africa in every few leagues a new government and a new language are found. An Indian missionary must learn at least three. Chinese presents difficulties nearly insuperable from the amazing number of its characters.'[7] But, Haweis reported, the language of Tahiti is easily acquired: 'I am assured a corporal of Marines, after three months stay on the island, spoke it fluently.'

How naive can you get!

The London Missionary Society ship *Duff* landed its first party of missionaries in Tahiti on 5 March 1797. Almost eighteen months later the missionaries reported to the LMS directors in August 1798:

Our time has principally been engaged in labouring to acquire a knowledge of the language of the country, which we find all Europeans who ever visited Otaheite have utterly mistaken, as to spelling, pronunciation, ease of learning and the barrenness of it.

We have already joined some thousands of words, and we believe some thousands yet remain; a knowledge of which we hope to attain through the blessing of God. We endeavour to speak a little to the inhabitants, as occasion offers, on the one thing needful, but our ignorance of the language will not suffer us to say much.

They reported further on 9 April 1799, more than two years after their arrival:

Our growth in the knowledge of the language is still slow, and in many cases uncertain; . . . the language abounds with vowels . . . many words consist of nothing but vowels, and each has a sound; but the natives utter the words with such rapidity, that it is with the utmost difficulty we can discover the true manner of spelling them.

Then on 31 December 1800 (having just heard of the capture of the *Duff* by the French on her second voyage) they wrote to the directors:

The public preaching of the Gospel to the inhabitants of Otaheite is not yet commenced, we not yet being sufficiently acquainted with the language of the country; though, we endeavour, as we are able, to drop the word of life to individuals . . . Though, to our views, the work of the mission seems to be nothing advanced with us, yet we see we have abundant cause to be thankful that the whole fabric is not destroyed.

Finally a letter in August 1801, four and a half years after their arrival, announces: 'We have the satisfaction of informing the missionary society that by the grace of God we hope, for the first time, publicly to address the natives on the next Lord's Day. Brother Nott will be the speaker.' The following year, Nott and Elder had sufficient language to undertake a preaching tour throughout the island. At one place they preached to forty, at another to forty-five 'several of them very attentive'. In 1806 they were working together on a Tahitian-English vocabulary of 2,100 words, exclusive of 500 names of trees, plants, fishes, birds and insects and several hundred more words about breadfruit, plantains, coconuts, etc. The many prefixes and affixes multiply the numbers of words greatly.

This early example demonstrates that sanguine expectations are rarely fulfilled, and that language learning sufficient to proclaim the gospel with clarity normally requires several years, particularly for unwritten languages with no available study materials. Those considering only short-term missionary service need to recognise the limitations of minimal language learning.

A first-century linguist: Paul the apostle

Language learning does not seem to have been much of a problem for the apostles. We are told that Mark acted as Peter's interpreter,[8] which could mean that Peter was much freer in Aramaic than he was in Greek, and needed John Mark to translate him into Greek. Apart from the twelve, who as Galileans may well have spoken Greek as well as Aramaic, most of those who took the gospel to the Gentiles were Hellenistic Jews. They were Jewish by birth, yet they were educated in Greek, and probably spoke that language by preference: the New Testament as we have it today is all written in Greek. Paul, Barnabas, Silas, Mark and Apollos all belonged to this group of men with their feet in two cultures. Timothy had a Jewish mother, but a Greek father. Priscilla and Aquila may have been a mixed marriage between Jewish man and Gentile woman. Luke was a Gentile.

Paul seems to have been an accomplished linguist. We see

him addressing the commander of the Roman troop that arrested him in Greek, and then switching to Aramaic to address the Jewish mob in front of the Antonia fortress.[9] He could make himself understood in Greek in most of his journeys: though on one occasion he and Barnabas were unable to understand the Lycaonian dialect of Anatolia in rural Lystra.[10] But even there it seems they could make themselves understood until the people remonstrated with them in Greek.

Paul must have had some acquaintance with Latin, certainly in written form. It is difficult to find any discussion in scholarly works as to how much spoken Latin Paul had. Philippi was a Roman city. Corinth had been a Greek city until it was razed to the ground by the Romans in 146 BC and lay derelict until Julius Caesar rebuilt it as a Roman colony in 44 BC, probably with an eye to the taxes that could be raised from ships and goods being towed across the isthmus on the *diolkos* (tramway). First-century (AD) inscriptions from Corinth are nearly all in Latin, the official language of the empire, rather than in Greek. Paul evangelised in Illyricum, ministered in Rome and envisaged working in Spain, all of which were more Latin speaking than Greek. As an educated Roman citizen, it seems probable that Paul could communicate in Latin as well as in Greek and Aramaic. All three languages were used in the official notice attached to Jesus' cross.

Although my more charismatic friends may reject the suggestion, I think there is much to be said for the view that the 'gift of interpretation' would be needed in the cosmopolitan ports of Corinth for the benefit of visiting Parthians, Medes, Elamites, Mesopotamians, Phrygians, Libyans and even Italians, who could not make themselves understood in church in Greek. It seems absurd to assume that no one in those days ever needed such help and interpretation. We still need it a great deal: in the past couple of years I have needed interpretation into Mandarin, Cantonese, Hebrew, Arabic, Hungarian, Russian, Ukrainian, Slovak, Portuguese, Spanish, German and Inuktituk. Interpreters certainly need the help of the Holy Spirit just as much as the person they are interpreting.

Actually the Old Testament gives rather more clues on language assimilation than the New Testament does. Both Joseph and Moses must have learned to speak Egyptian with great competence.[11] Daniel and the other aristocratic hostages of the Babylonians embarked on a three-year course of language and culture.[12] There was no way these Jews could have attained such leadership positions in foreign countries without good language assimilation in the second language.

A pioneer missionary linguist and translator: Henry Martyn

Henry Martyn was a genius. I include him because there is always room for people for whom languages and comparative philology are a consuming passion. Languages were his favourite means of relaxation, and he had to pray that the study of them might not distract him from prayer! In the six years between his arrival in India (1806) and his death in Persia (1812) at the age of only thirty-one, he completed three New Testament translations significant for Indian Muslims. More correctly, he himself completed an Urdu (Hindustani) translation, he supervised Mirza Fitrut's Arabic translation, and produced in Persia a complete revision and retranslation of Sabat's stilted Persian draft version. And all of this in tropical heat, while slowly dying of tuberculosis. It was said of Henry Martyn that 'he read grammars as other men read novels'. He reveals his insatiable passion for languages in a letter written from Cawnpore in 1809:

There is a book printed at the Hirkara Press, called Celtic Derivatives: this I want; also grammars and dictionaries of all the languages of the earth. I have one or both in Latin, Greek, French, Italian, Portuguese, Dutch, Hebrew, Rabbinical Hebrew, Chaldee, Syriac, Ethiopic, Samaristan, Arabic, Persian, Sanscrit, Bengali, Hindustani.[13]

I include Martyn not to deter the plodder (William Carey called himself a plodder), but to encourage the enthusiast, and because Martyn also displays important personal character traits which we shall look at in later chapters.

A nineteenth-century hare: Thomas Valpy-French[14]

If you ever visit St Ebbe's Church in Oxford, you will see above the table two stained-glass windows dedicated to a former curate and later rector of the church named Thomas Valpy-French, first bishop of Lahore. He came up to Oxford from Rugby and was made a Fellow of University College at the age of twenty-three. He left for India with the Church Missionary Society in 1850 aged twenty-five to found St John's College, Agra. He opened a mission on the North West Frontier in 1862, but was invalided home before the end of the year. However, he returned to Lahore and founded St John's Theological College there in 1870. He was Bishop of Lahore for ten years from 1878 and finally after retirement died trying to start a mission in Arabia in 1891.

He was known as the *haft-zaban padri* (seven-tongued man) as he spoke seven related Indian languages (including Hindi and Urdu) in addition to French, Latin, Greek, Hebrew, Persian and Arabic. This seems to suggest that once you get the hang of learning languages you can assimilate faster and faster! Even in the heat of India he reckoned to work for at least ten hours a day, and this facility in language was not achieved without hard work. His alarming advice to a recent arrival shows that he expected others to apply themselves with the same diligence:

> You must, of course, commence with Urdu or Hindustani, so as to be able to talk to your servants, to help in the services of the church and in the schools. You had better give some six or eight hours a day to that, and also spend two or three hours at Punjabi to be able to talk with villagers. You should also try to give two or three hours to the study of Persian, which you will find invaluable in the schools, and all your spare time (sic) to the study of Arabic so as to be able to read the Qur'an.[15]

If this advice scares you silly, it still forces you to realise that even one new language will not be assimilated without setting aside the majority of your waking hours to language study. We may enjoy privileges that our nineteenth-century predecessors did not, of air-conditioning and modern textbooks using the latest techniques for learning language, but we cannot escape the need to spend time and sweat, and to apply diligence and perseverance. It takes time to programme even the most well-organised human brain. This is why language study needs to be the top priority of the first one or two years of a missionary's life, and perhaps of the whole first term of service.

At a later stage we may no longer need to study full-time, and language is best learned by hearing it and using it in everyday situations. It was written into the Principles and Practices of the China Inland Mission by Hudson Taylor that new missionaries should spend 'several hours of every day out in the marketplace among the people'. Valpy-French himself was a superb model of such practical learning: 'I always spend from three to four hours in direct study of the languages daily, besides what I gain in teaching others and in conversation in the bazaars. It is essential for a thorough knowledge of the languages that they should be learned in this practical way.'[16]

Notice his use of the plural! Most of us will have to learn only one new language at a time, but countries which employ a national or trade language as well as major tribal languages may require us to tackle more than one – so in addition to Swahili, Portuguese, Indonesian or Tagalog (Philippines), you may need to add Masai, a Mozambique tribal language, Javanese or Cebuano.

At the Lahore Theological College, Valpy-French was known to translate Chrysostom or Augustine straight from Greek or Latin into the native Hindustani (Urdu). His students, who included Afghans, Pathans, Rajputs, Persians, Punjabis and Kashmiris (mostly brought up as Muslims), were expected to read Ezekiel in Hebrew and Ephesians in Greek. He and his colleagues lectured largely in Urdu with occasional use of Persian, Pushtu, Punjabi, Sanskrit and Arabic. He had few models of theological education available at that time, and most of us today would think his expectations too high.

Muslims appreciate beauty in literature, loving the recitation of the Qur'an, and Valpy-French found they would listen with equal reverence to the recitation of the prophets and the Gospels from the Christian Scriptures in classical Arabic. At the end of his life he scared the newly arrived Samuel Zwemer, when he started reading the Gospels out aloud in a coffee shop in Jeddah, the port of Mecca, but was heard with great reverence. A few weeks before he died in Muscat at the age of seventy-one, he wrote to his wife: 'I am pushing on very hard with Arabic, copying out verses to give to hopeful enquirers to carry home and preparing a tract on the leading articles in the Creed. . . . the work is a great effort and one has to hang upon God for strength.'[17] I can well imagine that this example is most frightening, and calculated to make us feel rather inferior. But my third example may be more encouraging.

A twentieth-century tortoise: Patrick McElligott[18]

Patrick grew up in a deprived Roman Catholic home in Deptford, in London's East End, and managed to gain just four O-levels, failing in French. He left school early at sixteen and started work. He trained at the WEC College in Glasgow, expecting to work in literature for CLC in Japan. Tested for language aptitude, the assessment was that he would find Japanese language study very difficult, and quite probably would not be able to learn it at all.

Back in England on his first furlough at the age of thirty, Patrick passed an O-level in Japanese, and started work on an A-level. He continued study throughout his second term of service, and on his second furlough sat for a London University external Bachelors degree, having had no tuition and attended no lectures in England. Past examination papers were his only guide, and by this time he knew some two thousand Chinese ideographs with their various phonetic readings. The exam lasted ten days and he passed. He must have done well for the next we hear, Patrick was working on a PhD in the poetry of Kobayashi Issa – being successful in 1984, nineteen years after arriving in Japan. Patrick demonstrates that even for those of moderate ability, perseverance wins the prize.

His drive to learn contrasts starkly with those who fall foul of the commonest threat in language learning, which is to plateau off once you have passed your language exams and make do with what you have, as long as you can get your general meaning across somehow.

William Carey, suspecting rightly that his nephew intended writing his biography, said:

Eustace, if after my removal any one should think it worth his while to write my Life, I will give you a criterion by which you may judge of its correctness. If he gives me credit for being a plodder he will describe me justly. Anything beyond this will be too much. I can plod. I can persevere in any definite pursuit. To this I owe everything.[19]

Readers may classify themselves as linguistic hares or plodding tortoises, but language learning is a field in which the plodder will always arrive successfully. I have known only one couple who totally failed to learn an Asian language (out of two thousand whom I knew over twenty years with OMF). Certainly people learn at different speeds. For example Alan Cole, who was lecturing in Classics at Trinity College, Dublin at the age of twenty-one, learned three Chinese dialects in four years: most people take that long to learn one.

A poor linguist who communicated: John Ethlestan Cheese

Some famous missionaries to Muslims have been brilliant linguists like Henry Martyn, Joseph Wolff, Valpy-French, Keith-Falconer and Temple Gairdner, but this man with the improbable name, who spent forty-six years of his life in the Middle East, was manifestly not a linguist. Cheese, though educated at Rugby (with William Temple) and St John's, Cambridge, was no scholar, being awarded only third class honours. During a curacy in the Isle of Wight he suffered a bad melancholic breakdown. Part of his cure was a tour in the Holy Land, and so in 1912 he arrived in the Middle East. Bishop Rennie McInnes of Jerusalem put him in charge of a school of Druse boys on the slopes of Lebanon near Beirut and he began to study Arabic for which no official provision seems to have been made. In consequence he developed a unique idiolect of English-inflected Arabic. Temple Gairdner said kindly that 'he speaks no known dialect of Arabic, but is intelligible'.

Although he had inherited family money he gave it all away so that he might live simply on £60–70 a year. On one occasion he requested at a steamship office in Aden that he might travel in the hold, registered as a piece of luggage. In consequence of internment by the Turks, during the First World War, he suffered a further bout of depression. Moved to Cairo, he endeared himself to simple people around the Old Cairo Mission Hospital. An Egyptian catechist said:

> I saw someone come in at whom one had to look . . . his face shone with piety and goodness . . . a slight man of middle height . . . simply dressed and wearing sandals. You would have said a monk or an ascetic like Sadhu Sundar Singh . . . we loved him and he was welcome wherever he went.[20]

His stooping figure and fair beard became known in the Arab world. He was the *weli*, the holy man, allowed to pass safely anywhere. He travelled on a *dhow* to Muscat, and whenever the crew said their Muslim devotions, he knelt down and continued much in prayer on the deck. Through friendship with a Somali street cleaner he became interested in that country, the more so when he discovered that they had only the Gospel of Mark in their language. En route he got stuck in Addis Ababa for eighteen months because they were without a British chaplain. A hospitable American Mission found his bed unslept in night after night, and when they finally enquired, explained that he had trained himself to sleep on the floors of native huts and was afraid of getting soft. He spent the next twenty-four years (this is commitment) as a wandering apostle to the Somalis. They were a half-nomadic, pastoral people, travelling by camel from pasture to pasture. Ethelstan travelled with them, gradually assimilating more of their language, walking when they walked, sleeping in their camps, eating their food and learning to milk a camel when thirst overtook him. A British official reported that when he asked Somali chiefs if they knew Ethelstan, they said: 'Of course, he is a Christian. We don't believe what he believes – he is wrong and we are right. But he is without doubt the holiest man in all Somalia.'

He attempted to translate more Scriptures into Somali in Roman script, but they never achieved the standard required by the Bible Society. He produced some tracts written by himself, and translated the first part of *Pilgrim's Progress* into Somali in which Christian became Hajji Osman, and this was printed.

He was knocked down by a car in Mombasa, had a minor stroke which affected his speech and his writing, and became increasingly deaf. In 1958 he gave away his few books, and falling ill the consul in Beirut put him on a boat to return to England, and he died quietly on the boat alone in mid-Mediterranean.

This man seems to have found the secret of communicating with Muslims – a life of holiness, simplicity and poverty, manifesting the presence of Christ, offering and accepting friendship. It is the holy life which provides the most convincing evidence of the truth of the gospel.

His life illustrates positively the truth that 'if I speak in the tongues of men and of angels and have not love, I am only a resounding gong or a clanging cymbal'. No amount of scholarly expertise in a foreign tongue is much use to anyone unless they can make friends and relate to other human beings.

Dr Leigh Ashton had served most of his working life as a

surgeon in Kenya, and came to help out in Thailand after retiring age. Somehow, with a minimum of Thai language, he communicated the love of Christ, and Thai people loved him for
it. I say this not to excuse younger people who have time and
energy to apply to language study, but to encourage late start-
ers! It is better to spend two years in full-time study and be
ninety per cent understood, than only one year and be sixty
per cent understood. Every additional month spent in diligent
study increases our ability to communicate the gospel clearly.

Language learning for wives and mothers

Husbands today are generally prepared to take a share of
domestic responsibilities to ensure that wives learn the language as well as they do. When we first arrived in Japan, we
took it in turns to put our firstborn through his evening bath
and get him settled down in bed. Even today some missionary-
sending countries have strongly prescribed roles for husbands
and wives, and it is noticeable when such women make much
slower progress with language assimilation. It may not seem
to matter when children are small, but once they are off to
school women are left with time on their hands, and if their
language progress has been good they can now play a much
fuller part in missionary work. But if their language study has
suffered because of domestic work, they may become frustrated, unhappy and may even insist on returning to the home
country because they have never been given time to learn to
communicate effectively. My wife was fortunate in that she
had not long stopped being a university student when we
reached Japan, and she was used to the discipline of study. For
our first four years in the country, that meant after the children were in bed, six nights a week, if we had no Bible class,
out would come the study books from 7–10 pm each night.

The timing of our babies by God's overruling providence was such that she always seemed to pass a language examination a few days before the next new baby arrived. In the event, in spite of bearing and caring for two babies, she took only one year longer to complete our mission's required (self-study) course than her husband. Our third child arrived very shortly afterwards!

In the early months, when a female visitor arrived, Valerie would sit with her by the stove while I tried to study or prepare teaching material through a paper door in the next room. There is no privacy in a traditional Japanese house and I could hear every word. A long paragraph of rapidfire, collo-quial Japanese from the visitor would be followed by a hesi-tant *Hai* from my beloved, struggling to understand and clearly failing. It was a classic example of a word that means 'I have heard you' rather than 'I agree' or 'I understand'. Another spate of fast-spoken, polite women's Japanese fol-lowed – followed by another *Hai* that I knew concealed lack of comprehension. I could understand some of it: should I intervene and take over? Not if I wanted my wife to make progress. I had to sit there and grit my teeth while she learned the hard way, and the best way. I had my reward in later years when I heard her chattering away in polite women's language on the telephone. Men in missionary conditions tend to learn more from books, and women more from hearing and using the language.

When the American Baptist missionaries Adoniram and Ann Judson first arrived in Burma in 1814 to join Felix Carey (son of British Baptist William Carey), their only language aids were the Gospel of Matthew and part of a grammar and dictionary started by Felix. Ann's comments about the lan-guage learning methods of herself and her husband provide an interesting contrast:

Could you look into a large open room, which we call a verandah, you would see Mr Judson bent over his table, covered with Burman books, with his teacher at his side . . . they talk and chatter all day long with hardly any cessation.

My mornings are busily employed in giving directions to the servants, providing food for the family, etc. At ten my teacher comes . . . I have many more interruptions than Mr Judson, as I have the entire management of the family. This I took on myself for the sake of Mr Judson's attending more closely to the study of the language; yet I have found by a year's experience it was the most direct way I could have taken to acquire the language, as I am frequently obliged to talk Burman all day. I can talk and understand others better than Mr Judson, though he knows more about the nature and construction of the language than I do.[21]

Judson completed a Burmese Bible by 1834 and a dictionary was published 1849, in the year before his death. Ann had died in 1826. She translated Daniel and Jonah into Burmese, wrote a Burmese catechism, and was the first person to translate any of the Bible into the Thai language, translating Matthew's Gospel into Siamese.

Every husband should see his partner's progress in the language as being as important as his own, and should try to relieve her of as many domestic chores as he can in the earliest months of language study. Ideally both partners should complete their formal language study requirements before starting a family. This was easier to achieve in days when new missionaries went out unmarried in their early twenties than it is today when many arrive already married in their later twenties or early thirties, often already with children. Where couples have the option of delaying the arrival of family they would be wiser to do so in the interests of the wife's language learning. If it does not work out that way all is not lost, for the young missionary mum who is able to bond with the local young mums at the nursery school or playgroup will have many practical learning opportunities.

There can be pastoral problems when a wife is more gifted linguistically than her husband. Instead of thanking God for such a competent partner and fellow worker, some spouses feel threatened, as though somehow their masculinity is in doubt. With bearing of children and caring for them, a wife faces, like Ann Judson, 'many interruptions' and the husband should rather thank his Lord for blessing him with such a wife, so well equipped for the work. Those coming from Christian traditions with a rigid interpretation of male headship and female subordination are more likely to have problems when the female partner proves more able linguistically or in spiritual giftedness than her spouse.

If you are still feeling uncertain about your capacity for assimilating a new language, look at these interesting examples from some languages to show you what fun language learning can be.

1. The relative ease of building up new language response reflexes

Many greetings and human exchanges are oft-repeated rituals: 'Good morning.' 'How are you?' 'Have a nice day.' 'Thank you.' 'Don't mention it.' If you spend time with people you will soon hear, and come to understand, and then (falteringly at first) to use some of the common exchanges of everyday life. These can be learned from books, but they are equally well learned by osmosis. We learn language by hearing it, understanding it and then using it ourselves. So to learn the 'Guten morgen', 'Buenos nochas', 'Selamat pagi', 'Ohaio gozaimasu . . . Konnichi wa' expressions may require no more than repeating back what we have just heard addressed to us. Or there may be stereotyped answers to stereotyped greetings:

'*Gochisoosama deshita*' (thank you for the honourable feast) requiring the reply: '*Osomatsusama deshita*' (it was nothing worth having!). Announcing one's return home '*Tadaima*' elicits the inevitable prescribed response: '*Okaerinasai*'. On departing the humble '*Itte mairimasu*' requires the honorific '*Itte irasshai*'. Such formal exchanges soon become reflex reactions. Such language learning is easy!

2. The enrichment (and fun) of using onomatopoeic words

The Japanese language, for example, is rich in words and phrases that express sounds and movements almost audibly. Thus dripping rain falls *poroporo*, while heavy rain pours down *zaza*, and the drenched dripping wet person is described as *bishobisho*. Steam trains puff along *pipopo, pipopo*, while electric ones standing at the platform make that characteristic *gatan gotan* sound. Milk churns collide with a clanging sound *gachan, gachan*, and the sound of sawing is *gorigori*. The addition of such words to an otherwise plain narrative gives it lots of extra sparkle: the child walking in becomes much more interesting if it toddles *chokochoko*.

3. Four character phrases in Chinese characters

The Chinese language uses four characters in a phrase to express colourful meaning (the Japanese took many of these over and modified some). For example: 'Same bed different dream': 'Same' contrasts with 'different' and 'bed' pairs with 'dream', and it describes perfectly two individuals involved in the same task or pursuit, and yet with differing aims in mind. 'Broken body, powdered bones': where the two pairs of characters reinforce each other to express total commitment of the individual to the point of death if necessary. A good word to describe attitude to language learning! 'Dragon's head, dog's tail' (though the Chinese say 'Tiger's head, pig's tail') provides a good description of any venture that begins with a bang and finishes with a whimper (like some sermons!).

4. Proverbs

These often provide a rich way of expressing yourself: for example, 'Eye medicine from the second floor', conjuring up the ludicrous picture of someone with an eyedropper trying to hit the patient's upturned eye from a considerable height, a totally inadequate solution to a problem. 'Even a monkey can fall' reminds us that even the expert may slip up sometimes. Only last week I picked up two more relating to the difficulties experienced by new Christians converted while overseas, now returning home: 'Nails that stick up get hammered down', and 'Water that is too pure contains no fish'.

5. Substitution frames

To see the way your brain is already programmed to learn language, let's make use of a common language learning device that by repetition of certain key words enables you both to learn new vocabulary and to grasp the way in which nouns and verbs hang together to make sense. We will use two rather basic words from the Malay language. (The closely-related Indonesian and Bahasa Malaysia are spoken by two hundred and fifty million people!) The words are *makan* meaning 'eat' and *minum* meaning 'drink'. If you start with seven subjects eating rice, and the same seven each enjoy six other foods, you will have used the Malay verb 'to eat' forty-nine times!

Saya (I)	*makan*	*nasi* (rice)
Kita (we)	*makan*	*roti* (bread)
Awa (you)	*makan*	*daging* (meat)
Dia (he)	*makan*	*ikan* (fish)

Bapa (father)	*makan*	*pisang* (banana)
Enche Ali (Mr Ali)	*makan*	*telor* (egg)
Amah (househelp)	*makan*	*nasi goreng* (fried rice)

And here are thirty-six ways you might use the verb 'to drink'.

Saya	*minum*	*ayer* (water)
Kita	*minum*	*susu* (milk)
Awa	*minum*	*teh* (tea)
Dia	*minum*	*kopi* (coffee)
Bapa	*minum*	*ayer seju* (cold)
Amah	*minum*	*ayer panas* (hot)

By the time each of the seven subjects have eaten each of the seven foods, you have certainly learned the word *makan*, and probably several of the other words. Similarly you have probably learned the word *minum* and you have some idea of four possible fluids you might drink. If you repeat the drill daily for a week, you will remember more, and that will be driven further into your memory the moment you enter a café and start deciding what you want to eat and drink. The fact that verbs precede their object, and the hint that adjectives come after the noun they qualify means that now you can specify in turn hot and cold water, milk, tea and coffee. We needed the phrase *ayer panas* when on holiday in Malaysia, when asking to be directed to hotsprings in a river where male Rajah Brooke butterflies could be found in large numbers!

My guess is that this was not really such a painful exercise and that you now have some glimmering about constructing language drills and feel rather pleased to realise that your brain already has the 'software' installed to help you learn language. Just think of all that unused capacity!

6. Picking up some easy vocabulary

We already know some words in foreign languages, because languages borrow words from other modern languages, especially English. And English has many words derived from Greek and Latin, and imported French words like mutton, beef, venue, creche, as well as recognisable French phrases. Most languages do this, even if they change the spelling. Thus Malay contains words like *basu*, *sekolah*, *kelabu*, *teksi*, *rumah sakit* not to mention *orang utang*. Japanese borrows words from many languages like *pan* for bread from Portugal (all Japanese words beginning with the letter p are imported words), *avec* from French and *arbeit* from German. Most words for clothing come from outside Japan, apart from native *kimono*, and many words get changed, often abbreviated or pronounced differently – *terebi* for television, *rajio* for radio, *masukomu* for mass communications, and so on. We already know Russian words like *vodka*, *aeroflot*, *pravda*, *Bolshoi* as well as names of places, novelists and composers, though often we have modified pronunciation too. And they borrow words we already know like *kiosk*, *bar*, *park*, *telephon*, *cofye* and *footbol*. All of these features of exchange between languages make our learning task easier.

7. How many characters can you learn in ten minutes?

I want to teach you some Chinese characters – which Chinese speaking different dialects, and Japanese and Koreans will all understand as well. That is a large number of people, nearly a fifth of the world population. Many languages require learning a new 'alphabet', whether it's Arabic, Hebrew, Hindi, Thai, Korean hangul (only twenty-two letters!) or one of the Indian scripts like Punjabi. It becomes most complicated when using the ideographs or pictographs used by the Chinese and their neighbours. In Japanese one uses Chinese characters, which mean the same in both languages, though they require different noises to represent them, and two syllabic scripts, *katakana* for all foreign words and *hiragana* for adding to characters to indicate tense, voice and so on. Compared with English and all its different vowels, it's easy because it is totally phonetic and the same syllabic symbol is always pronounced in the same way, and there are only five possible vowels which are always pronounced in exactly the same way. You may say that's all very well, but how many of these Chinese (Japanese) characters are there? Well, we once had a Korean scholar at London Bible College who reckoned that he knew 50,000. Actually there isn't anything to worry about. Really! It's just a rather clever code, as you might expect the Chinese to devise: a symbol at the left-hand side (a radical) tells you whether this is a kind of metal, fish, bird or tree, or something to do with feelings, water, motion, bamboo, pipes and flutes, and so on.

One, two, three are all obvious and easy, and so is ten, if you remember that the Japanese word for the cross of Calvary is literally 'ten-character-frame'. A single tree is a simple convention, and if you write two of them it means a copse, and if you use three, it means a forest (*mori*): what could be simpler than that? If you want to put a little crosspiece down at the bottom of the tree you now have the character for a root, or the origin of something (*moto* or *hon*). You could use that last one as a symbol on a map, and the conventional signs for mountain (*yama*), river (*kawa*) and paddyfield (*ta* or *da*) soon grow on you. So now if you know a Mr Yamamoto, Yamada or Morita, or own a Honda car, you now know how to write them in Japanese. If you add in sun and moon, which are both rough pictures certainly, but quickly written symbols – we can

Learning Japanese (Chinese) Characters

一	one	峠	pass (up and down a mountain)
二	two	目	eye
三	three	耳	ear
十	ten	口	mouth
木	tree	言	word (John 1:1)
林	copse	信	believe, trust
森	forest	人	man
本	origin, bottom	女	woman (carrying bamboo pole)
休	rest	安	peace (woman under a roof)
田	paddy field (本田 = Honda)	子	child (on mum's back?)
果	fruit	好	good, liking
日	sun, day (日本 = Japan)	門	gate (also as radical)
月	moon, month (十月 = October)	問	question (mouth at door)
明	brightness	聞	listen (ear at door)
心	heart	間	between (sun in door)
思	think	雨	rain (also as radical)
山	mountain (also as radical)	雪	snow
上	up	雷	thunder
下	down, below (下さい = please)	電	electricity

now add *Nihon* or *Nippon* which means the origin (root) of the sun, the place where the sun comes from if you live in China. And as Sunday and Monday begin with these two symbols you can begin to read a calendar already! And you can recognise First, Second, Third and Tenth months (because the moon symbol is used for months, and the sun character for days).

Man, woman (the liberated woman staggers under the weight of a bamboo pole) and child are three convenient symbols, and can be combined with others: woman and child together mean good, one woman under a roof means peace, and a man (abbreviated as a radical like this) next to a tree means to rest: put that together with the day and you have a 'rest day'. You can take the mountain as a radical, add up and down and now you have a symbol for a mountain pass.

Let's introduce you to a few bodily organs – a mouth, an eye, an ear and a heart (not very difficult are they?). You can use the heart as a radical for verbs of feeling – take your heart out to the field and that means think!

Now if we have a gateway (*mon*) – it looks like a pair of saloon doors in a western movie – and then insert a mouth, it means 'to question', or an ear (means 'to listen') or the sun (it means 'between'). The rain radical looks complicated until you get used to it, but you can see the raindrops falling, and if we add other symbols we can manage cloud, snow, hail, thunder and electricity.

Now what I would do at this point with a class is to test them by showing them twenty characters and asking them what they all mean. Nearly everybody scores at least ten, most get more than fifteen. You see what fun it is: like doing cryptic crosswords all day long and calling it work!

The joy of learning new languages

After reading all this, how do you feel about learning a new language now? Many people are apprehensive or even afraid of it all. But there is no need to panic! After all, the vast majority of babies learn to talk, whether they are very intelligent or not. Modern Language Aptitude Tests (MLAT) give a rough measure of anticipated speed of learning: they are quite good at distinguishing hares from tortoises. Some learn fast, some learn slowly, but hardly anybody fails to learn something. Remember that huge database sitting on top of our necks: with memory banks holding thousands of megabytes? Most of us use only a fraction of our total potential; that database is just waiting to be used!

1. The joy of being able to understand and speak it

It is an extraordinary privilege to meet a person from another country or culture, and to find the right words springing automatically to your mind and lips. It may take a few moments to tune in, but then you're off. When you have been privileged to learn a major world language, suddenly there are millions of people you could talk to, if you had the time! If you have learned Mandarin Chinese, you can now talk to more than a thousand million fellow humans; if you have learned Russian, not only have you added another quarter of a billion people you can talk to, but you have taken a running jump into several other Slavic languages. If you have learned Malay or Indonesian, at least another quarter of a billion warm, friendly people are open to communication. And if you have learned French, it's not only all the people in France and Switzerland, but all the many francophone Africans you can now engage with. Language learning is an intensely rewarding exercise of our God-given capabilities.

2. The joy of preaching Christ with it

After about two and a half years in Japan, I remember one dark winter's evening walking through deep snow to a rice-growing village on the Tsugaru Plain. The footpaths were frozen and crackled underfoot. The moonlight lit up the slopes of *Iwaki-san*, the great volcano that dominates the whole region. Because it was deep winter, the farmers could not work the fields and there was time to attend a meeting. They were all wearing padded jackets and trousers to keep out the cold, and there was a small charcoal burning *hibachi* in the room: if you got closer, it got warmer, but get too close and the fumes gave you a splitting headache. But after that meeting was over, I skipped home across the snow with my bag of Bibles and hymnbooks. All the way home I was leaping and dancing for joy, because that night I had preached Christ in a village which had never heard the good news before. I had seen some glimmerings of understanding in the eyes of my farming audience. There are still many places left in the world where you can do that, if you love your fellow human beings enough to take time to learn their language.

Realism about learning languages

The missionary goal may be expressed as achieving 'functional bilingualism', but sadly it has to be admitted that many fall short of this goal, especially if they are only able to serve for three or four years. We can usually make ourselves understood within the limits of our vocabulary, but cannot always understand what other people may say to us using a much wider vocabulary. We missionaries also have to be scrupulously honest in not pretending to or allowing others to attribute to us a greater fluency than we actually possess. One of the

'Famous Five' East India Co. evangelical chaplains, Claudius Buchanan, wrote in 1814:

> Beware, especially of giving too favourable an account of your ability to preach in the native languages, and of the effects of your preaching on the hearers. For instance, after you have made some progress in a particular language, and have committed to memory a few theological phrases, you will, perhaps, try to converse with the Natives on religious subjects. But in your account of such a conversation in this stage of your study, do not call it preaching Christ to the people. For it may be that the people scarcely understood a single doctrine of your address, and that, when they asked you a question, you could not understand or answer them. To preach Christ implies the preaching of Him fully, and to the understanding of the people.[22]

A recent letter from a missionary couple who have spent one year learning Portuguese prior to going to Mozambique reads:

> We can say with some confidence that we can now speak fairly fluently and fairly accurately in Portuguese. Unfortunately we can't yet do both at the same time, so it's a tough choice between fluent very poor Portuguese and fairly good Portuguese spoken painfully slowly.[23]

This is refreshing realism. 'Functional bilingualism' may be easier to achieve in languages written in Roman scripts or phonetic alphabetic scripts, but languages written in ideographs like Chinese and Japanese leave many floundering. Missionaries can preach and be understood, but cannot understand all the written material they may encounter. They can usually read the Bible, which often uses a simplified vocabulary anyway, but may not be able to read other books or documents without a laborious process with dictionary in hand. This explains why in early days in China missionaries were reluctant to invite national pastors and believers to their conferences, if that meant proceedings would have to be conducted in Chinese, when only the more senior and most linguistically gifted missionaries would be able to participate on equal terms.

Bonding and language learning

I recently came across the following story about Florence Young, who founded both the Queensland Kanaka Mission and the South Sea Evangelical Mission. She did join the China Inland Mission briefly in between and this beautifully illustrates the relationship between language learning and bonding, as well as the agonies of trying to speak an imperfectly learned language.

> The first Sunday after my arrival, without warning Miss Marchbank called on me to give my 'testimony'. I had never done such a thing in English, but in Chinese! However, we had learned an unwritten law – never to refuse to do what was asked. So I did my best. A very poor best it must have been, for the people all laughed. This was bad enough but worse was to follow. Probably Miss Marchbank did not realise that my time of study had been broken into by nursing and journeys. I had only had five months study of the language. Be that as it may, when the company knelt for prayer, to my dismay Miss Marchbank asked me in Chinese to pray. I knew what her words meant; but surely I must be mistaken. The Bible woman kneeling alongside touched me (and in Chinese said she had asked me to pray). I did pray and they laughed again. Oh, how humiliated I felt. But that evening one of the Bible women, dear Mrs Hong, with loving words tried to comfort me: 'Let your heart rest. If you eat our rice, you will soon speak our words.' Then she asked if I would like her to pray with me, and every night she came hobbling upstairs on her tiny feet and we prayed together.[24]

This was learning by doing, but the love shown by the older Chinese woman to the raw Australian recruit, I find most moving. National Christian friends want us and will us to speak their language with fluency and freedom. The early years of struggling to express oneself, and wondering if one ever will be able to do so, can be agonising. But personal friendship and relating to local Christians in their own tongue is by far the most effective way to learn. The laughter above was partly embarrassment, and your friends want you to succeed.

Another story about Chinese prayerful concern focuses on Jessie Gregg, who later held 183 Missions for women in fifteen provinces, travelling 28,000 miles by cart or mule litter: some 5,000 Chinese women went through the enquiry room and professed faith in Christ. She sailed for China in 1895 and arrived at first station Hwailu in Hopeh in 1896.

> I cannot say I found the language easy at first, but one old lady took me upon her heart, and daily told the Lord that there was a lady who had come but could not talk; and that she lived in the West Room of the courtyard and was 25 years old; would He kindly give her the *oil* of the Holy Ghost, for her tongue was very stiff and she couldn't get it round the Chinese words. *He did it*, and at the end of three years I had passed all the required examinations (Jessie's italics).[25]

Praise God for indigenous believers who love us enough to pray for us!

Language proficiency levels

Any classification is bound to be somewhat arbitrary, but they do give a notion of the progress which needs to be made. It is important to recognise the differing levels that exist. The following is based upon the Brewsters' LAMP (Language Acquistion Made Practical) course.[26]

0. *zero proficiency* means no ability in a language. And zero plus proficiency means you can use at least 50 words in appropriate contexts. Brewster includes 'plus level' at each stage which is more complex, but is omitted here.

1. *elementary speaking proficiency* is adequate to express elementary survival needs, routine travel and minimal courtesy and to answer familiar questions, which have been specifically prepared and rehearsed.

2. *limited work proficiency* means one is capable of giving simple instructions and explanations, with hesitant fluency in extemporaneous situations.

3. *minimal professional fluency* requires vocabulary such that you rarely grope for words, and comprehension is complete at normal rates of speech.

4. *full professional proficiency* where your speech is as effortless as in your mother tongue.

5. *native speaker proficiency* marks total fluency and idiomatic language (and usually requires a university education in the language and total immersion in the society for several years).

It is worth noting that short-termers rarely progress beyond Level 2 because they do not normally have time to devote to language study. The Brewsters make a shrewd comment:

It is not uncommon for people who speak English to establish themselves in roles overseas which make language learning virtually impossible. For example, the person who goes as an administrator subconsciously puts on an administrator front, and acts in an administrative way. If someone goes as a teacher, or a medic, or a missionary he has a high status role. His self-image compels him to behave in ways which conform to that role. . . . In language learning, the attitude of superiority that often goes (subconsciously) with the sophisticated role, must be laid aside.[27]

And that leads us into a discussion of attitudes in the following chapter.

Notes

1. Michael Blake, *op. cit.*, p.101.
2. *Ibid.*, pp.103–104.
3. *Ibid.*, p.106.
4. Archibald Fleming, *Archibald the Arctic* (London: Hodder and Stoughton, 1957), p.71.
5. *Ibid.*, p.116.
6. John Lyons, *Chomsky* (third edition) (London: Fontana, 1991), p.134.
7. Richard Lovett, *The History of the LMS 1795–1895* (London: Frowde, 1899), p.121ff.
8. Papias, cited by Eusebius, *Hist. Eccl.III.xxxix.15*.
9. Acts 21:37; 22:2.
10. Acts 14:11.
11. Genesis 41:45; Acts 7:22.
12. Daniel 1:4.
13. Richard T. France, 'Henry Martyn' in *Five Pioneer Missionaries* (London: Banner of Truth, 1965), p.250.
14. See my account in *Mission and Meaning, Essays presented to Peter Cotterell*, Billington, Lane and Turner, eds (Exeter: Paternoster, 1995), p.169ff.
15. Herbert Birks, *Life of T. Valpy-French, Bishop of Lahore* (London: Murray, 1895), p.47.
16. *Ibid.*, Vol. 1, p.74.
17. *Ibid.*, Vol. 2, p.372.

18. Patrick McElligott, *On Giant's Shoulders* (Gerrards Cross: WEC, 1994).

19. George Smith, *Life of William Carey* (Everyman Edition), Preface.

20. Constance Padwick, 'Unpredictable Impressions of the Life and Work of John Ethelstan Cheese' in *The Muslim World*, Hartford Seminary Foundation LVII No. 4 1967.

21. Alfred Mathieson, *Judson of Burma* (London: Pickering & Inglis), p.79.

22. Eugene Stock, *History of the CMS* (London: CMS, 1899), p.184.

23. John and Shan Barry, May 1998 letter to 'Queridos Amigos'.

24. Florence Young, *Pearls from the Pacific* (London: Marshalls, c1925), pp.78f.

25. Jessie Gregg, 'These Forty Years' in *China's Millions*, (December 1937), p.224.

26. Brewster, Thomas and Elizabeth, *Language Acquisition Made Practical: Field Methods for Language Learners* (Colorado: Lingua House, 1976).

27. *Ibid.*, p.7.

CHAPTER TWO

LAMBS BOND WITH WOLVES

Developing Empathy and Rapport

The one great secret of being an effective messenger and representative of the Lord Jesus Christ is to become like him as his disciples, not only in our character and lifestyle, but also in all our relationships with all other human beings. The good missionary makes friends with other human beings across ethnic and cultural barriers. Everything hangs upon our ability to relate to others – in a word to 'bond' with other people. While this is the overall theme of the book as a whole, this chapter tries to explain how such bonding takes place, to indicate some of the hindrances to bonding and to suggest approaches to achieving such a relationship.

The attraction of the *Dances with Wolves* story is the way John Dunbar relates to the Indian community. He identifies with the tribe and bonds with its members. From his initial suspicion and fear, and his feelings of loneliness and rejection, he moves into increasing acceptance and warm friendship. Dunbar's sense that here was 'a whole separate race of humans' and that 'he would never know them' are the initial fears of most of us when we first confront a new and apparently alien culture. You can be repelled by some cultural aspects.

The word 'Eskimo' was originally a derogatory word used by Indians meaning 'people who eat uncooked meat' describing a race of human beings fighting for survival in the Arctic without cereals or vegetables. In that context the Scottish missionary Fleming writes:

> I do not mean that I took delight in every aspect of life among the Eskimo. When I saw the family squatting on the skin-covered sleeping-bench at mealtime pulling and tearing at the raw flesh of a recently killed seal, the blood oozing out between their fingers and dripping from their hands and chin, I felt nauseated and repelled beyond measure. Yet I asked myself, Was this not the way our Anglo-Saxon forefathers in Britain ate only a few centuries ago? . . . such thoughts kept me humble and helped me to look upon my people with sympathy and understanding.[1]

At church services and student meetings when we first arrived in Singapore in 1957, I used to watch the faces of industrious, efficient Chinese and wonder if I would, or even could, *ever* get to know and understand what made them tick. And there was no language barrier, for those we got to know had all been educated in English, and spoke it well. Some could speak no Chinese at all, though many spoke Cantonese and Hokkien at home. But in spite of common language, there seemed to be a cultural glass wall between them and us. We wondered whether we could ever get through it. Initially we were still at the stage of 'all Chinese look alike': which exactly parallels 'all Africans look alike', and it comes as little surprise to realise that Asians and Africans often say 'all Europeans look alike'. Our early thought processes went something like this: 'Well, never mind, we are only here for six months – but because of a common language this ought to be easier than Japan is going to be, and even though we can talk in English, really relating to people is going to be difficult.' (We didn't know at the time that after ten years in Japan, we were to live thirteen years in Singapore.)

What actually happened was that the mass of strange faces began to resolve very quickly into recognisable, friendly individuals whose names we knew, and with whom there were the faint beginnings of relationship. The feelings of strangeness slowly began to dissolve, the more so because of kindness towards us on their side. Some people were kind enough to pick us up and take us to church in their cars (even forty years ago the elite Singaporean students appeared to be materially much better off than those in Britain), or bothered to talk and help us feel at home; and we began to perceive them as distinct personalities, even though initially we found Cantonese personal names difficult to remember.

In cross-cultural Christian ministry, human relationship is basic. The essential secret of effectiveness is friendship and bonding with national Christians. *Good missionaries are those who form lasting friendships: bad missionaries are those who, however hardworking, fail to relate to national Christians.* A Kenyan theological student once told me that when a newly-appointed expatriate teacher arrived at their college, Africans discussed between themselves, and watched to see whether the new missionary would 'become a brother' or not. What matters is not so much how we missionaries perceive ourselves, but more importantly how we are perceived by those among whom we are going to work.

There is a significant brief essay written by the Brewsters on missionary bonding.[2] However, in order to see what they are getting at, and the attitudes they are trying to correct I need to outline some of the drawbacks of the existing traditional system.

Staying out of the expatriate ghetto

John Dunbar would normally have lived inside a military fort along with other American cavalrymen, isolated from human contact with the indigenous population. His experience of cross-cultural bonding was only made possible because he was all alone and had no other human beings to relate to apart from the native Indian community. Expatriate minorities always tend to huddle together protectively to give one another mutual support in what, often albeit unconsciously, they perceive as a threatening alien environment. It is this fortress mentality that leads to the development of a ghetto syndrome. There is an excellent article on the subject of 'The Missionary Ghetto' by Charles Taber,[3] in which he suggests that the advantages of ghettos are all pragmatic and superficial and completely overshadowed by the disadvantages, which are unavoidable and virtually fatal.

Some nineteenth-century biographies show just how much the new arrival from overseas was expected to identify with and conform to the expatriate subculture. William Carey in Calcutta, Robert Morrison in Canton, Hudson Taylor in Shanghai and David Livingstone in Africa were all automatically entangled from the outset with other foreigners from their own or other nations, who expected them to identify with them in preference to the local people.

The missionary society always means well. They act kindly in attempting to shelter the newly-shorn missionary lamb from fresh cultural winds. They try to lower new missionaries gently in at the shallow end of the cultural pool to avoid the risk of their drowning! Almost certainly the new arrival will be enrolled in a *language school* along with other foreigners. The language teachers will be nationals, often quite westernised ones, and even if they refuse to speak any English,

English will probably be the common language of the student community, which naturally outnumbers its teachers. It will probably be arranged for the newcomers to live with, or close to, *senior missionaries* who can explain local customs and help them settle in. You may even be expected to live in that hideous anachronism, a *mission compound* (see below). Those responsible for budgeting the money will argue that if rooms are available inside the compound, why spend money to rent expensive rooms outside.

If mission offices and language schools are in major cities, there may well be a convenient *international church*. If you try to attend a local national church, you initially understand little apart from stage directions like 'Let us pray', 'Let us stand up', etc. and it is difficult to talk to anyone intelligently. The international congregation, on the other hand, offers comprehensible teaching which hopefully blesses us, and is full of friendly expatriates wanting to make us feel at home, offering us familiar food such as we enjoy eating (and better than we could afford on a mission budget), and good conversation in our own heart language. If we delay our arrival until we have children, the pressure to take them to services in our own native tongue will be strong indeed. Once we start attending an expatriate congregation in our own language it becomes increasingly difficult to cut the umbilical cord and move out into a local church using the native language(s).

It is much easier to identify in the rural outback, but the increasing number of growing cities make it harder to identify – with mission offices, language schools, international schools for children, international churches and lonely expatriates wanting to get together with other expatriates in the evenings and at weekends. The international community of people working in secular business firms or in embassies and consulates will hopefully include committed Christians eager to involve us in expatriate Bible studies to reach non-Christian expatriates. We will need to be strong-minded to insist on carving out time to start making friends with national Christians. Adoniram Judson, arriving in Burma, refused to conduct services for expatriates: he had to be single-minded; he had come to reach the Burmese, not to evangelise British colonial expatriates however spiritually needy.

I hope you are beginning to picture this cartoon of new missionaries living in an expatriate ghetto, occasionally plucking up courage to sally forth to distribute tracts and take prisoners, but then hurrying back to the safety of the foreign citadel, pulling up the drawbridge and lowering the portcullis. If such new arrivals make any national friends at all, they will be westernised individuals who speak English and like cultivating friendships with foreigners, and not always with the best of motives!

Worse, in this expatriate ghetto you may well pick up foreigners' criticisms of the national culture and lifestyle, and their 'us' and 'them' attitudes. In the old days words like 'Wog'[4] and 'Chinaman' were derogatory in tone, and even today one hears phrases like 'Chinesey' and 'Japanesey' that carry implied, if unspoken, criticism. There is a sad conversation early in E.M. Forster's *Passage to India* in which Dr Aziz, the lawyer Mahmoud Ali and Cambridge educated Hamidullah are discussing 'whether or no it is possible to be friends with an Englishman'.[5] They conclude that many of them 'come out intending to be gentlemen' and initially treat Indians as fellow human beings, but that before long the expatriate community gets at them, and they adopt arrogant and patronising attitudes of racial superiority. They comment that: 'They all become exactly the same, not worse, not better. I give any Englishman two years. . . . And I give any Englishwoman six months. All are exactly alike.'

Forster's characters are right: so often snobbish and racial attitudes towards local people are spread within the expatriate community. They criticise perceived indigenous shortcomings, just as the three Indians were criticising the British. Whether native or expatriate, we are all subject to group pressure to accept the 'us' and 'them' polarisation. This may not matter as far as secular expatriate cliques are concerned, reprehensible as it is, but for Christians commissioned as heralds of the king of kings it can be fatal to our future usefulness.

Fortunately in many parts of the world mission compounds are things of the past: but some of them survive as almost literal fortresses. I saw such a Presbyterian mission compound in Korea (when that country was still very poor and there was a great deal of thieving), surrounded by high walls with barbed wire, with a gatekeeper, a guard patrolling with a dog and bars on the windows. Even then it did not keep bold and ingenious thieves out. The missionary most appreciated by national Christians (and incidentally with the best language!) was a Presbyterian single lady who lived outside the compound and shared her tiny apartment with a Korean woman. There were other such compounds in Manila, belonging to a major service agency, with houses provided on site for all its members and English language services on the compound in English for its expatriate and national staff.

My advice to societies and to individual missionaries is to stay out of expatriate ghettos, the product of unconscious xenophobia and great hindrances to our effectiveness in Christian service. Keep your objectives clearly in mind: we must learn the native language(s), identify with national churches, make lifelong friends, and bond with indigenous Christians. You will fail to achieve your goals if you get sucked into the expatriate community, however kind and welcoming it may be. 'Any missionary strategy which minimises or places obstacles in the way of effective personal relationships is self-defeating . . . . [the ghetto] is a prison when it hinders him from taking the initiative in establishing social relationships with people.'[6]

The Brewsters and bonding

The concept of bonding was amusingly described by Konrad Lorenz,[7] who by crouching and quacking persuaded newly hatched ducklings to follow him as a kind of surrogate mother. The Brewsters draw the parallel of the new-born baby, who properly should bond with his parents, but who if left in hospital too long can bond with hospital personnel instead. Just after birth the new-born infant is stimulated, adrenaline levels are at a peak, and physiological and psychological forces prepare the child to become bonded to its parents. The birth is essentially an entrance into a *new culture* with new sights, new sounds, new smells, new positions, new environment and new ways of being held.[8]

This first birth is analogous to the rebirth experienced by the missionary entering a new culture. Like new-born babies they are bombarded with new experiences and ready to bond; how they spend their first few weeks is critical. As we have seen, the danger is that instead of bonding with national Christians, they may merely bond with the expatriate community and with fellow missionaries. The typical tempering of the wind to the shorn lamb for its protection is not helpful if the missionary lamb is to learn to dance with the gentile wolves and come to love and understand them.

Many years ago a parachurch organisation made what seemed like a generous offer to missionaries – a fully furnished caravan with air conditioning, water filtration, a built-in screen and full set of Fact and Faith films. It was a lovely hygienic little capsule, and, as the benefactors pointed out, if the situation became politically disturbed, you could just drive it away to some safer area or country! Any missionary thus equipped would resemble some alien from outer space making occasional sorties into human society, and after this foreign foray retreating into his space vehicle. Stephen Spielberg's ET may have longed to 'go home' but he did succeed marvellously in bonding with native American kids!

Other missionaries may be less well equipped, but still live in sub-cultural ghettos, venturing out sometimes into the hostile, alien world before hurrying back again to their safe refuge. This kind of Christian worker never builds significant relationships with the community, always failing to bridge the cultural gap. The same problem of alienation and what the Germans call *entfremdung* can occur even within our own country. Two of my contemporaries whom I much admired had, when I first knew them, the polish typical of ex-public school men. One played cricket for England, the other took first class honours in theology. Both of them were much altered by their experiences as Anglican clergymen: one in the East End of London and the other in Liverpool. They started to think differently and to bond with people of very different social sub-cultures. It is this kind of crossing of cultural boundaries and learning to live in new situations which is called for in all missionary work.

Expressing this in a more theological way, we need to implement the doctrine of a universal, multiracial church (which doubtless we embrace with enthusiasm in theory) with the actual human beings we meet in other nations. They may not belong to our social group, our national group or our ethnic group – but they are fellow human beings, made by the same creator. They are fellow believers, brothers and sisters in Christ. And so you must bond with them. The minister or missionary who complains, 'I am lonely; I have no friends' has failed to bond emotionally with those who belong to the same worldwide family in Christ.

To bond or not to bond, that is the question. It is a huge and significant issue. The first few weeks are critical. Plunge in at the deep end – live with the people, eat with the people, worship with the people, go shopping with the people, travel by train and bus, walk or use a bicycle. Those glass-windowed boxes on wheels that Americans and Europeans drive about in cut us off from meeting ordinary people. Jesus lived with his disciples – they walked together, talked together, ate together, took boat trips together.[9] The Lord Jesus himself is *the* supreme model of effective identification and bonding. If we use Marshall McLuhan's language, tribal man bonds more effectively than either Gutenberg man or electronic man. Missionaries have to merge these three paradigms.

Three differing roles[10]

We need to appreciate the differing roles that the newly arrived foreigner may adopt, as he or she seeks to cross cultural barriers.

1. Guest

Our kind and courteous hosts will always treat us as guests when we first arrive. The short-term visitor automatically tends to accept this role as a matter of course and to experience no other. Everyone is very polite to you, defers to you, treats you with great respect, takes good care of you, and even appears to invite you to express your opinion on various things. It is very pleasant; it flatters our egos and makes us feel special. But it underlines all the more that we do not belong: we are respected guests to be fêted. It is pure human kindness on the part of those who welcome us. But it can go to our heads. It is horrible really, for we are being treated as aliens and we remain aliens. We can even seem to be saying: 'Make a fuss of me. I am a great man, a significant woman, and even if I am not, I enjoy being treated as such!' You may have to put up with a little of this to start with, but get out of it as quickly as possible, without being rude or ungracious.

The guest is often asked how this or that compares with our home country's ways of doing things. If we are critical it just confirms how alien we are. People do not really want to hear unfavourable comparisons: the excellence of our own country is not a necessary constituent of the gospel. I did once hear of a man living in one of the Manila ghettos I mentioned earlier, who at his farewell meeting told his hearers that he was returning to 'God's own country'. Extraordinarily, he was not joking but quite serious: a very defective doctrine of creation manifestly for 'the whole earth is full of his glory'.

Sometimes things are said specifically to test us. An Inuit friend living at 73 degrees north in the Canadian Arctic made some comment to me about 'us primitive people'. I looked at him and grinned: 'Any human beings who can live and survive under conditions here are anything but primitive. You have to be extremely advanced human beings, courageous, adaptable, innovative and persevering. I am full of admiration for people like you. I doubt whether I would survive more than a few weeks up here on my own, if that!' (This courteous Eskimo was married to a lady from Palmer's Green in London, so he had come to understand our culture also!) The guest is treated with respect, whether we deserve it or not, but that respect stems from the kindness of our hosts rather than from any merits of ours.

We need to see that the 'guest' role, enjoyable as it may be, gives no lasting foundation for the building of genuine friendships between equals. It is a temporary pedestal from which we need to descend as rapidly as is politely possible! We have to crucify our desire to be affirmed and made a fuss of.

2. Learner

Dunbar can be seen learning from the Indians. He is much impressed by the speed with which they can break camp and the extreme mobility with which they can move off to fresh hunting grounds. To start with, all of us begin as cultural morons and linguistic idiots. We are all familiar with the pregnant phrase: 'You must be born again!' Entry into a new country or culture is indeed like starting all over again as a helpless baby. As human babies we make noises, but nobody can understand what we mean. Our parents and brothers and sisters make noises at us, and we do not know what they mean. All we can do in the early months is to contract our masseter muscles and smile. And the advice in most cultures is that if you can do nothing else initially to communicate at least you can smile at people just as a baby does. Writing in a valuable book on language learning, the Brewsters also say this:

> A person who wants to learn another language often has legitimate responsibilities to perform, and these should help motivate him to learn the language well. But in language learning, the attitude of superiority that often goes (subconsciously) with the sophisticated role must be laid aside. The learner must assume the role of a learner: he must act like a learner.[11]

This is a problem especially for those working with relief organisations, even Christian ones, and with other 'experts' working in co-operation with missions. They somehow remain part of the expatriate community rather than bonding with the local population. There are some glorious exceptions, but they are less common than those who remain always as 'foreigners' working in a 'foreign land'.

The attitude of the learner has to be 'Teach me, for I am a fool'. A Thailand tribal missionary got lost in the mountains trying to find his way to a village. Eventually somebody met him and put him on the right road. Everyone seemed very amused that anyone could be so clueless as to get lost. When the time came for him to leave they offered him a guide to show him the way back to the nearest road – a six-year-old child! Very humiliating, but those who are familiar with their own environment often find it hard to understand the helplessness of the stranger.

Being a learner makes one feel very vulnerable and unsafe. It is a good lesson in humility. As we try to understand the unwritten subtleties of a culture, we are always asking questions, just as small children do. Where? What? And above all, Why? A fellow staff worker of ours in Japan came to stay with us for a *miai* (literally 'look-meet'), a kind of orchestrated 'blind date' celebrated *en masse* by both families. Our friend lived in the Kobe-Osaka region. The Christian lady in question came from the far north of Honshu, Akita prefecture. Why did they not arrange a marriage with, say, the Secretary of the Graduates Christian Fellowship in Osaka, I wondered? Well, we thought of her, but she is very outspoken and would have to live with his parents, and so not such a good idea. Well, surely there must be a suitable Christian lady in the Tokyo area. What about that beautiful young woman whose sister got married last month? Isn't it her turn next? Yes, well, we considered her also, but she is sensitive about the same things as he is. Well, I asked in some exasperation, what on earth does this lady from the rural north have that none of the others do? Is she a gifted soul-winner? Well, we don't know yet, she was only baptised last month. It turned out that both parties originally came from families involved in fishery businesses in the north. At last it began to dawn on me that though both were Christians, it was also important the match should be socially appropriate. (It was incidentally a marvellously successful marriage: they remain special friends, whose family and church life we greatly admire.) This puzzling out of things, which everybody in the new culture takes for granted, and never thinks of explaining to outsiders, is part of the adventure of cross-cultural learning.

We should make progress as we become more familiar with a culture and how things are done, but it will take a long time to catch up with those who are native to a particular culture. The Penun tribe in the jungles of Sarawak have been nomadic, and are perfectly adapted to life in tropical rain forests: their eyes are constantly sweeping the environment to see all that an outsider would entirely fail to see.

The attitude of being a learner is not one that we should grow out of: the quality of *insatiable curiosity* is indispensable to the missionary who wants to understand his or her new culture, its history, traditions and ways of doing things. The more we understand, the better we shall be able to communicate gospel truth in new words and new metaphors in a way relevant to culture. Some years ago in the Bario Highlands of Borneo, I was expounding the Sermon on the Mount. After all, I thought, though I am very ignorant of the lifestyle of my hosts, if I stick to Scripture I can't go wrong. Then I began to realise that I could not even do that: how do these Kelabit tribal people 'store up treasure on earth' in this non-cash culture (at that time). I did not know. I had to ask – ownership of water buffaloes and ancient glass beads stored in old Chinese jars are the closest to 'capital' they had at that time. But I would not have known without asking. We must humble ourselves to become learners.

3. Friend

The process of identifying and bonding should lead us into friendship. We shall not get there overnight. Even when people in a particular culture are apparently outgoing and friendly, they still may not make friends lightly or easily. It takes time to trust a foreigner. Part of the problem is our inability to express ourselves in the appropriate words. We may have learned words to buy train tickets, or to ask directions to the post office, but our limited vocabulary makes it difficult at first to express feelings and friendliness. We still use words in the new language like blunt instruments, and subtleties and nuances (so important in cultures that convey meaning in an indirect fashion) are often beyond us. The new language learner just does not know how to imply something tactfully without actually saying it. We behave like linguistic bulls in cultural china shops, even when we are trying hard to be tactful.

Initially our communication will be limited, but as we get to know people over an extended period our friendship will deepen. Women are often better at making friends than men are. Sometimes it takes some family crisis, illness, bereavement or suffering and the opportunity to give or to receive help to deepen mere acquaintance into lasting friendship. Fleming, working in the Arctic, knew what it was to share in the hunger of the Inuit community when blizzards prevented the hunters to go out after seal.

> But because we had been so closely linked with the people in their days of strain and adversity, and because we had helped them to the limits of our own resources, we discovered a brotherhood of feeling and action which drew us together as nothing else could have done and made us feel an at-one-ness which we had not known before.[12]

Fleming also describes his developing friendship with Joseph Pudlo as they worked together:

> Our friendship that lasted through many years was broken only at his death. He had the honour of being the first full-time native catechist in the service of the mission. Together we travelled far and wide by sledge and dog team in order to reach hitherto unvisited tribes. It was on such expeditions that I came fully to understand and appreciate my fellow worker. It is sufficient to say that with each expedition my love and admiration for him increased . . . when he prayed aloud, the curtain that hid from my gaze the deep wells of his soul were drawn aside, and I became conscious of the richness of his spiritual experience and of the depth of his nature.[13]

The New Testament basis of friendship

Friendship is not just a technique for being effective in Christian work, but an intrinsic aspect of Christian character. Our first model in everything must be the Lord Jesus himself, not only in what he taught, but also in what he exemplified. The incarnate Jesus was an amiable, highly sociable and approachable person, relating to all sorts of people across the social spectrum. Matthew contrasts him with the ascetic John the Baptist,[14] remaining out in the desert. So well known is his capacity for friendship that he is criticised for it in that passage as 'the friend of tax collectors and sinners'. He may have retired to pray on his own 'a great while before day', but the general picture we have of him once the day begins is surrounded by people all day long. There are no fewer than seven dinner parties in Luke's Gospel, and Jesus is a popular after-dinner speaker. The wedding at Cana shows him giving a wedding present, astonishing both in generous quantity and lavish quality. He saved the face of a family in danger of disgrace before the whole village because of failing in hospitality.

Instead of gibes about Stingy Simon or Mingy Menachem, for years afterwards people would remember that they had never tasted wine like that before or since. The presence of this highly sociable and attractive person, the man Christ Jesus, brings joy to all that meet him.

Some church pastors hesitate to become friends with those in their congregation, fearing others will misunderstand this as favouritism. But the Lord Jesus himself chose twelve, whom he called friends (John 15:14–15). Sometimes he chose three of those to be with him on especially significant occasions like the transfiguration and in Gethsemane; and he was known to have special friends like Lazarus, Martha and Mary: 'Jesus loved Martha and her sister and Lazarus.'[15] Are we spiritually stronger than Jesus that we can afford to live without friends? A psychiatrist friend of mine[16] regards both 'tycoon type' and 'servant type' ministers as being in a psychiatrically perilous situation. The secure person is the 'member type', that is someone who has bonded into the church family, and does not regard themselves as pastoring a different species whom they are in danger of treating as literal sheep. Those Jesus was training to build his church, the twelve most of all, he treats as friends, and exhorts them to treat each other as friends.

> Love each other as I have loved you. Greater love has no one than this, that one lay down his life for his friends. You are my friends if you do what I command. I no longer call you servants, because a servant does not know his master's business. Instead I have called you friends, for everything that I learned of my Father, I have made known to you. This is my command: Love each other.[17]

There is a close relationship in Greek between the various words for love and for friendship. Christ is not only to be our own closest friend, but commands us his followers to give that kind of committed friendship to one another. As we develop such bonding between us as Christian friends, we are only being obedient to the command of our Lord. Perhaps we have never thought of developing friendships as being a mark of Christian growth in holiness.

It is remarkable how frequently words for friend and friendship crop up in the letters and ministry of the apostle Paul. In Ephesus some of the council of the Asiarchs were his friends (and non-Christian friends at that, or their conversions would have been recorded).[18] When the ship on which Paul is being taken under guard to Rome stops in Sidon, the centurion Julius allows Paul to go to his friends.[19] The unique word translated 'hospitably' is literally 'in a friendly manner' of the developing relationship with Publius of Malta.[20] We often think of Paul as a somewhat rugged, self-sufficient personality, but it emerges that he has a huge warm Jewish capacity for friendship: he is, to use a Yiddish phrase, 'a real mensch'!

The last chapter of Romans is remarkable in a letter addressed to a city that Paul had never yet visited: he knows no fewer than twenty-six people there by name, of whom nine are women. Indeed, Epaenetus, Ampliatus, Stachys and the woman Persis[21] are all, one after the other, singled out as 'friends'. This man has built up a network of friends all around the Mediterranean, and he keeps in touch with their movements. Elsewhere in his letters six more individuals are described in this same way: Timothy;[22] Tychichus;[23] Epaphras;[24] Onesimus;[25] Luke[26] and Philemon.[27] I find this impressive and compelling: this man knows how to make and keep friends. But he uses other words that express a sense of relationship: in the letter to the Philippians he speaks of having the 'same soul',[28] and later calls Timothy a 'kindred spirit'.[29] If we have expounded the command of Jesus to his followers to love each other, in the context where he speaks of friendship, correctly as a command to build a network of friendships between the members of the Christian community, then Paul provides us with a wonderful illustration of precisely that. Christians are not expected to be loners and alien outsiders but are commanded to demonstrate that warm capacity for human friendship that we have seen illustrated in the Scriptures.

So we do not have an option on whether to develop this capacity for friendship. Obedience to the commands of the Lord Jesus, and following the pattern set by New Testament Christians *compel* us towards friendship. We may not opt for committed diligence, while remaining detached and keeping other people at arm's length. We are there to model the Lord Jesus to those to whom we go: 'Follow my example, as I follow the example of Christ.'[30]

One of the chief and most lasting joys for missionaries is keeping in touch with their national Christian friends. The aged John says, 'I have no greater joy than to hear that my children are walking in the truth' (3 John: 4). We may not feel old enough to be that paternalistic, but we can testify to the joy we experience when our friends walk and revel in the truth, and lead fruitful lives of Christian service. It gives huge pleasure!

This ability to relate to people is crucial to evangelism. A Japanese friend describes it as the ability to 'touch the heart': that is, to establish empathy and rapport with other human beings. It takes both friendliness and an outgoing character, a genuine concern for other people, *and* an understanding of language and culture to achieve this successfully. It is not always easy to explain how this development of interpersonal relationships takes place, for there is something indefinable about rapport and empathy. Just as a friendly puppy makes friends non-verbally by enthusiastic tail-wagging, so we need to make plain by our facial 'tail-wagging' and outgoing attitudes that we like people, want to serve them and get to know them better.

A classic example of a rugged and dedicated pioneer who recognised his own inadequacy at forming relationships was the dour Scot, George Hunter, who lived in Urumchi in Xinjiang for nearly forty years. Mildred Cable writes frankly of these difficulties:

> By nature uncommunicative and at all times slow to share the deep things of life with others, he now lived surrounded by men to whom the most vital matters of his Christian life were but an occasion for idle curiosity or even light jest . . . for nearly a decade he lived alone and he carried this inward isolation so far that he even lost all natural desire for a companion, largely owing to the fact that among the Westerners whom he had met there did not appear to be one whom he considered suitable to share the life to which he had now completely adapted himself, and it never occurred to him to make friendship with a native of the country.[31]

Even when the younger Percy Mather finally joined him in 1914, and after enduring years of close companionship and shared hardships, and developing almost a father and son relationship, they retained the formality of addressing each other as 'Mr Hunter' and 'Mr Mather' a rigidity of a bygone generation that survived even to the 1950s as a traditional formality of the China Inland Mission.[32]

This raises the issue of how far such difficulties relate to our cultural traditions, and to our gender. Anna Ford once wrote that men are 'emotional pygmies', and it seems that women are much better at relating with each other than men are at relating with other men. 'Men are remarkably good at avoiding confrontation in areas of personal relations they would rather leave untouched. Men are successfully self-deluding in their behaviour towards others, and often lack the ability to empathise with even those closest to them.'[33]

Her whole book rather relentlessly rubs in this apparent weakness on the part of men to be in touch with their emotions, and incapable of discussing them even with their wives and those closest to them. Many of us are conscious of these difficulties in communicating even in our own language within our own cultures, and it seems we need to pray to our God (the God who communicates) that we learn how to relate across ethnic and linguistic barriers. In the final analysis we need to be swamped by the realities of our Christian theology: that we belong to a mission-hearted God who loves all human beings equally, and requires that we should learn to do the same. We are to learn to love all those whom he loves. If we feel inadequate in this area we need to get down on our knees and ask the Lord to share with us his heart, his love and ability to relate to every creature he has made. We need the gift of making friendships and building relationships across cultural frontiers. Yes, human beings rebuff the Lord on a regular basis, but he keeps on coming back to try again to establish relationship. All day long he reaches out to people. It is extraordinary that he does not stand on his dignity, and weird that we should ever try to stand on ours! We need that gentle vulnerability that is willing to share thoughts and feelings.

The iceberg of communication

Care and Counsel, sadly no longer in existence, produced a diagram of an iceberg of communication, with superficial comments about the weather or telling jokes just emerging above the surface.

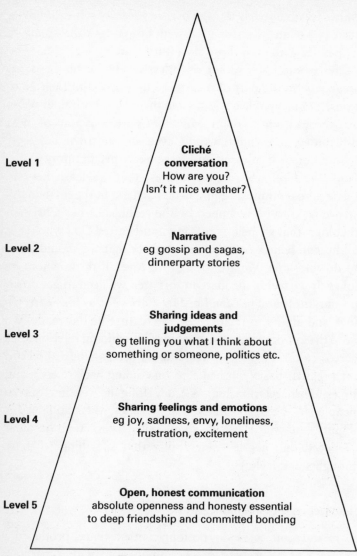

Level 1

Cliché conversation
How are you?
Isn't it nice weather?

Level 2

Narrative
eg gossip and sagas,
dinnerparty stories

Level 3

Sharing ideas and judgements
eg telling you what I think about
something or someone, politics etc.

Level 4

Sharing feelings and emotions
eg joy, sadness, envy, loneliness,
frustration, excitement

Level 5

Open, honest communication
absolute openness and honesty essential
to deep friendship and committed bonding

The iceberg of communication

There are several more layers of communication before we reach down to true heart-sharing. This establishes how superficial so many of our human contacts can be and how hard we have to work to establish real communication. The barriers of language often require us to initiate relationship in Levels 1 and 2 because we are not yet capable of expressing ourselves at any deeper level. We realise that without progress in language study we cannot make much progress in relationships. But this diagram helps us to realise how relationship deepens when some crisis in our own lives or those of others enables us to relate more deeply. I have modified it to apply to cross-cultural communication.

Secular models

We shouldn't be surprised that sensible people in the business world recognise these same principles. In my daughter's home my attention was caught by a chapter in Stephen Covey's book *The Seven Habits of Highly Effective People*[34] headed 'Principles of Empathic Communication'. It was full of good and helpful comments, seeing the key to effective interpersonal communication as: Seek first to understand, then to be understood. I was tempted to write it all off as business techniques for manipulation until I read:

> you first need to understand me. And you can't do that with technique alone. If I sense you are using some technique, I sense duplicity, manipulation. I wonder why you are doing it, what your motives are. And I don't feel safe enough to open myself up to you.

Some soul-winning techniques come perilously close to manipulation. Again and again as I read, I wanted to reinforce it by applying Christian motives and showing Christ himself as the perfect model to be followed. This is not made any easier for the missionary with less than adequate language, because one is struggling to understand the words being used. 'Most people do not listen with the intent to understand; they listen with the intent to reply. They're either speaking or preparing to speak. They're filtering everything through their own paradigms, reading their autobiography into other people's lives.'[35]

Covey suggests five levels of listening:

1. *Ignoring* and not really listening at all, preoccupied by something else.
2. *Pretending* with automatic 'Uh huhs' (which as new language learners we are forced to do quite a lot in the early stages).
3. *Selective listening*, as when we listen to the chatter of a pre-school child.
4. *Attentive listening*, focusing energy on what a person is saying.
5. *Empathic listening*, in order to understand how the other person really feels, fully, deeply and emotionally as well as intellectually. It's not just registering or reflecting or even just understanding the surface meaning of words. Instead of 'projecting your own autobiography' (which is what a lot of Pinteresque conversations are!) you give them space to explain their own frame of reference, the reality inside their heads and hearts.

This fifth category is an essential step to bonding. 'If I speak in the tongues of men and of angels, but have not love' expresses the same thing: there has to be good language learning to grasp the meaning of words, but even excellence in language of the tongue is not enough; it has to be the language of the heart.

Empathic listening is also risky. It takes a great deal of security to go into a deep listening experience because you open yourself up to be influenced. You become vulnerable. It's a paradox, in a sense, because in order to have influence, you have to be influenced. That means you have really understood.[36]

He even suggests three Greek words – *ethos, pathos* and *logos* (all biblical words incidentally) to which somewhat arbitrary meanings are attached, where *ethos* is personal credibility, *pathos* is your alignment with the emotional thrust of another's communication and *logos* the reasoning part of communicating. He says rightly that many people try to jump straight to left-brain logic without first establishing relationships.[37] These notions do not even get close to biblical values in relating and bonding with people.

Clearly, much that comes out of the so-called 'neuro linguistic programming' school is seen as techniques to achieve excellence and success in business and in life[38] (a kind of updated version of Dale Carnegie's *How to make friends and Influence people*). The motivation is utterly suspect. We would say that from a biblical perspective 'bonding' is truly and spiritually 'being human', especially when it is also consistently Christian.

Obstacles to bonding and gaining acceptance

1. An undefined role

The Comanche were puzzled by Dunbar. What was a solitary white man doing at a military fort on his own? He was certainly courageous to the point of foolhardiness, but laughable as a fighting force. He was cleaner than most whites, kept the fort cleaner, and rode a horse very well for someone who was not an Indian. He treated them with respect and friendship was developing. But why was he there? And were more white

men coming? And what would happen then? He was manifestly a soldier and must be associated with an oppressive,
invading power in some way. Bishop Hannington of Uganda
died a martyr's death, because the Muganda were convinced
that the *Muzungu* (white men) were coming to 'eat up' their
country. The threat of the Germans on the coast, and their
subsequent conquest of East Africa showed that these anxie-
ties were real, and no less so when the British took over their
countries from the Germans.

Looked at from the viewpoint of the indigenous observer,
the missionary can seem something of an oddity. Why is he
there? What are her intentions? What is their relation with a
colonial power? Are they agents of some intelligence organisation like the CIA? Who pays them and provides support?
Japan closed its doors to Spanish Franciscans and Portuguese
Jesuits in the sixteenth century because Protestant Dutch and
English told them that priests paved the way for soldiers and
a colonial takeover, as happened in Latin America and in the
Philippines. There was clearly some truth in this, although
thoughtful Jesuit missionaries had already recognised that
Spain and Portugal could never conquer China and Japan as
they had done in South America.[39] Even in Latin America the
Jesuits had tried hard to defend native Christians from the
secular European colonists (as in *The Mission*). US President
Ford's ingenuous promise that the CIA would not use missionary organisations as information sources 'any longer' was not
entirely helpful either. It prompted some missions to give fresh
reminders to their members not to give information to their
own or other national intelligence organisations.

In Buddhist countries the common perception is that missionaries are trying to gain 'merit' for themselves by good works, that
is for their own benefit rather than anyone else's. Religious acti-
vism is seen as a form of salvation by works. Literature distribu-

tion is perceived as one form of this self-benefiting activity. Two missionaries in North Japan helped keep a neighbour's roof in place during a typhoon by hanging onto opposite ends of a rope slung across the roof: they had hoped this practical act would open doors for them. However, the local newspaper reported that the two had 'left the work of God' in order to assist!

How can the missionary be regarded as a useful and helpful member of society? Patrick McElligott (see chapter 1)[40] working as a church-planting missionary was asked if he would coach boys at the local school at football and referee matches on Saturday afternoons. He wanted to refuse because he was too busy and needed to prepare for Sunday. He accepted for a trial period, and then found everybody's attitude to him transformed. The boys were grateful and related to him, but their parents also felt under obligation to him for helping their children. After that church planting took off! Dunbar was accepted when he alerted the tribe to the buffalo herds, assisted in the hunt, saved the life of Smiles a Lot, and later helped repel an attack by murderous Pawnee Indians. T.E. Lawrence of Arabia (who once taught Sunday School at St Aldate's, Oxford, and whose older brother was a missionary doctor with the China Inland Mission)[41] won acceptance by saving a man's life from dying of thirst at the risk of his own and by helping the Arabs to defeat the Turks. In South Thailand, Malay peasants would not have valued a doctorate, but a Maori missionary from New Zealand won acceptance when he remained seated upon an unbroken horse for half an hour, and showed that he could cut up a cow faster than any of them could!

2. Failure to give acceptance (see also chapter 5 on relating with national Christians)

Certainly we need to gain acceptance, but we also need to *give* acceptance to national Christians and fellow workers. This requires the missionary to be humble and to expect and recognise the gifts and guidance of the Holy Spirit. It has always been a problem for Christians to recognise God' s working in those of a different ethnic group. After Peter had persuaded his critics in Jerusalem of the Holy Spirit's work in the house of Cornelius, their almost comical response seems to mingle reluctant astonishment with near incredulity: 'So then, God has granted even the Gentiles repentance unto life.'[42] We all find it hard to believe that others have received the Holy Spirit just as we have.

So there needs to be a two-way process of mutual acceptance; Wind in His Hair and Kicking Bird needed to know that Dunbar accepted and respected them and their culture. Racial prejudice and feelings of cultural superiority, or even the national Christian's suspicion that the expatriate might have such attitudes, are enemies of true fellowship among Christian believers in a multiracial church. Prejudice works both ways: on the one hand it is indigenous suspicion and prejudice against foreigners, and on the other hand our own innate sinful pride and stupid feelings of ethnic superiority. We need to anticipate this and to overcome it by God's grace.

One of the advantages of the language learning barrier is that we have our noses rubbed in our cultural and linguistic ignorance. We pass through two or three years of self-imposed silence when we are only too aware that we can contribute nothing because we cannot yet communicate clearly. This sense of uselessness can be a sore trial to the Christian worker, especially for one who has been active in evangelism and teaching, and much used by God.

We have deliberately isolated ourselves in a world in which we are unable any longer to communicate and fulfil our God-given calling. We natural extroverts, prone to rush in where angels fear to tread, are forced into silence by our inability to use the foreign language with competence. Jesus says: 'For whoever exalts himself will be humbled, and whoever humbles himself will be exalted.'[43] The danger is that as we become more fluent, and able to preach the gospel, we become arrogant again and begin to feel indispensable, and fail to regard our national brothers and sisters as 'better' than ourselves.[44] That is why we need to maintain the attitude that the apostle took in Corinth: 'I did not come with eloquence or superior wisdom. . . . I came to you in weakness and fear, and with much trembling.'[45]

In short, with all this emphasis on what we need to do both to study and to bond with national Christians and non-Christians there is always the danger that we may forget our continuing constant dependence upon God to enable us through his Holy Spirit. We all need to recognise that it is the chief harvester himself who is the real missionary. He enables us to communicate, opens blind eyes, gives new birth and causes the church to grow.[46] We human co-labourers are often little more than privileged spectators of God at work. We are like small children 'helping' mother and father in the kitchen or garden: it's just a way of keeping us out of mischief while our parents actually get on with the job! It is God who is pleased to work, eager to work and we are his unskilled and clumsy assistants who keep on dropping things.

This aspect of the missionary attitude to local Christians is such a barrier to bonding and so important that the whole of chapter 5 is dedicated to it.

The struggle and its reward

For some people it is a costly thing to identify with other cultures and especially the poor and needy. It is disappointing when one hears today that some are reluctant to go to work in Eastern Europe and the former Soviet Union because the standard of living is low, and Christian workers are reluctant to take their families to live there. If that had been the attitude of our evangelical forebears, China, India and Africa might never have been evangelised at all. There are some interesting reactions to Hudson Taylor's insistence that China Inland Mission workers should adopt the Chinese dress of that time. 'I attribute a great deal of the quiet which we have had, to our wearing Chinese dress; we go about and are taken little notice of. When we were in Shanghai, every dog was barking at us; but no sooner had we put on Chinese costume, than the dogs left off barking at us.[47]

Hudson Taylor himself, writing in 1867, explains the motives behind all this:

> To get close access to the hearts of the people is our great aim: to win their confidence and love is our daily object. To effect this we seek as far as possible to meet them – in costume, in language, in manners. And to use this course, is not only advantageous; it is indispensable; no female in foreign dress could visit here as our sisters do in Chinese costume . . . it is an undoubted fact that one of the principal objections which the Chinese have to Christianity arises from it being esteemed a foreign religion. Why then not remove as far as possible its foreign surroundings?[48]

At a public meeting in London in 1884 the Lord Mayor read an extract from a report presented to Parliament by the British consul in Hankow (an interesting secular testimony):

> The China Inland Mission does little locally, but its members are now to be found living quietly, and making the name of foreigner a title of respect, in every part of the interior. They have been

sneered at by their own countrymen, for the first members of the Mission were not all of high position either with regard to education or culture, and poorly paid, and assuming Chinese dress and mode of living, it seemed they were more likely to breed contempt than to increase the strength of our position . . . they have taken Christianity throughout the land, and made the Chinese understand that listening to its teaching does not lead to their denationalisation. They come nearer to their hearts than their foreign-dressed and foreign-living brethren, and made them feel that they can still remain Chinese though they adopt the Christian faith . . . that not only men, but ladies, both married and single, are able to live year after year, hundreds, nay thousands of miles from foreign centres, without appeals from them for Consular intervention, is proof sufficient of their prudence and good conduct.[49]

And even today there are parts of the world where it is wise for missionaries to behave discreetly in observing the dress code regarded as appropriate in Islamic countries for example. Sleeveless dresses, low necks and bathing costumes will certainly give great offence in more conservative areas. Missionaries in Bangladesh grew beards and their wives wore the veil when it was culturally appropriate.[50]

The essence of such approaches is to remove everything that may seem foreign and alien in Christian practice so that superficial external barriers to becoming a Christian are removed. The Christian church is seen as indigenous, and part of its own culture. But there is also something distinctively Christian in following the apostle Paul, who became all things to all men in order to win some (1 Corinthians 9:22), and even more our teacher and Lord who identified with our human race, and chose to live in a poor, oppressed little country. There is a spiritual blessing in similarly identifying. Another early China missionary, Miss Bowyer:

I cannot help rejoicing that in every step I have taken towards assuming the dress and customs of this people, the Lord has given me a blessing in my own soul. It is so sweet to feel that He accepts it as done to Him. I do increasingly feel that the more heartily we can throw ourselves into the habits and customs of those around us, the more we shall experience the Divine blessing on our souls.[51]

It seems appropriate to give almost the last word to Bishop Fleming, summing up:

When first the winter came with its cold and bitter winds, I had looked forward with considerable trepidation to life in a snow village . . . I had learned that it is the common necessities that have priority value – food, shelter, light, heat, useful work and friendship . . . I also realized that only by living their life, and meeting them on their own ground, could we accomplish what we had set out to do. Beside, I had already come to love the people, and now I was to have the opportunity to share the most demanding part of their life . . . (and then in the igloos) in the long evenings as a member of this household watching the doings of young and old under the flickering flame from the blubber lamps, I knew I had come a long way from the River Clyde. I had learned to sit where they sat. I had found the peace I had sought in serving this once remote people who had now become my friends. I was glad that I had obeyed the Master's command 'Go tell.'[52]

Mary Ann Leisk was the orphaned daughter of Scottish parents in Batavia. She was the ward of Mary Ann Aldersey in Ningpo from 1840. She arrived in China at the age of fourteen, alongside Burella and Maria Dyer (the future Mrs Hudson Taylor) and married William Russell of CMS in 1852, later the first bishop of North China. She was said by Eugene

Stock to be one of the noblest missionaries in China, 'a mother in Israel indeed'. She died in 1887:

> deeply lamented by the Chinese of Ningpo, of whom she had been from her childhood the never-failing friend, whose language she spoke like one of themselves, who was more 'in touch' with them than any other missionary, and whose tender consideration for them, even for their failings, approached almost to a fault.[53]

One of the most moving examples of total identification short of the incarnation of the eternal Son of God is that of the remarkable Flemish Catholic missionary Joseph Damien De Veuster (1840–1889)[54] who volunteered to serve in a leper colony in the Hawaian islands. His earlier letters spoke of 'these lepers', but his later letters of 'we lepers'. It would be difficult to imagine a more thoroughgoing identification for a human missionary than this.

Paul's precedent of being self-supporting

If our perceived function is to proselytise and promote a new religion, we may not be regarded as being very helpful. It is here that the so-called 'tent maker', self-supporting mission-ary has great advantages over the church-supported evangel-ist. People often fail to realise that being church-supported is a relative novelty of the past two hundred years, impossible until the development of international banking. Before that all missionaries had to support themselves: the Jesuit Matteo Ricci did so by making clocks and maps, and giving clavicord lessons in Pekin; Jesuits in Japan were supported by a share in the silk trade with China; the Moravians all supported them-selves using their trade skills or by running a retail business, as did the early LMS missionaries and the first English CMS missionaries in New Zealand. So called 'mission stations' in the nineteenth century were usually self-supporting agricultural projects.

William Carey first supported himself in India by working as manager of an indigo plantation, and later supported his family and all the translation work at Serampore by lecturing in Calcutta College. Robert Morrison worked as an interpreter for the British East India Company in Canton. Henry Martyn and others were paid as chaplains in India. Miss Aldersey opened the first Chinese girls' school in Ningpo in 1844. Valpy-French opened St John's College, Agra, and later St John's Theological College, Lahore: in both places he was seen to be doing a definite job. On the whole, nineteenth-century missionaries were perceived by nationals to have other roles besides that of proselytism and planting churches, and because of this they were probably more acceptable and therefore more successful. The lack of a clear role constitutes a problem both for the missionary and for the national observer trying to understand why this person is here at all!

We often think of Paul as a model missionary, but most of the time he was a self-supporting one.[55] Luke tells us that he made tents in Ephesus and Corinth, but Paul's own letters show him working to support himself and others as a matter of principle. It is implied that he and Barnabas supported themselves on the first journey (1 Corinthians 9:6, 18); and that on the second journey he worked in Philippi, Thessalonica and Corinth; on the third journey in Ephesus and probably also when in Rome (Acts 18:3; 20:34; 28:30; 1 Corinthians 4:12; 1 Thessalonians 2:9). In this last reference, Paul says, 'working we proclaimed.' The participle 'working' defines the conditions in which the preaching was done. For us working and preaching are two mutually exclusive alternatives, but Paul seems to have been capable of preaching at the same time as he was working.

All these people were seen to be doing something materially productive to support themselves that earned them respect, status, recognition and acceptance in the eyes of society. Medical missionaries, doctors and nurses also enjoyed this. In Thailand the Presbyterian Dr Samuel House (in Thailand 1847–1876) and Dr Dan Bradley (in Thailand 1835–1873) were widely accepted because of their medical ministry. However, House's commitment to evangelism is clear. 'He [House] felt that whenever someone died who had not been led to Christ, he had failed his Master. A man of intense sympathy and understanding, House suffered whenever he could not relieve the suffering of others.'[56]

The great plus of the self-supporting expatriate in China or anywhere else is that they have a clearly-defined role and source of support: their witness to Christ may carry greater credibility, simply because they are not being paid to evangelise. The problem for those of us who are evangelists and church planters is that we are apparently paid by churches elsewhere in the world to make converts and start churches: in consequence people think we do it for money! While people in their homelands may know that most missionaries get a laughably small income, that is rarely evident to those among whom they are working.

Summing up then, to gain acceptance we need to find things to do that are not just for our own self-gratification nor even to replicate our own Christian sub-culture, but are seen to be of benefit to the ordinary people among whom we are living. As his language improved, Patrick McElligott found himself invited to lecture to parent-teacher associations on subjects like 'Home education: love between parents – a key to our children's future'. The relevance of what he was saying was clear to secular audiences, and he was able to reinforce them with a more overtly Christian message at such public lectures.[57] Many tribal missionaries provide a measure of unskilled medical help, dishing out antibiotics where appropriate to save life. One well-qualified physician trained tribal people as paramedical workers able to recognise and treat all the commonly occurring illnesses, as well as to recognise conditions that needed to be taken to the coast for hospital treatment. The usefulness of such work was clearly perceived by those who benefited from it.

There is possibly a lesson here for all professional religious workers. The agonies of *The Rector's Wife*[58] are partly solved when she gets herself taken on to do a job in her own right. The breakthrough often comes when minister or church can do something for society. In north London, our local minister served as secretary to the parent teacher association, and so came to know and be known by many other parents with children in the same school. There is a mining community of a thousand people in Queensland and a local Baptist church with more than a hundred members. The housing all belongs to the mining company or to the government. The pastor lives in a government house for he is a local schoolteacher: he also happens to be a trained chef. In this small community, the church provides the catering services: anybody wanting to arrange a wedding or family celebration requests the church to organise it. If some congregations were raptured, nobody would notice they had gone, but this one would certainly be missed. It is such involvement in the community and impact upon it that we need to aim at in every culture.

Notes

1. Thomas and Elizabeth Brewster, *Language Acquisition Made Practical: Field Methods for Language Learners* (Colorado: Lingua House, 1976).

2. E.T. and E.S. Brewster, *Bonding and the Missionary Task* (Pasadena, CA: Lingua House, 1982); also reprinted in Winter and Hawthorne, eds, *Perspectives on the World Christian Movement* (Pasadena, CA: William Carey Library, 1981), pp.452ff.

3. Charles R.Taber, 'The Missionary Ghetto' in *Practical Anthropology*, Sept–Oct 1971, Vol. 18, No 5.

4. Originally a quite respectable title, WOGS meaning 'Warranted on Government Service' for civilians employed in Egypt by the British Raj, it began to be used in a critical and derogatory way, further illustrating the way the colonial ghetto reacted against those without its walls.

5. E.M. Forster, *Passage to India* (Cambridge, 1924), pp.7–8.

6. Taber, *op. cit.*, p.194.

7. Konrad Lorenz, *King Solomon's Ring* (London: Pan Books, 1957), pp.62–63.

8. *Ibid.*, p.3.

9. See P.T. Chandapilla, *The Master Trainer* (Bombay: Gospel Literature Service, 1974), pp.17–18.

10. I owe this general insight here to Ruth Stoick Anaya, formerly a Pentecostal missionary in Kenya, and a missionary in residence at Regent College in 1990.

11. Brewster, *op. cit.*, p.7 (this book is often conveniently referred to as LAMP and will be here).

12. Fleming, *op. cit.*, p.83.

13. *Ibid.*, p.146.

14. Matthew 11:18–19.

15. John 11:5.

16. Dr Montague Barker, whom I have heard expounding this psychiatric problem of those in full-time Christian ministry: psychiatric dangers to which Christian workers are

exposed if they adopt clerical attitudes, rather than humble human ones.

17. John 15:13–14.

18. Acts 19:31.

19. Acts 27:3.

20. Acts 28:7.

21. Romans 16:5, 8–9, 12.

22. 1 Corinthians 4:17.

23. Ephesians 6:21; Colossians 4:7.

24. Colossians 1:7.

25. Colossians 4:9.

26. Colossians 4:14.

27. Philemon 1:3.

28. Philippians 2:2, *sumpsuchos*.

29. Philippians 2:20, *isopsuchos* that is literally 'same soul' or perhaps 'soul brother' in contemporary idiom.

30. 1 Corinthians 11:1.

31. Mildred Cable and Francesca French, *George Hunter: Apostle of Turkestan* (London: China Inland Mission, 1948) p.49.

32. *Ibid.*, p.52.

33. Anna Ford, *Men: A Documentary* (London: Weidenfeld and Nicholson, 1985), p. 251.

34. Stephen Covey, *The Seven Habits of Highly Effective People* (London: Simon and Schuster, 1992), pp.236ff.

35. *Ibid.*, p.239.

36. *Ibid.*, p.243.

37. *Ibid.*, p.255.

38. See, eg, O'Connor and Seymour, *Introducing NLP* (Harper-Collins, 1990).

39. Andrew Ross, *A Vision Betrayed: The Jesuits in Japan and China, 1542–1742* (New York: Orbis, 1994), pp.xii, 42–43.

40. Patrick McElligott, *op. cit.*, p.231ff.

41. J.S. Reynolds, *Canon Christopher* (Abingdon: Abbey Press, 1967), p.346 and also the records of the China Inland Mission (OMF).

42. Acts 11:18.

43. Matthew 23:12.

44. Philippians 2:3.

45. 1 Corinthians 2:1–3.

46. 1 Corinthians 3:6, 7, 9, 10.

47. Rudland, 1866 quoted in Frank Houghton, *The Fire Burns On* (London: China Inland Mission, 1965), p.117.

48. *Ibid.*, p.119.

49. *Ibid.*, pp.123–124.

50. Philip Parshall, *New Paths in Muslim Evangelism* (Grand Rapids: Baker, 1980), p.115.

51. Houghton, *op.cit.*, p.117.

52. Fleming, *op. cit.*, pp.68–80.

53. Eugene Stock, *History of the CMS* Vol.II, p.295, Vol III, p.560.

54. Anderson, *Biographical Dictionary of Christian Missions*, p.166.

55. See my longer exposition of this in *A Task Unfinished* (London: Monarch/OMF, 1996).

56. Donald Lord, *Mo Bradley and Thailand* (Grand Rapids: Eerdmans, 1969), p.41.

57. McElligott, *op. cit.*, p.301ff.

58. Joanna Trollope, *The Rector's Wife* (London: Black Swan, 1991), subsequently made into a BBC television series.

LAMBS FACE CULTURE SHOCK AND STRESS

For potential missionaries the prospect of 'culture shock' lurks like a bogeyman hiding on the dark corner of the staircase. In this chapter three things are underlined:

1. We all adjust to 'life changes' through normal human experience anyway, with minimal difficulty. It's part of our human condition, and *homo sapiens* is an extremely adaptable species. Adapting to culture change is really 'no big deal'.
2. Moving out into another culture inevitably results in an accumulation of extra stresses, but these are easily recognisable and readily absorbed.
3. Being made aware beforehand, and enabled to recognise the symptoms of cultural stress in ourselves, greatly reduces the degree of trauma experienced.

John Dunbar finds himself all alone at an abandoned frontier post, outnumbered by savage people wanting to steal his horse, his only mode of transport. They find him naked and defenceless, and repulse his first approach to their encampment. He has lost the supporting structures of the US cavalry, his status as a military hero, his ability to command and communicate: he is definitely the odd man out, all alone among hostile and alien people. Even when they begin to accept him, he can still make enormous cultural gaffes such as when asserting ownership of his hat, or baulking at the offer of raw buffalo liver still warm from the slaughtered beast. But let's start at the beginning.

In our familiar home environment we function on a kind of automatic pilot. We scarcely need to be more than slightly conscious to get out of bed, shower, shave, eat breakfast and travel to work. We are not normally particularly aware of being European, white, black, Catholic, Protestant, male, female, British, American, etc., nor do we have to think much about dress (if we are male anyway!) or what words to use.

But in a new culture we suddenly become acutely self-conscious and have to start thinking about every action we perform and every word we speak. All the normal cultural cues have disappeared; all those behaviour patterns we have learned and become familiar with since childhood have disappeared. Once in my student days I was travelling to a children's beach mission with a fellow student, an African from Kenya. We stayed overnight at my Aunty Olwen's home in Wales. Next morning she brought me a jug of hot water for a shave (in those days there was not always hot water in the taps). As I thanked her, I added, 'Is there some hot water for Tombo?' She put her hand to her mouth, reddened rather charmingly and said, 'Oh does he need it? I thought they just grew wool on their heads!'

I was reminded of this one morning several years later, when I tottered out of my first Japanese student conference to get my regular morning shave. Oddly, nobody else was looking for a place to shave. When at last I found a wash basin in a toilet, there was no hot water. This seemed very odd. Surely

Japanese do grow some facial hair? Surely older male students and staff workers would need to shave? The penny finally dropped late that afternoon when a stream of students poured into the baths and I realised (something I would never have found out in my own home) that Japanese men shave for dinner during their evening bath (unless they use electric shavers). At the conference I was suddenly floundering. Living in our own home in Tokyo, I had been able to stick with my familiar British schedule, but our reflex patterns are suddenly broken when we venture into the wider world.

The southern English are 'no touch' people, and seem to shake hands with reluctance except when being formal. I soon discovered when visiting Germany, Holland or Switzerland that I had to get used to shaking hands when arriving and leaving, even before going to bed at night and coming down to breakfast in the morning. I came to appreciate this custom, because there was conscious recognition of every other person present in the home. Whether adult, teenager or child: nobody got left out. Conversely, other Europeans visiting Britain find it equally difficult. The English are notoriously casual about greetings. They float in and out of conversations without introductions or farewells. German and French actually have expressions for the 'Englishman's farewell', just because it rarely happens – the English just quietly drift away from the scene!

When Africans greet each other it can be a prolonged performance. So Africans say, 'Europeans [meaning the British] are people who do not greet each other on the street.' Other cultures are much more tactile than ours. An Ecuadorian lady, commenting on the relative coldness of Canadians (whom the British find extremely warm and friendly), said that in her own culture she would embrace others in greeting several times every morning. Filipinos tend to hold your arm when speaking with you, like Coleridge's Ancient Mariner. It was stupid of me to be taken aback by Greek men greeting me by kissing me vigorously on both cheeks. Cultures at the opposite extreme avoid physical contact, and one might be excused for thinking that the Japanese bow is a reversion to the foetal position, though they express affection by eye contact. After living several years in Japan, I remember being acutely embarrassed when a Korean professor put his arm around me.

Travelling by sea from Yokohama to near Vladivostock, our children seeing a vast Siberian in a red sweater with his arm around a young woman, exclaimed, 'What *is* that man doing to her, Daddy?' for they had never seen such public demonstration of affection while growing up in Japan. Valerie and I felt we must conform to this custom in public, though when we were leaving after four years she took my arm on the ship in Hong Kong saying, 'Isn't it nice to be able to do this again!' But this too has changed in Japan over the half century, reminding us that cultures are never static. Perhaps the variety of body language between different cultures is what confuses us most.

No big deal?

We have established the self-evident fact that cultures differ from each other and that amusing conflicts can occur. But surely this isn't anything to get apprehensive about? Will we really commit such dreadful cultural gaffes that we shall have to abandon our cultural bridgehead and scuttle away back home with our tails between our legs? After all, huge numbers of people from wealthier countries pay out large sums every year to take holidays abroad in what to them are 'foreign' countries, and nobody ever seems to talk about 'culture shock' in that context. This may be because holiday visits are brief and temporary, and because tourists staying in western hotels never really get to grips with the real culture, but are treated with false deference, pampered with food and other treats. They are cushioned from the harsh realities and exploited for their money.

Even if we have never been outside our own country, we are aware that when we attend a conference, start a new job or enter a hospital as a patient, we have to make conscious adjustments to new surroundings and new people. Going to live overseas is a more long-term situation requiring greater adjustment. The stress we may face when we start living abroad is not because citizens of other countries are so astonishingly alien and different, but because we have lost some of our familiar landmarks and so feel slightly disorientated. Many books and films glory in the adaptability of human beings to adjust to new situations: *Dr Zhivago* and *Gone with the Wind* are classic examples. Zhivago, Scarlet O'Hara, Melanie Wilkes and Rhett Butler are the survivors. They are able to adjust to the most devastating changes in status and material circumstances. The problem for Ashley Wilkes is that he finds it almost impossible to adjust. Even fairy stories show their heroes, like Jack of beanstalk fame, adjusting to a new situation in a castle of giants. *Gulliver's Travels*, *Robinson Crusoe*, *Swiss Family Robinson* and the *Chronicles of Narnia* are all stories of how people learned to adjust to totally new environments, and we enjoy them as classic adventures.

Life change stress

Change is a feature of modern life. We have to contend with unemployment, and mobility in finding new work, as well as all the changes due to health and bereavement that have always been a normal part of human experience. The reader may be familiar with the table of stress factors[1] in adjusting to normal life changes. Consider the following table.

Death of a spouse	100	Change of work responsibilities	29*
Divorce	73	Son or daughter leaves home	29
Marital separation	65	Trouble with in-laws	29
Prison term	63	Outstanding personal achivement	28
Death in close family	53	Spouse begins or stops work	26*
Personal injury/illness	53	Begin or end school/college	26*
Marriage	50	Change in living conditions	25*
Losing one's job	47*	Trouble with boss	20
Marital reconciliation	45	Change in working hours	20*
Retirement	45	Change of residence	20*
Illness in close family	44	Change in school/college	20*
Pregnancy	40	Change in recreation	19
Sex difficulties	39	Change in church activities	18*
Business readjustment	39*	Change in social activities	18*
Change of financial state	38*	Moderate mortgage or loan	17
Death of close friend	37	Change in sleeping habits	16
Change to different work	36*	Change in frequency of family reunions	15
More marital strife	35	Holiday	13
Large mortgage/loan	31	Christmas	12
Foreclosed above loan	30	Minor violation of law	11

This table attaches arbitrary numerical quantities to various losses, stresses and bereavements that take place in human lives in an attempt to quantify the comparative stress they create. We may question the validity of this arbitrary quantifying of stress, which will vary from person to person, and place to place, but would still have to agree that some events are extremely stressful. We immediately recognise how many of these events will affect someone moving out of their home and work in their original country to do something entirely different in a foreign country (marked with *). It takes little imagination to appreciate that going abroad to work with churches there in any capacity may introduce a succession of stress factors which pile up one upon another all at once. People vary enormously in the amount of stress that they experience. It is this extreme, cumulative life stress of changing countries which may produce some measure of what is often described as culture shock. By its very nature, leaving behind family, home, possessions and status in one country to enter another country with a very different culture is bound to cause a whole new set of life stresses. The list above applied to a newly-arrived, cross-cultural missionary may add up to around 300. A score between 150 and 300 is supposed to mean a fifty per cent chance, and over 300 an eighty per cent chance of a major health change – disease, surgery, accident or mental illness! Even though we may question the number crunching aspect, it does feel a bit scary, doesn't it?

In the new environment, memories of the old country and those who live in it begin to fade and become difficult to visualise, even though everything in that home country is seen as special and is longed for. In spite of communication with family and friends by letters, telephone, email, photographs and cassette tapes, the two worlds seem far apart – Alice has come through the looking glass; Lucy (and later her siblings) have come through the wardrobe into Narnia. We know intellectually that the parallel world still exists and that life there continues much as always, but we are distanced from it and only our immediate world seems real. When we do return 'home' the process is reversed, and now it is the 'field' that seems unreal. Two separated geographical areas on the same planet can sometimes seem like two different worlds, even when airline flights connect us so much more closely.

Paul, prior to his defection from Judaism, had been recognised as a promising, up-and-coming member of the younger generation. What he lost as a Pharisee might be compared with what Christian workers would lose should they become involved in divorce or marital unfaithfulness. Paul would seem to have lost his reputation, status, friends, and may have been disowned by his own family. He says, 'I have lost all things' (Philippians 3:8) and the fact that this is for the sake of 'Christ Jesus my Lord' may not necessarily make it any easier for him or us to bear. The sense of loss and stress is considerable.

The cross-cultural experience may be likened to being born again, starting all over again as a baby who can only smile and try to understand the sounds being made by adults. The new missionary seems to be a linguistic moron, a cultural idiot with no status and no contribution to make. For someone who has been active in Christian work and leadership that can be quite traumatic. In our own country we may have had status and respect within a circle of people who know and value us. Now we have become nobodies, almost un-persons – useless, helpless parasites in a new society. For example, illustrating loss of status: a former student at London Bible College had been managing director of his own software company. Now as a new missionary in Hong Kong he had lost all that status. In his church at home he had been an elder; now he was just a stupid, negligible foreigner speaking poor Cantonese.

I used to give out tracts in the main street of the city of Hirosaki in North Japan, bowing politely each time (a thousand bows was about my limit for one afternoon) and a young peasant woman grimaced and refused my offered pamphlet. I felt more than somewhat affronted: did she not realise that I was a graduate of Cambridge University, and had come all this way to offer her the good news? She almost certainly did not, and it would have meant nothing to her anyway! All the things that once gave us status have gone. We have to go back to the beginning and establish a new set of relationships. It's like the game of snakes and ladders when we land on a snake and slide back to the bottom, or Monopoly when we land on a Park Lane hotel, lose our fluid capital and have to sell all we own to pay our debts.

Loss of self-esteem

The underlying problem of the newly-arrived is loss of self-esteem. We all need to carry with us some sense of self-worth. Admittedly, some individuals have a very low self-image, but screening and selection of missionary candidates usually excludes people for whom this is an obvious problem. Almost by definition, those selected as suitable missionary candidates are already achieving something in their own native church subculture. Up till this point we have become used to receiving affirmation and approval and have been confident that we were doing a good job. The gratifying consequence is that we have got used to feeling that we are worthy, competent, capable, significant and successful people. Like Little Jack Horner we suffer from the 'What a good boy am I' syndrome. And now suddenly, at one stroke, all of this is taken away from us. Transfer to an unfamiliar environment makes us feel like failures. Even extroverts, who have never had problems of self-worth, develop them now. Paul Tournier makes these comments about normal human motivation:

> All are constantly motivated by the single aim of making themselves appear in the best possible light. They are all, and always, on the watch, anxious lest their weaknesses, their faults, their ignorance, their fads or their failings be discovered; anxious to distinguish themselves, to be noticed, admired or commiserated with. Some do it openly and naively, and are considered vain. Others conceal it better, but are no less vain.[2]

When you and I move into another culture, most probably we will stop feeling good about ourselves. We start falling short of our expectations. We start to doubt, asking: 'Will I ever be able to succeed here?' The root problem is one of self-esteem: and this is often harder for the single person than the married person whose realistic partner helps to keep their feet on the ground. We all have human defence mechanisms for protecting our esteem. These reactions have been variously and alliteratively described as fright, fight and flight, to which we might perhaps add fake!

Missionary role stress

However, normal 'life change stress' may become exaggerated by an individual's false expectations of a heroic missionary role. Many missionaries start by trying to live up to a Christian superman image, arising from the totally unrealistic expectations of other people and of themselves. At home they have been fêted and put on a pedestal. They have devoured nineteenth-century hagiography – books about missionaries who knew no fear, had no faults, who never raised their voices to the children, who prayed for hours at a time. They began to believe some of this adulation, and that their famous predecessors were somehow clothed in moral and emotional asbestos. But now they are experiencing sweat, mosquitoes, prickly heat, screaming kids, incomprehensible language, senior missionaries who seem to fall far short of the anticipated spiritual ideal, and worst of all – themselves! Will I be able to live up to my own and other people's high expectations? And then doubts begin: Have I made a mistake? How did I get myself into all this? Perhaps I am not altogether suited to this life after all? These are normal, common reactions.

People have told us that language learning requires sustained hard work. They tell us that being a missionary requires great professional competence, and the ability to perform under pressure in unstructured situations. The task also requires a deep spirituality that shows endless patience when provoked, and invincible courage to continue to work in dangerous places without flinching. This totally fictional 'bionic Christian', lauded in some biographies, naturally makes us wonder how we can model all this in front of skilled and able national colleagues, and how we can live up to these expectations of being 'spiritual leaders'. Some people attempt it by putting on a mask, pretending to be spiritual supermen or wonderwomen, like David's 'mighty men' with faces like lions, swift as gazelles upon the mountains. Yet all the while we know in our inward hearts that we are not. The problem is that our home church's expectations, and indeed our own, may be very high – but frequently our actual performance falls far short. Some try to maintain the stiff upper lip and soldier on, striving and pretending to be the omnicompetent superhero. It is actually hypocrisy for an element of deceit has crept in. We may discern the manipulating hand of Satan exercising Screwtape craftiness.

The solution is to be honest with ourselves, facing up to our own limitations, fears and weaknesses. A flight on an airplane today no more transforms us into missionaries than a sea voyage did in the past. We need to repent of humbug, praying and admitting frankly that without the Lord's help and grace we can never achieve anything at all. It is the person who humbles himself whom the Lord can bless, not the self-inflated success seeker. As always, Scripture provides the bracing antidote. 'God opposes the proud but gives grace to the humble.'[3]

By now the reader should begin to see that we are piling

up a considerable amount of stress: life-change stress and loss of self-esteem (because of fear of failure to cope in the new culture) are compounded with the unrealistic expectations of what the ideal 'spiritual giant' of a missionary is going to be. Complicate this further with the stress of suddenly becoming culturally deaf and dumb idiots, and we begin to understand the explosive mixture called 'culture shock'.

But it shouldn't be! We do not, as Ted Ward says, talk about 'marriage shock' though we recognise that considerable adjustments need to be made when people get married – or 'parent shock' when two people realise that now the first baby has arrived life will never be the same again. Adjustments are necessary following marriage or childbirth, and it is perfectly reasonable that when we move into a new culture, adjustments are also necessary.

The symptoms of culture shock

In any new situation we may experience vague feelings of not belonging, and alienation, but rarely of inadequacy to the point of mental distress. Some people feel victimised and get depressed. They blame their situation on their host culture and become angry and hostile. Symptoms may include:

1. **Homesickness** often linked with longing for favourite foods and comforts not available in new culture.
2. **Withdrawal** by avoiding contact with people of the new culture as far as possible, and escaping to structured situations like cinemas and formal restaurants, especially choosing to hang around with our own ethnic group of expatriates.

3. **Boredom and need for excessive amounts of sleep.** There's a lot of yawning, enjoying naps and prolonged siestas, and general sense of lassitude, though paradoxically insomnia at night is also a possible symptom.

4. **Compulsive eating and excessive drinking.** This is partly a self-comforting mechanism and partly an escape mechanism. Racial minorities – Eskimos, North American Indians, the Ainu in Japan – often retreat into drunken stupor as an escape from reality. Expatriate minorities always seem to congregate in bars!

5. **Escape Activity.** Spending much more time than usual, not only eating, drinking and sleeping, but bathing, grooming, day-dreaming, reading magazines, playing cards, reorganising our equipment. These are simple escape mechanisms.

6. **Irritability, short-temper and quarrelsomeness.** This also stems from the general sense of unease and disorientation. Husbands and wives quarrel and sulk. There are arguments with other new missionaries, especially of other nationalities (theirs is a different culture too). There is a critical attitude towards those running mission homes and language schools. It's all symptomatic of culture shock more than sin, though one may open the door to allow the other to enjoy a field day.

7. **Physical ailments.** Headaches, stomach problems and unexplainable fits of weeping can also occur. Many first-year ailments may be due to lack of resistance to local bugs, but some are psychosomatic, but seem nonetheless real to the afflicted person.

8. **Hostility towards host nationals** and stereotypes of them. There is much talk about 'these people' and blaming 'them' for everything. In the initial euphoria only good things were screened in, now unfavourable aspects loom over everything.

The stages of culture stress

Culture shock is not an all or nothing experience. The onset may be rapid or gradual, but it is experienced in a series of recognisable and overlapping stages. What follows represents what happens to a normal balanced person who experiences initial stress, but ultimately copes very well. Initially there may be no culture stress, and the individual reacts with interest and fascination to the new cultural scene, much as a tourist does.

1. *The honeymoon stage*

This is the time of fascination with all the sights and sounds of the new culture. Everything is novel, interesting, intriguing and exciting. The new arrival is still a detached observer, still insulated by his or her own culture. No attempts are yet being made to cross frontiers and bond with the new culture. Their status, role and identity are the same as though they were back home, or a tourist on a visit. If they were to write a prayer newsletter home in this first few weeks, everything (and perceptions are screened and selected) would be described as marvellous, absolutely fascinating. All this stuff about 'culture shock' is rubbish! The new arrival is still a tourist who has not unpacked. The individual is greatly stimulated with fresh experiences and is possibly even euphoric. The artistic Lilias Trotter, founder of the Algiers Band, is typical of this in an opening letter:

> As the night darkened the phosphorescence became wonderful, making a firmament of green starry flashes on the water besides the silver ones overhead. We went below for a time, and on coming up there was another far-stretching cluster of golden stars, the lights of Algiers! When the pilot's boat came up, it broke the path of living fire, and flakes of it dropped

from the oars and ropes till we were almost besides ourselves with joy.

It made a lasting impression, for elsewhere she wrote again of that night in 1888:

> We steamed into the Bay of Algiers, the water below shimmering with phosphorescence, the crescent of the shore set with gleaming lights, and the glorious southern sky above full of its quiet stars. Next morning, seen from the deck, the Arab town rose in a creamy mass in the sunrise against the dead, deep blue. Three of us stood there, looking at our battlefield, none of us fit to pass a doctor for any foreign missionary society, not knowing a soul in the place or a sentence of Arabic, or a clue for beginning work on untouched ground. We only knew we had to come. Truly if God needed weakness, He had it![4]

To be fair, judging by her delightful writing, her deep artistic sense of beauty never left her and she remained euphoric for the next forty years! This woman went on to build the first international and interdenominational team in North Africa, now merged into Arab World Ministries.

2. The fright stage

Fear of the unknown is a common human reaction to a new culture. Somerset Maugham has his Dr McPhail reflecting on his stay in the Solomons:

> The natives, blithe and childlike by reputation, seemed then, with their tattooing and their dyed hair, to have something sinister in their appearance; and when they pattered along at your heels with their naked feet, you looked back instinctively. You felt that they might at any moment come behind you swiftly and thrust a long knife between your shoulder blades.

You could not tell what dark thoughts lurked behind their wide-set eyes.[5]

One missionary newly arrived in Singapore, and staying in far from primitive conditions, arrived at breakfast the first morning complaining, 'I couldn't sleep a wink.'

'What's the trouble?'

'There are reptiles in my room!'

'What sort? Where are they now?'

'On the walls. They kept on hiding behind the pictures!'

'Ah! Geckos! Yes, they live there, and very useful too, as they live on insects that perch on the walls.'

The unfamiliar can be alarming even when there are no real grounds for anxiety. So emotional anxiety to the extent of fright is not uncommon in unfamiliar surroundings or when facing an unfamiliar experience.

I was once a passenger travelling alone in a small boat down from the extreme south of Thailand into Malaysia. The local Thai-speaking missionary had arranged it, so there couldn't be anything wrong with it. But no sooner were we out from the jetty than one of the Malay boatmen made gestures asking for a cigarette. I shook my head. Another rubbed his stomach, signalling food. I had none. Then they signalled money. But the fare had already been paid. Malay pirates were notorious. Oh dear! Fifty years ago they would surely have slit my throat. This is getting scary – is he reaching for a knife? No, he's handing me an umbrella to keep the sun off! Phew! Relief. They were just trying it on. Hopefully, people don't normally bother to give a sunshade to someone whose throat they are about to slit. It had an amusing sequel, for as we approached our destination port, another boat drew up alongside and they transferred several sacks of rice hidden under the planking.

Then we sailed innocently into port. I was providing cover for a smuggling operation. So if not pirates, they were at least smugglers!

On another occasion I was forced to realise how frightening it can be when one has no language to ask or understand what is happening. I was in North Thailand to attend the funeral of an experienced Swiss missionary who had just been murdered on a tribal trail. The local Thai-speaking missionaries had all gone ahead, and I was put into a local taxi all on my own without a word of Thai language. Within a few hundred yards, the driver swung off the main road onto an unmade-up road through the mountains. What was he doing? What could I do? It might be OK, but I was scared silly. I was there because of one murder. So I, shamefully, pretended I had forgotten my money – and gestured and signalled I must go back. Then I took the bus instead! In both these events the settled missionary on the spot knew that everything was fine: but the visitor without the ability to talk to people in their own language was, understandably, scared. Some fears may have more reason than mine – like a newly arrived couple in Indonesia travelling on a bus who suddenly spotted two men with knives out collecting money and rings from passengers behind them.

The fear of the unknown produces a feeling of disorientation. We are unable to predict what other people will do, and do not know how to handle a situation, and this leads to an overwhelming sense of incompetence. There are too many stimuli without clear meanings and we become locked into impotency and finally get overload. Thus the rather pleasing definition that 'culture shock is an overloading of the human information processing system that blows the fuses'!

3. The fight stage

Before long the novelty wears off, and the realisation comes that one is going to be here for a long time and needs to come to terms with it. Cultural reality cannot be screened out indefinitely, and cultural differences begin to intrude. It begins with minor frustrations, though sometimes insignificant difficulties begin to loom like major catastrophes.

a) Irritation. This can be illustrated from my own culture shock experience recently in Canada. (What! Do you mean to say that you even got culture shock in Canada? I certainly did, and it was worse because I was not expecting it.)

First. I tried to find a place to put my letters in a mailbox, but circle it and tap it as I would, there was no slit for inserting my letter. A Canadian, who obviously thought I was acting suspiciously (my paranoia?), explained that it was for use by the mailman to store the letters he was distributing! We don't have this problem in England. Why don't they label mailboxes more clearly?

Second. Our new bank expected me to pay for cheques. Ridiculous! Who ever heard of doing that in this day and age? And why can't your bank arrange to pay money each month to my landlord for me? Because she uses a different bank. So I have to physically go there? Ridiculous! Why can't your bank do things like banks in England?

Third. Why can't I get any petrol out of this wretched pump? Why doesn't it automatically go back to zero? I have to do *what*!? Pull this lever up first, and then it works? Well, I've never had to do that before! It's stupid. Not like in England.

Fourth. The last straw on a Friday afternoon. 'You mean that if I come to you on Friday afternoon there are no doctors to treat me? I have to go to hospital because I am not signed on with you? This is crazy. Don't your doctors swear the Hippocratic oath here? Are the sick just left to die on the steps of the surgery?

Brrrh! So what is wrong with me? It seems very like culture shock!

Fight manifests itself commonly in a whole variety of hostile reactions, among which critical feelings about the host culture are common. A mother returning to Mexico after a period back in the United States writes of her reactions on re-entry with her family. She had already lived there for seven years, and work, home and children's schools were all in Mexico. Even so, cultural stress appears:

> But as we drove into town I noticed the people hadn't cleaned anything up. The garbage still was tossed into the street. It was dusty. The big mudhole at the corner hadn't been filled in. We drove up to the church. Sure enough the outside faucet still leaked and made a trickling stream the whole length of the church. I found myself thinking. 'This would never happen in North America!' Within three minutes the kids were filthy . . . Our kids are getting an awful lot of attention. I'm not sure I'm too happy about it. An old man coaxed David with a toy to come to him and then grabbed him to paw over his blond hair and white skin. David screamed. He also grabbed Becky as she was passing by, and even though she was crying he wouldn't let her go. I was really angry. I think I am going to teach her to bite. Then I realised I was suffering from culture shock that Sunday evening. I had a headache.[6]

However, this missionary mother's response was at the mild end of the scale. Some new arrivals become short-tempered and combative, picking verbal fights with marriage partners, fellow new missionaries, language school teachers and senior missionaries. This may be totally out of character on previous showing, but is an anticipated result of cross-cultural stress.

b) Aggressiveness. We can become bad tempered, like the tourist who gets angry because it doesn't work out the way he or she is used to. First time I had a haircut in Singapore, the Chinese barber suddenly gave me a karate chop on the back of the neck! 'What's all this about?' Our English barbers don't do this! A very British couple once arrived to stay with us in our Japanese home. We were used to Japan as it was then, but they were not!

'Could you please show us to our bedroom?'

'Well, that is rather difficult because nobody has bedrooms until bedtime. We all live in the rooms all day, and they only become bedrooms at night!'

'Well, perhaps you can show us to the bathroom.'

'Well, we only have one tap and that is being used for cleaning the potatoes at the moment.' 'Well, the toilet perhaps?'

'Yes, that's fine. It's not a flush, of course. Just a hole in the floor, so be careful not to drop anything out of your pocket. Fishing for it is not very pleasant. Sorry about the maggots, by the way. But it will be emptied out next week.'

People can get quite upset when bathrooms are not like what they are used to. In Thailand just a great jar of unheated water on a concrete slab, and a pan on a stick to bail it out and pour all over yourself. What – no electric shower? In Jakarta when we went to the dark bathroom in the morning, the shower hid scores of lurking mosquitoes – a frenzy of handclapping and body slapping followed, attempting slaughter! What an opportunity for the frantic release of frustration and aggression. What was worse was that we had forgotten to adjust our watches and had an extra hour to wait till breakfast. Culture shock!

c) Ethnocentric comparisons. Unfortunately this stage is sometimes made worse by nationals asking us to make comparisons, so please remember that they only want us to make favourable ones in terms of their own culture – and there is always something to praise! We have to be careful to avoid the commonly criticised stereotypes of local people: 'They are liars', 'lazy', 'dirty', etc. Most Asians washed more frequently than the English in those days, with our once or twice weekly bathnight.

A lecturer, who had been teaching in Sweden, came to teach in London. Nothing was right about Britain. In Sweden, it appeared, they pay far less tax. He said it was impossible to live here in Britain. Well, the other faculty members manage. No, you should all complain to your government! He resigned before the end of the first term because of acute culture shock.

Just today I read in Ted Ward's book that Americans were people of 7-4-76. Well, I thought, I never knew before that Americans had rebelled against England on my birthday – 7 April. Wait a minute, they celebrate 4 July! Why, it's 'the wrong way around'! We may be told that we drive on the 'wrong side' of the street. Apparently we even eat the 'wrong way'! In culture shock we often describe 'different' ways of doing things as 'wrong' ways of doing things. I remember once getting terribly worked up because American hymnbooks print the words between the lines of music instead of separately. Why do they have to do it differently from us? Culture shock!

d) Homesickness. This often seems to focus on the stomach. If only I was home. As a Brit, how I would love to enjoy a breakfast with porridge, bacon and eggs, marmalade and Marmite. The South African longs for mealies, the American for wieners and hamburgers, the Japanese for tempura and the Australian for 'barbies' and Vegemite.

e) Expatriate ghettos. Fellow countrymen or other expatriates are not always helpful. Those who have failed to identify, or who cannot communicate, cluster together in protective groups, with an us-them orientation that will be totally unhelpful to our own integration with the host culture. Beware of them dragging you down into an anti-host country, critical attitude. It is interesting that often minority groups like Eskimos and Indians in Canada, and Ainu in Japan compensate by using alcohol to reduce their stress. And so do expatriate Europeans – sitting in bars and hotels drinking. It's a form of culture shock associated with culture rejection.

f) Mechanisms to assign blame or divert attention. These are aimed at justifying failure by apparent rationalisation. All our problems are the fault of the car, the tennis racket or the language teacher! There may be attempts to divert attention – by illness, accident or quarrelling with other missionaries. Attack mechanisms may produce frenetic activity, the workaholic syndrome. The suffering person tries to compensate – by developing some new interest, by speaking in tongues or whatever.

4. The flight stage

At its worst, this stage moves to thoughts of premature retirement and immediate resignation. Sometimes only fear of loss of respect prevents such drastic remedies. Only recently, I realised that I first suffered from 'culture shock' as a ten-year-old boy on a scholarship at boarding school, aware that my parents' marriage was not entirely happy. I was horribly homesick, frequently in fights with other kids, and finally writing to my parents tear-stained letters begging them to take me away from school and let me come home. Mercifully they did not do so, for that wonderful school provided the stable structure that home could not, especially when the war forced my mother and siblings to leave London.

There are a very few people who fail to survive such culture shock. For most people the flight stage involves milder forms of escapism. Day-dreaming, watching television, withdrawal, repression and regression. Interestingly all these symptoms can appear, with greater or lesser degrees of severity, in new missionaries in language school. Fortunately almost all of them recover if given time and sympathetic counselling.

5. The recovery stage

Just as the degree of severity of culture stress varies with different individuals, so also does the speed of recovery. Some symptoms may persist for a time, especially if not recognised for what they are. Some Christians have problems controlling their nationalism, race prejudice and xenophobia. If these faults and sins are not rebuked and spiritually mortified (ie put to death) they may persist, and can seriously impair the Christian worker's usefulness. We will meet people who persist in the 'us' and 'them' mentality, who say derogatory things about national Christians, or who are happier in an expatriate ghetto than they are with the people they have ostensibly come to reach.

There is a place, of course, for robust and refreshing realism like that of Paul speaking to Titus about Crete: 'Even one of their own prophets has said, "Cretans are always liars, evil brutes, lazy gluttons." This testimony is true.'[7] The rest of the letter speaks to Titus of the life-changing power of the gospel, so that even Cretans will be subject to rulers and authorities, obedient, to be ready to do what is good, slandering no one, being peaceable and considerate, and showing true humility toward all people. We may have to be realistic about some national traits which are more than caricatures: for example, love of gambling, endemic bribery and corruption, acceptance of displays of anger, or an over-passionate concern with personal 'honour'. But at the same time not everybody follows the crowd and is totally programmed by an ungodly society. The gospel has power to transform Christian believers in any and every nation.

Everything begins to calm down and starts going well; people start to feel at ease, and know what is expected most of the time (there may still be the odd relapse or bout of cultural stress). They have finally unpacked mentally and emotionally, not just physically.

Is all this beginning to make sense as part of a total picture of the way that all human beings have to adjust and adapt to changing circumstances? The missionary moving overseas is just one example of a very common human phenomenon.

6. Aids to help adjustment to cultural change and stress

We turn now from symptoms to treatment. How may we adjust to the various life stresses and cultural stresses of the kind we have been describing?

a) Empathy. Part of our problems arise because we lack the language fluency to talk with people at any depth. We can talk about the weather, and travel and shopping, but often not about ideas and feelings. Empathy may begin by making friends with a cultural bridge-person, that is someone from the host-country, who can interpret and explain what is going on. As newcomers we are learners, and we have to recognise that we need to be dependent upon others. We have to learn to trust people and believe in their underlying good will. This is the quickest way to feel safe and to understand: when we start to build relationships (which is the first step to evangelism anyway!).

b) Observation. We need to gather information by reading books about our new country and culture (preferably written by nationals), by talking with national friends and by observing how nationals relate to each other. I used to find Japanese committees painfully cumbersome and time-consuming, but as I observed them in action I began to appreciate the way they worked. Unlike our committees, which depend upon argument and confrontation between outspoken individuals, the Japanese committee expects every person to have their say first. Having heard every other person's view, everybody speaks again and modifies to meet other views that have been expressed. This circular movement continues until the group reaches deadlock or, more commonly, agreement where everyone has been persuaded. It avoids the confrontational approach of westerners, and nobody loses face. It takes three times as long to reach a decision, but everybody present is now committed to implementing it. In the days when every *samurai* councillor would have been wearing swords, and sensitive to any implied criticism, it was doubtless a very wise way to discuss issues while maintaining harmony!

Try to work out why the other culture does things the way it does, and make up alibis for them. Why did our Japanese house help always hang laundry symmetrically over the line, so that it hung double and took twice as long to dry – clipping it under the line on each side? Look for logical reasons behind the strange and unfamiliar. Have a guess! It's simple, really. Bamboo laundry poles are too thick for clothes pegs!

This is a kind of detective game. Follow the example of hosts in how they eat. Don't keep on asking, 'What do I do next?' which only draws attention to our foreignness and the differences. Just observe and copy. Or close your eyes and try to reconstruct the room where you are sitting. How is it heated? Are there any power plugs? Where do the windows open? What is that little metal flower on the ceiling? Why that arrow on the hotel ceiling? We should always keep asking ourselves 'Why?' like a child does.

c) *Exploration or transactional learning by experiment*. Do something and see what happens. This is how a child learns. This is not just observing the environment but inter-reacting with it.

d) *Transfiguration*. Ask yourself: what is beautiful? What would you want to paint? Photograph? Write a poem about? What has God given to these people that is different from anywhere else? In Filipino homes I noted that they used translucent shells to make lampshades, and even made windows with thin square shells, as panes held in a wooden frame. I became fascinated by straw pictures; banana-leaf pictures; batik pictures in Nepal and Borneo, and by African and Eskimo stone carving. Japanese and Balinese art are quite different from each other: one leaves empty space and the other fills every centimetre with detail. Even at the most allegedly 'primitive' tribal level, the beauty of boxes and bags made of woven grasses is delightful. Whatsoever is lovely and worthy of praise should be appreciated. Natural beauties are to be found everywhere: damsel-flies over the paddy fields, butterflies in the jungle, kingfishers along the Thailand roads and telephone wires, pitcher plants in the forest, fishes among the coral. God has given us all things richly to enjoy. The writings of Lilias Trotter about Algeria, and the paintings she made to illustrate them, show how much there is to enjoy and to praise. Above all, the beauty of human beings themselves, as in this description by Fleming of a Communion service with Inuit on Baffin Island:

As I looked into the round, tattooed face of the dumpy little women and the bronzed weather-beaten faces of the men, I was filled with an unspeakable longing to serve them.[8] [He goes on to appreciate an elderly Inuit matron.]

Mary was a true daughter of a race that had never come close to civilisation, as we understood it. Yet this elderly widow woman had great dignity, was highly intelligent, a born organiser and a kindly and sincere spirit. Outside her family circle she was looked upon with respect and admiration. On one occasion when I complimented her on the excellence of her sewing her tattooed face, which had a multitude of wrinkles, lighted up with a flush of pleasure, her eyes sparkled and, smiling at me without embarrassment, she replied 'Certainly I sew well for you, because you are my own adopted son.'[9]

e) Refusing frustrated or hostile reactions. We should never blame the natives for our own ignorance and strangeness. We must resist the temptation to say, 'Stupid natives' and to blame totally innocent people to compensate for our own sense of fear and incompetence. It's not their fault at all! Learn to rely on things that are locally available, not things that have to be imported and so are in short supply. Use local transportation and accept its relaxed schedules. One main event per day is all that is wise to plan. Anticipate long turn-around times, and try *explaining* delays rather than *complaining* about them. Remember that calm, peace and urbanity are respected, while anger, impatience and blowing one's top are despised, and regarded as evidence of immaturity and sin. Enjoy the Taoist story of the foolish man running from his shadow and the sound of running footsteps in pursuit (his own). Foolish man, if only he had rested in the shade of a tree, he would have lost his shadow and the sound of running footsteps! Jesus and his disciples never looked at their watches!

f) Seeing the funny side. Humour is a great saving grace, and if we can laugh at our problems they will largely vanish away. As we begin to feel more at home and at ease, we can laugh at our own mistakes, and with the local people too. It is extraordinary what can mystify us. How to pull the curtains at night in Switzerland when I can't find any. How to plug the sink and stop the water running out in Eastern Europe. (We started to carry a squash ball around with us.)

An American missionary friend came over to see our children celebrate Guy Fawkes Day in Japan. The bonfire was a great success and the kids danced and screamed around it, but the fireworks were damp and useless. Then we heard the sirens of circling fire engines. A helpful neighbour, hearing screaming kids and seeing flames, had called the fire brigade. I was raking out the embers when they finally found us, and I had to apologise to a succession of fire officers of increasing rank and each time try to explain again what we had been celebrating. What missionary wants to even mention a festival that involves Protestants celebrating catching Roman Catholics trying to blow up Parliament? It had its comic side, but we never celebrated it again!

7. The bicultural stage

The aim and end of all this is to achieve the ability to function in both our home and the receptor cultures with equal ease and confidence. Once achieved we can enjoy it for life. It's now thirty years since we stopped being permanent residents in Japan, but each time we return every two or three years we feel immediately at home and delighted to be back. This is one of the great privileges of the bi-cultural person: to appreciate and delight in two or more very different cultures and no longer to think of them as alien and foreign. The greatest pleasure is meeting with old friends made over many years.

It goes without saying that functional bilingualism is part of this: we have to be free enough in the language to be able to initiate and develop relationships using that language, along with the language of the heart and helpful, sympathetic acts.

A spiritual response

Now, we might ask what difference it makes being a Christian in facing such stresses. We must not be simplistic about this and talk as though Christians wear a kind of all-weather survival suit which non-Christians do not. Christians are not immune from road accidents or from illness. C.S. Lewis wrote a classic book called *The Problem of Pain* in 1940, but when he suffered the life stress of the loss of his wife Joy, he experienced all the normal human responses that he outlines in his later book, published in 1961, *A Grief Observed*. We cannot as Christians claim immunity from normal human feelings, from bereavement or suffering. The rain descends, the wind blows and the floods come on the house of the wise man who builds on the rock, just as much as on the foolish man who builds on the sand. Indeed we shall only make things much worse if we deny that we are suffering stress because we wrongly think that it represents some kind of spiritual failure. David does not hesitate to write psalms about his stress when being pursued and persecuted (Psalms 3; 7; 10; 18; 31, etc.). Elijah suffers a kind of nervous breakdown in the anticlimax after his great victory at Mount Carmel (1 Kings 19:3–9). Paul does not hesitate in his letters to describe his stresses. Listen to them in 2 Corinthians:

> we were under great pressure, far beyond our ability to endure, so that we despaired even of life (1:8); I wrote to you out of great

distress and anguish of heart and with many tears (2:4); I still had no peace of mind, because I did not find my brother Titus there (2:13); this body of ours had no rest, but we were harassed at every turn – conflicts on the outside, fears within. But God who comforts the downcast [another translation says 'depressed'] comforted us by the coming of Titus (7:5–6).

Despair, anguish, fears and even depression seem to be authentic apostolic and Christian experiences, so we who seek to follow in their missionary labours should not feel that we are unspiritual if we also share in their sufferings. We have to experience stress first if we are to appreciate that the Lord has delivered us right through it all. And we ought to remind ourselves that our Lord Jesus himself suffered extreme stresses: 'being in anguish, he prayed more earnestly, and his sweat was like drops of blood falling to the ground' (Luke 22:44). The writer to the Hebrews stresses Jesus' humanity by saying: 'During the days of Jesus' life on earth, he offered up prayers and petitions with loud cries and tears to the one who could save him from death ... he learned obedience from what he suffered' (Hebrews 5:7–8). So what can we say? That when we do face these stresses, as we surely will throughout our lives in these mortal bodies and with these mortal minds and our mortal emotions, we may pray for the Lord to give us peace in our inmost hearts, as Paul also describes in 2 Corinthians. Please savour these promises.

'The Father of compassion and the God of all comfort (ie making strong) who comforts us in all our troubles' (1:4).

'He has delivered us from such a deadly peril, and he will deliver us. On him we have set our hope that he will continue to deliver us' (1:10).

'but we have this treasure in jars of clay [scruffy, disposable earthenware pots!] to show that this all-surpassing power is from God and not from us' (4:7).

'For we who are alive are always being given over to death for Jesus' sake, so that his life may be revealed in our mortal body' (4:11).

'Though outwardly we are wasting away, yet inwardly we are being renewed day by day. For our light and momentary troubles are achieving for us an eternal glory that far outweighs them all' (4:16 17).

'He said to me: "My grace is sufficient for you, for my power is made perfect in weakness." Therefore I will boast all the more gladly about my weaknesses, so that Christ's power may rest on me' (12:9).

In other words, the very fact that as we cross cultural borders we may be called to suffer a few (or many) of these stresses, may be a fresh opportunity to experience the blessing of the Lord's faithfulness in making us strong. He will deliver us through all these necessary hardships. Instead of shrinking from them in favour of the relatively greater security of our familiar comfort-zone, we should embrace them cheerfully as a road to greater blessing. Those who come through tribulations and distresses are always stronger in their character than those who have been carefully protected and wrapped up in emotional cotton wool!

Because we are fixed on this rock, our house will stand and will surely not fall. Prayer is an expression of our faith and trust in him, and will deliver us in life-stress situations from the collapse which could afflict those who have no rock, and no confidence in our Saviour.

Conclusion

People vary enormously in the degree of stress they experience when moving house within the global village. Laid-back people may have very little, while perfectionist, 'control-freak' types may have more of a struggle. My hope is that having read this chapter, understood why we may feel stressed, recognised some symptoms, and appreciated the stages through which most people pass, we shall be pleasurably surprised at how easily we overcome these stresses. So *relax*: for most people it's 'no big deal'; it's a matter of attitude. If we see it all as a fantastic privilege and adventure, it will help us greatly; and seeing it as part of our Christian commitment to the Lord and the human race will help even more.

Daniel was forcibly deported from Jerusalem to Babylon in 605 BC, in the first of the three deportations (see Daniel 1:1–4; 2 Kings 24:1–2). There was a second deportation eight years later in 597 BC (2 Kings 24:10–14) but it was nineteen years before Jerusalem was finally sacked in 586 BC (2 Kings 25:2–21). As Daniel was probably only a teenager at the time, the stress he faced must have been considerable. He was then given a compulsory three-year induction course into Babylonian language and culture (Daniel 1:4–5).

We are told that he survived the whole period of the Babylonian captivity until the first year of King Cyrus (539 BC). Though he was probably too old, by then over eighty, to return to Jerusalem with other exiles, he was still prophesying in the third year of Cyrus (10:1). This gifted young Jew, overcame his culture shock with the Lord's help (1:17), and understood the culture and bonded with it so well that he became a senior civil servant under first Nebuchadnezzar and then Darius. He seems to have remained and worked in Babylon, an alien culture to his own, for upward of sixty-eight years. If you do as well, you will deserve to be congratulated perhaps, but then your God is the same as the God of Daniel, is he not?

Further reading

Ted Ward, *Living Overseas* (New York and London: Macmillan Free Press, 1984), pp.98–129.

Derek Williams, *Prepared to Serve* (London: Tear Fund and Scripture Union, 1989), pp.53–61.

Myron Loss, *Culture Shock* (Indiana: Light and Life, 1983).

Richard Dawood, *How to stay healthy abroad* (Oxford: University Press, 1989).

William Smalley, ed., *Readings in Missionary Anthropology* (Pasadena: Wm Carey, 1974).

Notes

1. After T.H. Holmes and M. Masusu, 'Life Change and Illness Susceptibility' in *Stressful Life Events: their nature and effects,* B.S. and B.P. Dohrenwend, eds (New York: Wiley, 1974), pp.42–72.
2. Paul Tournier, 'The Dynamics of Success' in *Leadership* 11, Winter 1981.
3. 1 Peter 5:5 quoting Proverbs 3:34.
4. Constance Padwick, *The Master of the Impossible* (Sayings, for the most part in parable, from the letters and journals of Lilias Trotter of Algiers) (London: SPCK, 1938), p.vi, 51.
5. W. Somerset Maugham, 'Rain', *Short Stories* (London: Heinemann, 1976).
6. Missionary Monthly (Reformed Bible College, Grand Rapids) December 1983.
7. Titus 1:12–13.
8. Archibald Fleming, *op. cit.,* p.150.
9. *Ibid.,* pp.149–150.

CHAPTER FOUR

DIFFERENT BREEDS OF LAMB
INTER-RELATE

Something for you to do: You will get more out of this chapter if you first attempt the test quiz at the end. While it will be a fun thing, its serious purpose is to remind us just how ignorant we are of other people's countries, languages and cultures.

Difficulties between missionaries of different cultures

Many people still carry in their heads a mental caricature of the missionary, looking remarkably like David Livingstone when he met Stanley in Ujiji in 1871. Even today we tend to talk generally about 'missionaries' as though they were a homogenous group. But they never have been. The first Roman Catholic missionaries included Spanish, Portuguese, Italian and French priests. The early Protestants were Germans, Dutch, English, Scots and American. During the war years when Japan attacked Pearl Harbour they interned all American and British missionaries in China: the Germans, Swiss and Scandinavians were left at liberty for they were either Allies or neutral. Dr Fritz Eitel was a German doctor of the Liebenzeller Mission. Being at liberty he took food parcels to his American and British friends belonging to enemy nations who had been interned or imprisoned by the Japanese invaders of China. When the Japanese were defeated, the British and Americans were released, and I think the Germans were interned briefly. But fellowship between people of differing nationalities was significant and important.

Even today many people still have a mental image of missionaries as white men and women: but if you were to visit Thailand now, you would meet English, American, Chinese, Japanese, Indian, Korean, Swiss, Dutch, German and even Brazilian! Thus missionaries themselves come from many different races and nationalities, and may speak quite different mother tongues, even if they have to communicate with each other in English or in Thai! This is a very good thing because it shows that the Christian faith is not an American or European religion, but a universal faith whose representatives may be of any race, colour or nationality. That this group come holding hands together all one in Christ Jesus is a wonderful witness.

I first recognised the great benefits of internationalism when attending an early IFES Conference organised by the Fellowship of Evangelical Students in Hong Kong at the remarkable Dao Fong San centre – a Christian centre in what looks like a Chinese temple, founded by the Norwegian missionary Karl Reichelt. It was there that I first began to see why the Lord had allowed us all to belong to many races and nations. National stereotypes can be most misleading, but do arise out of distinctive cultures. It was an Asian conference using English as a common language, but there was no single Asian type. Each separate racial group made its own distinctive contribution to the total conference – our corporate experience would have been the poorer if we had lacked any of them. I began to get a glimmering of why it was that the creator had put boundaries between us,[1] so that we all grew up with distinctively different cultures, yet in such a way that we all needed each other to achieve completeness. At a later conference under different sponsors when a rather militant Korean gentleman was being stridently divisive, it was a quietly-spoken Indonesian woman who restored peace and harmony by her wise words. We are meant to be different, and we can help each other because we are different in our thought patterns and cultural norms.

Today's missionary lamb will, at the right kind of training college, have taken courses on how to relate to wolves, have discovered what the wolves believe, and will have embarked on studying the language of the wolf-pack. The culture stress of living as one of Christ's lambs among the Gentile wolves will have been anticipated. What comes as more of a shock is the realisation that one of the biggest difficulties is relating to some other breeds of sheep coming from different national and ethnic sheepfolds.

It is encouraging to know that today's missionary force is not only multinational, but also multi-ethnic. Checking on a current directory of members of just one missionary society, I discovered no fewer than twenty-four nationalities: Americans, Australians, Belgians, Brazilians, British (including Scots and Irish), Canadians, Chinese (HK), Dutch, Filipinos, French, Germans, Indian, Indonesian, Italians, Japanese, Koreans, Malaysians, New Zealanders, Singaporeans, South Africans, Swedes, Swiss, Thai and Taiwanese. Of these, about a quarter grew up speaking languages other than English. They are drawn from every continent except Antarctica, and enjoy a wide representation of different races, except black Africans. Over fifty would be Chinese by race, and actually far more if Americans and Europeans of Chinese extraction are included.

Now this multi-ethnic missionary force provides a great demonstration of the universality of the gospel. But that is not yet widely understood, and the questions people ask at missionary meetings often reflect the outdated notion that all missionaries are white colonialists. Being such an international team, while deeply enriching, has its drawbacks. While we will have read a great deal about the culture and thought patterns of the countries to which we go, we are often totally clueless about the cultures and thought patterns of our fellow missionaries. It shows, believe me! Putting it in a nicer way, it means that in the twenty-first century, not only must missionaries identify and bond with national Christians in the host country, but they must also effect some bonding and cross-cultural communication with fellow missionaries from other cultures. This is what this chapter is about.

1. Missionaries do not always agree with each other

This has always been the case, as Scripture itself shows us, even in the earliest days of the church. There was the famous occasion 'When Peter came to Antioch, I opposed him to the face, because he was in the wrong' (Galatians 2:11). Then, following this and leading up to the Council of Jerusalem, we read: 'This brought Paul and Barnabas into sharp dispute and debate with them' over the circumcision issue (Acts 15:2). Then, later in the same chapter, Paul and Barnabas 'had such a sharp disagreement [Greek *paroxysmos*] that they parted company' (15:39). These conflicts were important. In all three cases principles were at stake. And they illustrate how missionaries may have difficulties in personal adjustment with one another.

This is not necessarily sinful, but just part of being human. In all three disagreements those participating were of the same race, all Jewish men, though Paul and Barnabas were Greek educated and Greek speaking. Most of the Christian Jews who evangelised the eastern Mediterranean were Hellenistic Jews, people of two cultures, just as overseas Chinese today are people of two cultures. There were conflicts between the more conservative, traditional, Aramaic-speaking Jews and the more liberated, cosmopolitan, Greek-speaking Jews beginning in Acts 6. If, tongue in cheek, we say that it is perfectly biblical for missionaries to disagree, we are emphasising that it is normal and human for conflicts to arise between men and women of principle, which need to be resolved. They are not necessarily sinful, though it is always easy to regress into the corporate 'acts of the sinful nature' as the Galatians did (Galatians 5:19–21), and a deliberate choice has to be made to display the 'fruit of the Spirit' instead (Galatians 5:22–26).

2. We prepare for our target culture and language, but have little preparation for communicating with fellow missionaries

We know it will take us many years, a whole missionary lifetime, to understand the language, culture and ways of thinking of the foreign country in which we are working, but, as I mentioned earlier, we often fail to appreciate that our fellow missionaries also come from a wide variety of different cultures and thought patterns.

The great John R. Mott once commented that 'it takes ten years to get a new idea into the head of a Dutchman, but once it's there it takes a hundred years to get it out again'. Several questions arise from this: can this really be true as a general observation on a whole nation? Was it charitable of Mott to say this, and did such an understanding make it easier or harder for him to establish rapport with Dutch men and women? And if it's true that there is no smoke without fire, do we know what experiences gave rise to such a comment?

Currently there is quite a lot of criticism of Korean missionaries because they have a very distinctive culture of their own which few others understand. The problems might not all be solved, but at least if others understood the cultural background, some of the reasons for the problems would become clear.

On my first speaking trip to Italy, I reviewed what I thought I knew about Italians and was appalled at all the prejudiced notions that I had unthinkingly accepted. It went something like this: Italians eat lots of fat and greasy food, and this produces fat opera singers. They are politically corrupt and rotten with criminal elements. The Sicilians are vengeful and engage in vendettas, but Italians generally are cowardly, and surrender easily as they did in World War Two. (Had I forgotten the Roman conquests and empire?) In general they are superstitious, in bondage to the Roman Catholic Church, and overseas become comic waiters, racing drivers or work for the Mafia. I was dreadfully and stupidly prejudiced, but many of us live our whole lives without having to correct such stereotypes. Fortunately, once I met Italian Christians I was able to revise my prejudices.

The whole point of one of the questions in the quiz was to tempt you, having first shown your factual knowledge of national sports and languages, to express some of your stereotypes about other nations. With one class of students in Vancouver I read back to them what individuals had written about other nationalities, some of them so prejudiced as to be unprintable! They came up with things like this: 'Australians are crude, cocky and addicted to beer and sport.' 'Americans are brash, shallow and uncultured.' 'Brits are unemotional, arrogant and insular.' 'Germans are efficient, proud and cold.' Well, I asked the class, if you really believe that kind of thing about people of other nationalities, are such attitudes going to help you relate to and work alongside your fellow missionaries? Such prejudices wreck fellowship before you have started.

If you have attempted the quiz as suggested, I hope it will have demonstrated just how ignorant we can be in purely factual matters about the home countries of our fellow workers. But history, culture and thought patterns lie at a deeper level. How much do we really know about the thought patterns of Dutch, Koreans, Japanese, Afrikaners, French-speaking Swiss, Irish or even Americans?

We all need special grace in being considerate of others, and recognising that they may think and look at the world quite differently from ourselves. Some races hardly ever touch another human being, while others usually talk to each other while firmly grasping the other person's arm. We even vary in the distance we stand away from each other when we speak: some ethnic groups stand much closer than others do. I once had to deal with complaints in Singapore from Singaporean ladies working in the office, that a Swiss accountant stood far too close to them when he spoke to them. It wasn't sexual harassment, and he was quite unaware of what he was doing or that it was offending cultural rules. In his own country nobody would have thought his behaviour remarkable, but he was giving offence and we had to ask him to stand a foot further away!

3. Insularity and ethnocentricity

The Japanese have a four-character phrase *shimagunikonjoo* – which means the 'island country syndrome'. And we British, who live on the opposite side of the European-Asian landmass from the Japanese, have a similar problem. Mainland Europeans always laugh at the English for talking about travelling to 'Europe' or to the 'continent' as though they did not belong to it! But countries with much larger land masses can be just as insular. In the United States and Canada there is so much local news in the papers that the rest of the world gets pushed out. We are told in great detail about what is happening in baseball, American football, Hollywood and the White House, but not much about the rest of the world. Hong Kong is unusual in its interest in stock markets and business in other parts of the world!

I remember my horror the first time I opened an atlas in Japan. I had grown up with a school atlas. It began with a world map with the British Isles coloured in red in the centre, the Americas to the west and Europe and Asia to the east. The world map would be followed by several pages of maps of the British Isles, and then the rest of the world. But opening a Japanese atlas – would you believe it? The world map had the Japanese Islands in the middle coloured in red, the Americas in the far east and the British Isles in the far west. It was followed by several pages of maps of Japan. Where were the maps of Britain? We did not even get a page to ourselves, but had to share it with the rest of Europe! The Australians for fun (surely they can't be serious?) publish maps of the world upside down in order to get themselves in the central position. North Americans cut Europe and Asia in half to get themselves into the 'centre', with Europe in the far east, and Asia in the far west. We all put our own country in the centre. China actually calls itself the Middle Kingdom or Central Country. At an agricultural college near Christchurch, New Zealand, I came across a huge map of the South Island on the wall, five feet long – every famous sheep farm was marked on it by name! And the North Island? Some wag had added a tiny map of the North Island the size of a postage stamp. That's ethnocentricity!

I once heard a Lebanese Christian say, in introducing himself, 'I come from the Middle East, my country is in the middle of the Middle East and my village is in the middle of my country. My house is in the middle of the village, my bedroom is in the middle of my house, my bed is in the middle of my bedroom, and I sleep in the middle of my bed!' That is rather extreme ethnocentrism, but he was only fooling. Yet all of us, without thinking, assume that our own country is the best, and is at the heart of everything. In Africa they have a proverb which says he who has never travelled thinks his mother is the only cook! And in Wales, that Mrs Jones has never travelled further away than the back of her own oven!

The result of this is that we all think our experience in our own country defines the 'correct' way of doing things. Which side of the road is wrong and which is correct; how to use a knife and fork; how to speak the English language even. Some Canadian houseparents in Japan taught the children in the school for missionaries' children that 'the proper, polite way to eat' is using only a fork, while English people think it quite wrong to eat bread, butter and jam with the main course. When these differing cultural patterns encounter each other, they can be allowed to grate if we are stupid enough.

4. Beware caricature stereotypes of other nationalities

It is very easy to accept stereotypes and caricatures of other nations. It is far from true that all Americans are loud and all English people reserved with 'stiff upper lips'. People from the north of England are much more friendly, while the Welsh and the Irish can be as passionate as any Latin. The difficulty here is that we do not want to replace one stereotype with others. Every person in each nation is different. We may recognise that certain features are normally characteristic of particular cultures, but must always be ready to recognise that it may not be true of a particular individual. It is ridiculous to create an American stereotype: there are widely varying accents, temperaments and cultures. They may be Irish, Polish, Swedish, Italian, German, Slavic, Chinese, Jewish or native Indian Americans. People from New England may well be even more conservative (generally speaking) than conservative southern English (generally speaking!). It is equally stupid to talk about 'the enigmatic Asian' – Koreans, Japanese, Chinese, Filipino, Thai, Malays, Cambodians are all utterly different from each other.

So we must be careful to avoid national caricatures formed of a composite identikit of all the worst characteristics we have ever encountered, or more likely just read about or seen in films or on television. My attitude to Italians, referred to above, is typical. Nearly everything I thought I knew was negative and uncomplimentary: a nation of fat cowardly criminals stuffing themselves with starchy food and singing beautifully at the tops of their voices. It was sinfully stupid and once I started to meet real Italians in the flesh, I had to revise it very rapidly. Contrary to my prejudices I found that I liked Christian Italians very much indeed.

5. International missions with an Anglo-American subculture

Most older international mission agencies were founded in Britain, other European countries or North America. For this reason, the English language tends to be the 'official' language and American and British ways of doing things tend to dominate. Ironically, these two often disagree strongly with each other as to what is 'correct' English, and, generally speaking, have different views on eschatology, ecclesiology, evolution, economic policy and the etiquette of business meetings! What Americans and British alike fail to realise is that they both rather arrogantly expect all other nationalities to adjust to them. Mission members from Germany, the Netherlands, Scandinavia, Switzerland, South Africa and all the Asian countries have to make huge adjustments to the cultures of the majority nations. For them English is a second language and communication difficult. The British and Americans are often blissfully unaware of the problems they create for everybody else. Thus missionaries coming from minority home countries are having to face two kinds of culture shock at once. They are trying to adjust not only to the national culture, but to a mission sub-culture at the same time.

In one's own home one can follow one's own national customs. When I visited Japanese missionaries working in Thailand, the moment I entered their home I might have been in Japan. We did not *wai* like the Thai or shake hands like Europeans: we bowed to each other, and we ate Japanese food. The mission hospital in a Swiss physician's home was just like going to stay in Switzerland. This is very helpful for the children of missionaries: it means that at home families can maintain their national identities.

For single people it is much harder, for they are often sharing their homes with missionaries from other cultures than their own. A Chinese lady missionary was sharing a home with a German and an American. They decided to take turns to prepare meals for each other. But the other two objected when they were offered Chinese food for breakfast! But the Chinese lady said, very rightly, this is my culture, this is the kind of food that I am used to preparing and cooking, and that I like to eat for breakfast as well: so please adjust to me as I adjust to you! It calls for a sacrificial sensitivity when single people of different nationalities and races set up house together.

6. Don't abandon national distinctives for a monochrome hybrid culture.

Does this adjustment mean all of us are to abandon our own distinctive cultures and accept instead a kind of monochrome digest of all our differing cultures? God forbid! The very variety of our cultures and backgrounds brings great interest and enrichment to our lives. God not only 'from one man . . . made every nation of men, that they should inhabit the whole earth', but he also 'determined . . . the exact places where they should live' (Acts 17:26). In allowing us to develop distinctive cultures, our creator gives us the opportunity of mutual enrichment. Some cultures have features that are an improvement on others. Think of the restaurants all over the world selling Chinese food. A perfect house would have a Japanese bath, a Korean heated floor, an American kitchen, Turkish carpets, Canadian quilts, a German car and so on!

Scripture says that in heaven there will be a great multitude, which no one can number 'from every nation, tribe, people and language' (Revelation 7:9). This suggests that even in heaven we shall be recognisable by our different cultures: 'the kings of the earth will bring their splendour' into the holy city, and 'the glory and honour of the nations will be brought into it' (Revelation 21:24, 26). The sinful and impure will be excluded, but all that is good from human culture will have a place in the world to come. We should start enjoying each other now.

So we are not to abandon our distinctives for a kind of monochrome culture; we are to remain recognisably Chinese, Japanese, British, American while appreciating the good things in other people's cultures. We should not criticise them for being different from our own, but revel in the differences that enrich each other before our creator.

7. Avoid customs and language offensive to others

Paul wrote: 'Do not cause anyone to stumble, whether Jews, Greeks or the church of God' (1 Corinthians 10:32). Both in religion and culture, Jews and Greeks were different from each other, but we are to avoid unnecessary offence, thus Paul instructs people living in cosmopolitan ports where many ethnic groups might be encountered. The eating of pork is offensive to Muslims – missionaries and Christians in Pakistan and Bangladesh therefore refrain from cooking and eating bacon and pork. They are free to eat, there are no food restrictions for us, but in order to avoid offence they refrain. North Americans celebrate the old autumn feast called Hallowe'en (a little like the Chinese feast of Hungry Ghosts) when commercial interests sell masks, and children go round the houses begging for sweets. But to Germans and Swiss this is a most offensive pagan spirit ceremony. Not all are happy with the way many westerners celebrate Christmas and Easter with many features that have nothing to do with the birth or death of the Lord Jesus Christ. We curtail our freedom to avoid offending other people.

Amusingly, words that are acceptable in one country may not be in another: I was shocked when a spiritual Australian lady lent me an Australian poem 'Songs of a Sentimental Bloke' in which the word 'tart' was used to describe young women generally, whereas in England it would mean a prostitute. Americans can use the word 'bugger' very freely, whereas in England it would mean someone was being accused of sodomy. Conversely, an English person will call their best friend 'a silly ass', which is apparently very offensive in the United States. Whether people are addressed by their first names or not is a custom from country to country. In Germany strangers will be addressed as *Sie* and one only calls them *Du* after being invited to do so. It is only those in *du* relationship one would address by their first names rather than Herr Schmidt, Herr Muller, etc. In England very close friends may sometimes be addressed by their family names as a special mark of intimacy, a sort of mocking of formality. In other countries getting it wrong can seem like deliberate rudeness. Getting the word wrong can sometimes be very funny, like the chaplain from St Andrews in Scotland who preached on Naaman being a great man with his master, *but* he was a leper. His homiletical structure was fine, but his choice of words was unfortunate in the North American context:

1. Every man has his own 'but'.
2. Your 'but' is different from everyone elses' 'but'.
3. You can't see your 'but', but other people can.
4. What are you going to do about your 'but'?

Unfortunately, until it was explained to him that 'butt' was an American synonym for gluteus muscles, he didn't understand why his audience was rolling about with laughter.

8. Thought patterns are different as well as words and acts

Some nations are very gentle, avoid confrontation, are always indirect and are careful to 'save the face' of others. Some are blunt and outspoken almost to the point of rudeness. Even approaches to discussion and conversation may be different. A group of missionary trainees in Singapore discovered that the British and American approach to argument was different. A common British device was flatly to contradict something that was said: 'What nonsense. Twaddle. Rubbish!' in order to provoke a good argument. However, some Americans thought this was very rude and unsanctified and just retreated, their feelings hurt. In Korean culture age and relative seniority are greatly respected: given three men present, the youngest will not venture to speak until his two seniors have voiced their opinions. This is true in other Asian cultures. In western cultures there is less deference given to age and who speaks first depends more on temperament than seniority. In Japan it was important to discover who was the senior, because the level of language would have to be more polite by the younger when speaking to the elder. But westerners labour under no such restrictions: the weight of opinion depends on experience, not necessarily upon age. The extent to which women participate in discussion will also vary from culture to culture.

9. *Religious mores also vary greatly between cultures*

The church in any given country is influenced by its own culture. For example, Scots and Swiss have very different attitudes towards Sunday. In the north of Scotland, where I was deputising for the minister of a local church who was on holiday, we were warned never to use the car on Sunday, and though we might go for a walk, never to go anywhere near the beach. In Switzerland, evangelical Christians are happy to go to church in the morning and ski in the afternoon! The Swiss enjoy a good glass of wine, but when we made our first visit to the Bernese Oberland we discovered that a woman who cut her hair was regarded with suspicion. English people were horrified that Mrs Billy Graham wore make-up, and yet one can meet Americans who have scruples about drinking coffee.

Asian countries have different standards too. In Japan a very committed Christian nurse was doing her language study, and was in an early lesson practising saying yes and no.

Teacher:	'Ocha o nomimasu ka?'
Missionary:	'Hai, nomimasu.' (Yes, I drink tea).
Teacher:	'Koohi o nomimasu ka?'
Missionary:	'Hai, nomimasu.'
Teacher:	'Beeru o nomimasu ka?'
Missionary:	'Hai, nomimasu.' (Yes, I drink beer.) The teacher hoped she would produce a negative, so she tried again!

| Teacher: | 'Sake o nomimasu ka?' She must say 'Ie. Nomimasen' (No!) to that, surely? Well, being a very honest lady who had tasted sake on one occasion, she replied: |
| Missionary: | 'Hai, nomimasu' (Yes, I drink sake.) |

The Christian teacher was shocked because Japanese Christians in most evangelical churches are never supposed to drink sake. Drinking spirits is a social issue in Japan, and causes much suffering to families, so the church abstains. In Singapore most Methodists are teetotallers, and 'give no offence to the church of God' would mean that the missionary would also abstain. In Sarawak alcohol was a social evil: the Muruts (or Lun Bawang) were drunk 100 days a year, and whole villages for three or four days at a time. Babies died because their mothers were too drunk to suckle them. In that situation the missionary would be careful to be a total abstainer, even if he or she otherwise felt liberty to drink a glass of wine or beer in moderation.

Conclusion: the blessings of internationalism

Faced with all these problems of the international community, forming mission agencies of only one nationality with its own language and cultural traditions might seem much simpler. The Scandinavians, Germans and Swiss have tended to follow the national pattern where they can communicate in their own languages and operate in terms of their own culture. This is not unreasonable: after all, why should they have to work in English and an Anglo-American mission sub-culture?

Occasionally a missionary society made up of only one nationality – all German, all French, all American, all Korean – may well come into headlong collision with the national church, for the missionaries are all of one mind, and may all hold the same opinion in accord with their own national cultural background. On the other hand, in an international, multi-racial group it takes much longer to reach a common mind. There are bound to be several varied points of view, and the national church can accept which advice seems wisest to them from among a wide choice of options.

This chapter began mentioning what for me was a most significant conference of student workers from various Asian countries held in Kowloon. The Hong Kong FES staff and students were the hosts under the leadership of Chan Hay Him. All of us were struck by the wide cultural differences between us, and yet how in God's providence each made a different kind of contribution. Each group was so different. The Hong Kong Christians were efficient and well organised and laid on an excellent conference in Shatin. The Filipinos were warm, cheerful people; not such capable organisers perhaps, but people of real faith. They were very short of funds and several had not been paid any salary for several months, but they knew the work they were doing was important, and they hung on in faith. The Koreans and the Japanese were both quite intellectual in their approach, but the Koreans were very passionate and made no attempt to hide their feelings, while the Japanese hid their feelings well. The main speaker was an Indian – passionate and emotional even, but extremely penetrating in his thinking.

There was just one Vietnamese present, slight in physique, somehow sad and most serious. People were suggesting to him that he should leave Vietnam and go to the United States for theological study, or that he should move to Thailand and work on a Vietnamese Bible translation from the relative safety of that country. But we were all deeply moved as he said: 'I must go back to my country.' We saw in this small man an indomitable commitment and readiness to sacrifice that was a challenge to us all. And so we began to see something of our creator's purpose in allowing us all to have different histories and different cultures: each of us has something to contribute to the totality of the Christian church, all of us can give something that is unique and God given. One national group alone might lack the breadth of traditions and experience of the whole group, but working together each cultural tradition has something to offer to the whole. After all, God's ultimate purpose is to bring this great multitude together in heaven, and it is wonderful to taste something of the possibilities here on earth.

So while communicating cross culturally with Christians from so many different countries and cultures may cause a few problems, we begin to see that it also has enormous potential for mutual enrichment.

Note

1. See Acts 17:26.

QUIZ ON OTHER COUNTRIES
How international do you think you are?

(If possible try to complete this in fifteen minutes)

1. Name the main language or languages (used for at least primary education) in the following countries:
Canada
Great Britain
Philippines
South Africa
Switzerland

2. What is, and with which country would you associate, the consumption of:
Birchermuesli
Biltong
Hagelschlach
Yuudoofu
Pine Sauce
Hushpuppies
Pulgogi

3. In which country would you celebrate:
Anzac Day
Day of the Covenant
Merdeka
Orangeman's Day
Guy Fawkes Day

4. Give the most characteristic national sport of the following:
Brazil
Canada
Ireland
Japan
New Zealand
Scotland
Switzerland
United States

5. Please sum up the major national characteristics of:
Australians
Americans
Dutch
Germans
Irish
Scots
Swiss
Welsh

6. Please explain the meaning of, and state with which country you would associate:
Ningnong
Nosh
Verkrampte
Galah
Grits
Robots
Split nair dyke
Greeting
Drongo
Balut

7. How good is your geography? (No books or maps to be consulted)

In each of the following simple outlines please show the approximate position of the cities and towns requested. Ignore your own continent.

Australia: Melbourne, Adelaide, Perth, Sydney, Auckland and Brisbane

More outlines follow . . .

Europe: Paris, Glasgow, Belfast, Dublin, Edinburgh, Berlin, Madrid, Athens

India: Calcutta, Bombay, Colombo, Delhi, Madras, Karachi, Kathmandu

Latin America: Bogota, Caracas, Sao Paulo, Quito, Buenos Aires, Lima

United States: New York, San Francisco, Seattle, Washington, Toronto, Boston, Los Angeles, Miami

To check your answers, please see the Appendix.

CHAPTER FIVE

LAMBS RELATE TO INDIGENOUS WOLVES

A common problem for missionaries is failure to identify our chief aim and the focus of our ministry. After all, why have we become missionaries? What is our goal? It is certainly not to further our own careers and development. Our chief aim, as part of our love and service of God, must be the planting and perfecting of local churches which are both thoroughly biblical and recognisably ethnic. The expatriate is not there to reproduce his own denomination or his own form of ethnic Christianity, be it British, American, German or Korean. Just as the doctor's ruling passion is the health and well-being of his patients, and the engineer's the beauty and durability of what he builds, so the missionary's ruling passion, second only to devotion to our Lord, must be our concern for the beauty, health and durability of new churches. We are not there to further our own careers, or to achieve great exploits for our own sake – mere self-gratification, all the more ugly for being done under the cloak of spirituality. Therefore these precious individuals of whatever tribe, tongue or nation must be our abiding concern: prompted by a biblical love for all human beings certainly, but raised above an idolatrous philanthropy because carried out in dependence upon God, and with the goal of pleasing him.

Two good models

1. Dixon Hoste

Although numbered among 'The Cambridge Seven', Hoste was not himself a Cambridge man, though his older brother William was. He was an artillery officer, and it is not difficult to anticipate that members of the English ruling class at the end of the nineteenth century might encounter problems in relating to very different Chinese people. However, Phyllis Thompson outlines the way in which Hoste's Christian experience enabled him to break through these cultural barriers: 'More and more I see that there will be need of much love and forbearance and willingness to be the inferior, if one is to really get across the gulf there is between us.[1]

Hoste realised that by reason of his Christian heritage and upbringing he had a contribution to make to the infant church in which God had placed him; and that the most effective way of making that contribution would be through the church leader. He knew all about the role of the leader in a military organisation. On one occasion he drew on a rowing metaphor: 'It was a cox that was wanted. Pastor Hsi was perfectly well able to stroke the boat, and he had got plenty of men to pull behind him. What was wanted was a little man to sort of steer.'[2]

Building relationships across cultural barriers is not something achieved all at once:

> He completely won the confidence and love of his Chinese colleague. But it was not won quickly or easily. Not only had he to exercise much patience with the Chinese leader, but to endure the

quiet disapproval of some missionaries who could not understand his attitude and felt he should have taken a stronger line. But when one day, Pastor Hsi came to him burdened to tears about some church problem, and said, 'Ah! Pastor Hoste! I couldn't get on without you!' he thought to himself. 'Well! It's been worth it!'[3]

2. Christopher Maddox

Maddox was a missionary surgeon who served as hospital superintendent first in China, then in Thailand and Laos. Though a typically reserved Englishman he was known and appreciated because of his ability to relate to local people whether Christians or not.

> Many are the Westerners who have attempted (and still do) to initiate what seems a worthwhile work in a distant country, only to give up in discouragement at the seeming impossibility of securing co-operation from government departments, satisfying local bureaucracy, and dealing on a day to day basis with local workers. It was not simply a matter of long experience, but of two-way respect. Chris regarded Chinese, Thai and Lao colleagues as colleagues, and there was on his part a presumption of trust, not a presumption of suspicion. Conversely, the remarkable extent to which Chris won the respect, on both the individual and an institutional level, of the people among whom he worked is shown in the fact that in several instances he was on good terms with government departments and rebel guerrilla leaders at the same time. Some missionaries felt that he was more prepared to listen to nationals than to his own missionary colleagues, and were suspicious of a Christian who was looked on favourably by Chinese Communists and Pathet Lao guerrillas.[4]

Here was a man clear thinking, forward looking, efficient and dedicated to the work with a sacrificial passion. He was seen by some as an abrasive martinet, and yet showed that he could relate with others across cultural boundaries. He was awarded honours by both the Thai and Lao governments, as well as an OBE by the British government for his refugee work.

> There was a feeling abroad that Chris favoured the Thais to the extent of valuing their opinion above that of his own colleagues. He was keen to demonstrate to the Thais that he was prepared to regard them as trusted colleagues, every bit as able as Westerners, but 'If you want something from Chris, make sure you get a Thai to ask him,' was a sentiment voiced more than once.[5]

Now an elderly widower, he is still living in Thailand and working to get both secular and Christian education for Thai and Lao believers.

These are two extreme examples of more than usually reserved Englishmen who overcame their natural temperaments to relate and bond with national Christians. This was achieved only by the grace of God and the fruit of his Spirit. Whatever kind of temperament and personality we have inherited and developed, the Lord himself will enable us also to do this, if we ask him.

The difficulty of maintaining our aim

Much of our upbringing has inculcated in all of us a (foolish) belief in the superiority of our own race and nation. 'The English, the English are best, I wouldn't give tuppence for all of the rest' chortled Flanders and Swann. Canadian interest in the Gulf War focused upon what a handful of Canadians were doing, while American newscasters always tell you how many people who died in an aircrash were Americans. Coming from a Welsh background, with a father who assured me that 'The Scots are the salt of the earth!', I was never in danger of assuming English superiority. Yet my school lessons before and during the Second World War endeavoured to teach me that the British Commonwealth was the most altruistic empire there had ever been, giving self-rule and dominion to Canadians (even though some of them still spoke French!), Australians, New Zealanders and South Africans (many of them Afrikaners). Nobody pointed out to us that all these regimes were in the hands of colonial whites rather than the indigenous inhabitants.

We are all the victims of our own upbringing and education, like Japanese schoolchildren after the destruction of the Japanese empire, who were assured in their textbooks that Japan had sacrificed itself in order to achieve independence for former colonised nations of East Asia – Indonesia, Malaysia, Philippines and Indochina. Though hopefully we sometimes recognise nationalistic jingoism, we have all been inculcated with patriotism and love of country, and 'loyalty' to one's own group of people, right or wrong. American internal unrest over participation in the Vietnam War was because the younger student element of the population had the temerity to question unthinking patriotism. Military training aims to brainwash soldiers into obeying all orders without asking if they are right or wrong.

If nationalism under the guise of love of country is blatant, then racial prejudice is more insidious. We have long regarded other races as primitive, backward, lazy, stupid, barbarous and unreliable in a way that ours is not. There are exceptions. The Chinese and Japanese are respected for being industrious, but this is seen as obsessive behaviour and somehow suggests that they are not as balanced as we are! There is a commonly held idea that it is impossible for Indians or Africans, now independent of western tutelage, to run their own affairs efficiently without corruption or tribalism. Such problems of hidden prejudice may seem less acute for non-Caucasian missionaries, but every single one of us needs to recognise that we have all unconsciously absorbed attitudes of assumed superiority over other nations and races. This creates a huge barrier to effective working and bonding with fellow Christians in those countries. It helps if we can recognise this insidious racial superiority and take steps to minimise its subtle influence on our ministries.

When I was seconded to work with the Japanese evangelical student movement, KGK, the Japanese General Secretary to whom I was answerable read widely in four languages – German, Dutch, English and Japanese. This was a blessing to me personally, because there was no way I could ever think of myself as intellectually (or spiritually) superior to him. Yet a stream of Bible-college trained missionaries were arriving in the country who assumed, on the strength of having read (or possessed) Halle's *Handbook to the Bible,* that they had come 'to head up the work' solely by virtue of being missionaries from Europe, the United States or Canada. My General Secretary friend used to quiz such people as to whether or not they had read Roland Allen! He had read more missiological books than they had.

At times it was tragic when able national Christians were not given responsibility because of the tacit assumption that, almost by definition, missionaries were somehow a higher order of beings. It needs to be drummed into every prospective missionary in training that 'even in missionary flesh there dwells no good thing'. One deeply spiritual missionary, who was the founder and leader of an excellent high school movement, once assured me, 'I have to keep praying and studying the Scriptures to stay ahead of my Japanese associates.' It was said in all seriousness, by a very committed man and yet the assumptions were painful. Was it not an aim of his work that his younger national colleagues should overtake and make more progress than himself? Sadly, some of his most gifted protégés finally left him in order to develop their gifts within other organisations because they felt stifled under his paternalistic leadership. After criticising the apostle Peter for fraternising with the uncircumcised and finally convinced by his testimony that the Holy Spirit had been active in the whole series of events, the Jewish Christian leaders in Jerusalem seem to agree with almost comic reluctance, and against their better judgement: 'Then God has given even to the Gentiles the repentance that leads to life' (Acts 11:18, NRSV). Again and again throughout mission history, Catholic and Protestant, we discover this reluctance to believe that Christians belonging to other races and nations receive the Holy Spirit in the same way as ourselves. Roland Allen was clear about this.

> Now if we are to practise any methods approaching to the Pauline methods in power and directness, it is absolutely necessary that we should first have this faith, this Spirit. Without faith, faith in the Holy Ghost, faith in the Holy Ghost in our converts we can do nothing. We cannot possibly act as the Apostles acted until we recover this faith. Without it we shall be unable to recognise the grace of the Holy Spirit in our converts, we shall never trust them, we shall never inspire in them confidence in the power of the Holy Spirit in themselves. If we have no faith in the power of the Holy Spirit in them, they will not learn to have faith in the power of the Holy Spirit in themselves. We cannot trust them, and they cannot be worthy of trust; and trust, the trust which begets trustworthiness, is the one essential for any success in the Pauline method.[6]

Do you see from this how essential it is to think biblically about the work of the Holy Spirit in Christians, and how important that we crucify our national pride and prejudices? It is appalling that our own unrecognised racial and national pride may hinder the progress of the gospel and the growth of national church leadership. As we begin work in other countries and cultures, we need a second 'conversion' experience – to recognise that just as we ourselves have been transformed in behaviour and belief by the work of the Holy Spirit in us over a few short years, he can perform similar and indeed 'greater works' in the lives of national brothers and sisters. Yet this 'conversion' does not happen easily or without struggle. Part of this chapter involves arguing our way through a succession of Christian doctrines so we may be intellectually and theologically convinced of this, and thus able to fulfil our missionary calling.

Racial jokes

It is interesting to reflect on the philosophy behind racial jokes, which seem common to many cultures. For example, there were two Scotsmen, two Welshmen, two Irishmen and two Englishmen stranded on a desert island. The two Scotsmen started a bank, the two Welshmen started a choir, the two Irishmen started to fight, and the two Englishmen were not yet speaking to each other for they had not yet been introduced. There is an equivalent Asian story about two Chinese, two Koreans, two Japanese and two Filipinos. The Chinese started a restaurant, the two Koreans started a church, the two Japanese started a golf club and the two Filipinos just talked and talked to each other. The joke is nearly always against the last of the group though sometimes against all of them.

There is a European Community story about heaven and hell. In hell the policemen are Germans, the cooks are British, the engineers are French, the lovers are Swiss, and everything is organised by the Italians. In heaven, on the other hand, the policemen are British, the cooks are French, the engineers are Germans, the lovers are Italians, and everything is organised by the Swiss. Notice that this type of joke depends upon national stereotypes. All over the world people tell jokes about other nations or groups of people. In Switzerland it's the Bernese who are supposedly very slow; within the British Isles it's the Irish; in America the Poles or the Swedes; in South Africa, an Afrikaner called van der Merwe. Racial jokes seem to exist, if not to put down the people who are the intended target or butt of these jokes, rather to bolster belief in our own superiority or to laugh at it gently!

The Lord Jesus once told a story about a priest, a Levite and a Samaritan. Everybody thought it was going to be a racial joke against the Samaritan, but he turned the story around so it was the Samaritan who was the real neighbour to the injured man. This parable of Jesus challenges us as Christians to adopt a new attitude towards people of other races, and we shall look at the theological truths that teach that in a moment.

The essential quality for a cross-cultural missionary

However gifted I may be as a speaker, however able a linguist, however well thought of by my own church, however good at relating to my fellow missionaries, if I have not love for my national brothers and sisters I am nothing, I am useless, I am as sounding brass and a tinkling cymbal.[7] Love is not a vague, abstract, cuddly feeling, but a basic underlying attitude towards other people. Good missionaries are those who make friends, bad missionaries are ones that never do. It is as simple as that. Love means more than this, but certainly includes the ability to relate and make friends with national Christians.

When I was a student, I was very interested in going to East

Africa as a missionary, and for almost five years was a member of a weekly prayer meeting for East Africa. I was thinking about applying to a particular missionary society – until an African student told me that Africans were never allowed into those missionaries' houses but were kept on the front step or the veranda.

Dr David Tsutada was a gifted and committed Christian leader in Japan. He had been a schoolboy overseas in Singapore, and graduated from London University, so had considerable experience of foreigners. During the Second World War he had suffered for his faith and been imprisoned with other Holiness pastors by the Imperial militarists because they would not stop preaching Christ's second coming, when every knee including the emperor's would have to bow before Christ. On one occasion KGK had a problem over a member of Dr Tsutada's church who had been invited to join our staff without anyone first consulting the church. I was sent on a diplomatic mission to apologise, 'because Tsutada-sensei likes Englishmen!'. Sent thus by my colleagues into this formidable lion's den, I took the opportunity to ask him what he would feel about Koreans, Indians and Filipinos coming as missionaries to Japan. I was both shocked and amused when this heroic man of God said, 'Well, we are used to English and American missionaries, but we cannot take the Australians – these kangaroo people!' Even the most holy men and women among us are not immune to racial prejudice. And it works both ways – it's not just western nations that have racial prejudices. The people of the Middle Kingdom saw all the rest of the world as marginal barbarians or 'foreign devils'. Chinese who want to marry non-Chinese soon discover the strength of the prejudice against them: it is the Chinese parents who need counselling, said a Chinese pastor in Vancouver.

The vast majority of human beings have an inbuilt sense of national and racial superiority to everybody else. The

Cheyenne Indians called themselves 'the human beings'; everybody else was not! The word *inuk* means human being, and in the plural *Inuit* human beings, used by the Eskimos as the name of their own tribe, as compared with the 'big eyebrows' who came up into their territory after whales and seals. In our own home countries it seems absolutely self-evident to everybody that our nation is superior to every other. The French, the Germans, the British and the Americans all feel like this about themselves. The difficulty arises when we take these prejudices with us into other countries. Yet we are all afflicted with these deep-seated racial and national prejudices. The word 'them' is a dead give away! Sadly we do sometimes hear missionaries speak in an 'us' and 'them' way and use derogatory adjectives like 'Chinesey' or 'Japanesey'. Chinese in Taiwan call mainlanders 'red bandits' and the Japanese 'dwarf bandits'. The French call the Germans 'pigs', the British call the French 'frogs', and the Australians call the British 'poms'. Black and white races also have derogatory names for each other. We grow up in a world of racial prejudice and suspicion: we seem to think that other people are not human beings in the same way that we are. And even when we try to conceal that prejudice it comes out. One of the most telling accounts I have ever read is that of Dorothy Parker's short story *Arrangement in Black and White*,[8] which I have enjoyed reading to classes of students. The story concerns a woman who attends a party in honour of a popular black singer of negro spirituals, but whose husband Burton is so prejudiced that he does not come. She herself protests loudly that she has no prejudice at all, and yet unconsciously it stands out in everything she says and does!

Well, I think you're simply marvellous, giving this perfectly marvellous party for him, and having him meet all these white people, and all. Isn't he terribly grateful? . . . I don't see why on earth it isn't perfectly alright to meet coloured people, I haven't any feeling at all about it, not one single bit.

She gabbles on about her husband's 'southern' attitudes while all the time revealing her own:

[Burton's] really awfully fond of coloured people. Well, he says himself, he wouldn't have white servants. And, you know, he had this old coloured nurse, this regular old nigger mammy, and he just simply loves her. Why, every time he goes home, he goes out in the kitchen to see her. He does, really, to this day. All he says is, he hasn't got a word to say against coloured people as long as they keep their place.

Following this revelation of her husband's open mindedness (!), she explains herself.

Now me, I don't feel that way at all. I haven't the slightest feeling about coloured people. Why I am just crazy about some of them. They're just like children – just as easygoing, and always singing and laughing and everything. Aren't they the happiest things you ever saw in your life? Honestly, it makes me laugh just to hear them. Oh I like them. I really do. Well, listen. I have this coloured laundress, I've had for years, and I'm devoted to her. She's a real character. And I want to tell you, I think of her as my friend. That's the way I think of her. As I say to Burton, 'Well, for Heaven's sakes, we're all human beings!' Aren't we?

When she finally meets the guest of honour, she speaks slowly with great distinctness as though speaking to the deaf, and unconsciously patronises him. He takes it all with courtesy and grace. The story speaks to all of us, for despite our defensive protests, we have all inherited underlying prejudices. The work of the missionary is undone and rubbed right out when it becomes clear that we are patronising and fail to accept those of other races as human beings just like ourselves. Sadly, because of earlier unhappy experiences inflicted by other westerners, they expect us to conform to such negative stereotypes. If we do, our witness goes down the drain and our usefulness is permanently diminished.

If the missionary brings with him or her an inner sense of racial superiority, it is almost impossible to conceal. The new arrival is scrutinised: will this person turn out to be just one more prejudiced foreigner or a consistent Christian? The situation is complicated further because there is often a reciprocal sense of solidarity among national Christians that make them treat the newcomer as an alien, a foreigner, somebody different from us. In Japan, everyone knows that foreigners have big noses, their eye colour is different, they have double eyelids and are culturally clumsy, inept, ridiculous figures. Even the children shout at aliens in the street: 'Weird foreigner, weird face.' If you feel you are being regarded as a ridiculous alien, some counter reaction is likely, unless we are protected by God's grace and his Spirit. And we usually know if we are being humoured, asked innocent questions which are really a testing of our attitudes, our commitment to Christ and to his people. One of our greatest problems in bridging the cross-cultural gap is the hostility against westerners because of the shameful way our own compatriots may have behaved during previous centuries of imperialism.

Henry Martyn found this. Whatever his profession, and however great his love, Martyn was an Englishman, and no one could expect Indians to love their oppressors or their religion. 'Here every native I meet is an enemy to me because I am an Englishman. . . . The manifest disaffection of the people, and the contempt with which they eyed me, confirmed my dread.'[9]

All of us face understandable prejudice against us because of our nationality – British in India, Dutch in Indonesia, Americans in the Philippines and Japanese over much of South East Asia. We have only to read of the dreadful way in which the aboriginal peoples of Australia and the Maoris of New Zealand were treated by greedy colonists, to feel deep shame and guilt. Money-making and land-grabbing whites wrecked the work of missions: 'Missionaries learned from bitter experience that the greatest handicap to the success of their endeavours was the pernicious influence of the degrading habits of their unconverted fellow whites.'[10]

This problem was recognised by CMS petitioners to Parliament in 1838, unsuccessfully opposing British colonisation in New Zealand:

> adverting to the disastrous consequences to the Aborigines of uncivilised countries, in their rights, their persons, their property, and moral condition, which have uniformly followed European Colonisation in every country wherein it has been carried out. . . . That many of the Charters for the Colonisation of North America professed in like manner to embrace the propagation of Christianity among the Natives as part of their plan. . . . Notwithstanding, the result of these schemes of Colonisation was, to deprive the Natives of their lands, to demoralise their condition and well nigh depopulate the country, they cannot anticipate any other than like consequences in the case of New Zealand.[11]

Subsequently what they feared happened in New Zealand. In spite of the Treaty of Waitangi, the promises of which were ignored, dispossession was carried out at the point of British guns in the Maori wars. This resulted in the collapse of Anglican and Methodist churches that previously had been drawing sixty per cent of Maoris to attend. We should hang our heads in shame at the behaviour of our forebears and compatriots. The gospel can never be proclaimed in an historical vacuum, and both the crusades and European imperialism alike are shameful episodes that hinder us forming meaningful relationships with our fellow human beings, and so hinder the progress of the gospel.

A biblical theology of race

It is important to remind ourselves of the Christian teaching to which we all give intellectual assent, and yet which seems somehow to take a nosedive into cover when we meet people of other nationalities. While there may be no total cure for this disease, studying biblical doctrines afresh and applying them to our relationships with those of other races and nationalities may nudge us toward appreciating and adopting Christian standards. In the final event, prayer for the Lord's help and the grace of the Holy Spirit is what we need most.

The doctrine of God

God is no respecter of persons: he is after all the creator of every human being of every race. He is utterly even-handed and fair, so much so that he does not even favour the righteous and the just. Whatever else the benefits of being a Christian believer, sons and daughters of the one we have the privilege of calling Father, it seems he shows no favouritism in the blessings he chooses to bestow. The story of the labourers in the vineyard who were equally rewarded whether they worked all day or only a part of it, was not an odd glitch in God's dealings with humanity. He makes his sun rise and his rain fall on just and unjust alike (Matthew 5:45). Believers and unbelievers alike experience the same blessings and the same trials (Matthew 7:24–27). He treats all of us in every race with absolute justice and impartiality. It is his desire that all human beings should be saved and come to the knowledge of the truth, that none should perish and all come to repentance (1 Timothy 2:4; 2 Peter 3:9). It is clear that not all will repent, but God responds to all who call upon him, whether Jew or Greek.

What is so extraordinary is that such teaching should emerge from the sixty-six books of the Bible, written principally by Jews. After the opening twelve chapters of Genesis, the whole focus of the rest of the Old Testament is upon the small nation of Israel. Yet most of their prophets have messages to deliver to other nations, and the psalms with which they worshipped make repeated references to the nations, peoples, all the earth and so on. We might expect the Old Testament to be totally ethnocentric, yet this concept of the impartiality of God towards every tribe, tongue and nation comes out clearly in both Testaments. It could be argued that much of the New Testament is an attack upon ethnocentricity. Though the action of the Gospels takes place within Palestine, and, according to Matthew, work among Gentiles or Samaritans was proscribed for the twelve (Matthew 10:5), Jesus consistently attacks prejudice against Samaritans, and commends Gentiles for their faith.

Rather than a centripetal movement of all nations inwards to Jerusalem to worship, the centrifugal force of the Holy Spirit sends the apostles outward to all nations. Stephen's remarkable speech, twice as long as Paul's longest address, shows that the God of Abraham can have dealings with human beings in Mesopotamia, Egypt, Arabia and Samaria, and there is holy ground outside the Holy Land. In the epistles, racial exclusivism is attacked: if 'Jews first, and then the Gentile' describes the past history of God revealing himself to humankind, the future teaching for the church is 'neither Jew nor Greek'.

The simple question we must ask ourselves is always: How does the God, to whom I belong and whom I serve, regard these people I am now meeting? The teaching of the Bible is clear. The passage about the way God treats the wicked and the unjust is found in the context of how we should react towards enemies and persecutors. This is how we demonstrate our relationship to the Father, by treating even the most hostile human beings as he himself does (Matthew 5:43–48). We are to be perfect in our attitudes to unchurched or even anti-Christian people, precisely because God himself shows his perfection in his attitude to them.

Notice then that our attitude to people is not determined by our *methodology* – because this is a tactful tactic, the worldly-wise method of the skilful salesman. It must be rather determined by our *theology*, because of the character of the God to whom we belong.

The doctrine of incarnation

The eternal Son of God was made flesh (Asian flesh incidentally) and dwelled among us. He chose to become incarnate as a Jew, not as a European. It is not only the fact that he once became a human and lived among us, but also that he still bears that human form in the glory of heaven, which has to determine our attitude towards all human beings. Christ took our human form and made it sacred. There is something special about the human form of existence since God himself chose to make himself visible by taking human form and likeness. Believers of every race are now transformed in Christ, and we need to view them all in the light of their belonging to him.

More, Scripture commands us to 'show proper respect to everyone' (1 Peter 2:17). Perhaps the most striking passage is the famous parable about the sheep and the goats (Matthew 25:35–46). The words 'I was a foreigner and you invited me in' and 'I was a foreigner and you did not invite me in' are especially significant here.

Once in London I was dreading a difficult interview with an Ethiopian student. He was about to tell me that the Lord had personally told him that he was to continue at college for seven years, even though he kept failing all his exams! It was as though the Lord said, 'Mike, you have read Matthew 25, haven't you? And do you see the implication: you are to treat him as though it was me on the other side of the desk from you!' It made all the difference to that interview and my sense of respect for the student. 'Whatever you did for one of the least of these brothers of mine, you did for me' (Matthew 25:40). Every human being we meet is to be spoken to and treated as though it were the Lord himself who stands before us. We must seek to apply all these biblical principles of grace and love in our dealings with others. Even though I am an alien and will be treated as one, I will go the second mile; I will love them all fervently, because Christ himself does.

The doctrine of humankind

The creator has made us all of one blood (AV) or 'From one man he made every nation of men' (Acts 17:26) so that we all share in a common humanity. There are some minor genetical differences between races. Africans can run faster than most other races, as is demonstrated at every Olympic Games. Jews are on average more intelligent than other races, as their leadership in the sciences and the arts alike make clear. It is less well known that Asian races sweat less and only excrete about one tenth the salt that Caucasians do, while the Rhesus negative blood factor occurs in only about one in a thousand Asians, but one in eleven Caucasians. But these are minimal differences. When we are born as babies, we all make the same noises! We are born as human beings without culture or language, prior to learning all that our environment, parents, siblings and schoolmates teach us. We need to see all human beings – rich and poor, intelligent and mentally slow alike – as equally human and worthy of respect and love.

This is not just the product of a tolerant humanism or kindly philanthropic feelings. The Christian's attitude is determined by Christian doctrine: not only by what the Bible says about the character of God himself, but also by what the Bible says about the nature of humankind, male and female, irrespective of race or nationality. All men and women of every race have been made in the image of God, and we should honour them accordingly. There used to be a television advert, for thermal underwear I think, in which everyone so protected was surrounded by a kind of protective glow, a perceptible aura. The Christian doctrine of humankind means that we need to see all human beings surrounded by a special aura.

The doctrine of salvation

Jesus shared our humanity in order to give himself 'as a ransom for all men' (1 Timothy 2:6). Every human being is precious, because Christ died for them.

> Since the children have flesh and blood, he too shared in their humanity so that by his death he might destroy him who has the power of death – that is, the devil – and free those who all their lives were held in slavery by their fear of death. . . . For this reason he had to be made like his brothers in every way in order that he might become a merciful and faithful high priest in service to God, and that he might make atonement for the sins of the people.
>
> (Hebrews 2:14–17)

And (*pace* those who teach that Christ only died for the elect) Jesus 'is the atoning sacrifice for our sins, and not only for ours, but also for the sins of the whole world' (1 John 2:2). The person of our own race, or those of other races, whom we may find that we dislike or against whom we may have an apparently justifiable grouse, is none the less someone for whom Christ died. How can I ignore, dislike, shun, despise or hate such a person on whose head God has set such a precious price? It is in the context of, and as a consequence of the death of Christ that Paul urges the Corinthians: 'From now on we regard no-one from a worldly point of view' (2 Corinthians 5:16). Until we ourselves were so redeemed and reconciled, we may well have regarded others from a worldly point of view, because we had not till then understood the significance of the death of Christ. Because Christ died to bring a free offer of forgiveness and adoption to each and every human being, we have to look at them differently.

The doctrine of the Holy Spirit

The Holy Spirit indwells Christians of every tribe, tongue and nation. Some people have been stupidly reluctant to recognise that 'natives' can be taught by the Holy Spirit just as much as any of the rest of us. 'They have received the Holy Spirit just as we have' (Acts 10:47). Peter's argument to his critics following the Cornelius affair was

> The Spirit told me to have no hesitation about going with them. . . . As I began to speak, the Holy Spirit came on them as he had come on us at the beginning. . . . So if God gave them the same gift that he gave us, who believed in the Lord Jesus Christ, who was I to think that I could oppose God?   (Acts 11:12, 15, 17)

Peter's subsequent argument at the Council of Jerusalem concerning converted Gentiles whom some Jewish Christians persisted in regarding as dirty dogs was essentially the same:

God, who knows the heart, showed that he accepted them by giving the Holy Spirit to them, just as he did to us. He made no distinction between us and them, for he purified their [dirty Gentile doggy] hearts by faith. . . . We believe it is through the grace of our Lord Jesus that we are saved, just as they are.
(Acts 15:8–11).

However unworthy we may be, we are all saved by grace, and however dirty and unholy we may be, we are made clean by the Holy Spirit (in the Welsh language 'the clean Spirit' as opposed to unclean spirits).

The outworking of biblical teaching

The early Protestant missionaries owed a great deal of what they knew of other countries and peoples from Captain Cook's journals. His Admiralty instructions read: 'You are likewise to observe the Genius, Temper, Disposition and Number of the natives, if there be any, and endeavour by all proper means to cultivate a friendship and alliance with them.' Even this highly secular source recognised the importance of friendship.

Henry Martyn, that earnest and dedicated linguist, who was a model of life-imperilling commitment, displayed a capacity for friendship that attracted even non-Christians.

India has always had more than its fair share of beggars and 'holy men', whose living, whether by misfortune or profession, depends on the charity of others. To such men the kind-hearted chaplain soon became known, and his house became a regular rendezvous. He let it be known that once a week, on Sundays, he would distribute food and money, and they came by hundreds, young and old, male and female, bloated and wizened, tall and short, athletic and feeble; some clothed with abominable rags;

some nearly without clothes; some plastered with mud and cowdung; others with matted, uncombed locks streaming down to their heels . . .[12]

Montstuart Elphinstone, ambassador to Kabul, was a fellow passenger with Martyn when Elphinstone was on his way to become British resident in Bombay. He said of him:

> We have in Mr Martyn an excellent scholar, and one of the mildest, cheerfulest and pleasantest men I ever saw. He is extremely religious, and disputes about the faith with the Nakhoda, but talks on all subjects, sacred and profane, and makes others laugh as heartily as he could do if he were an infidel. . . . A far better companion than I reckoned on, though my expectations were high. His zeal is unabated, but it is not troublesome, and he does not press disputes and investigate creeds. A man of good sense and taste, and simple in his manners and character, and cheerful in conversation.[13]

A much later model of simple lifestyle and sacrificial identification was John Ethelstan Cheese, an Anglican minister interned by the Turks during the 1914–1918 War (see chapter 1). His stooping figure and fair beard became known in the Arab world. He was the *weli* the holy man, allowed to pass safely anywhere. He spent twenty-four years as a wandering apostle to the Somalis. They were a half-nomadic, pastoral people, travelling by camel from pasture to pasture. Ethelstan travelled with them, gradually assimilating more of their language, walking when they walked, sleeping in their camps, eating their food and learning to milk a camel when thirst overtook him.

Another man who succeeded in breaking through the barriers of ethnic and religious prejudice was the CMS missionary to Egypt, Temple Gairdner. One Muslim told how Gairdner bicycled over every day for a fortnight, staying two hours:

> When we came to the chief points of dispute between the two religions, he would not teach me till we had prayed together. 'In prayer, things are explained' he told me. And he taught me to keep silence awhile before entering into prayer. I felt he loved me for myself, not because I might become a Christian only, and in this I found he was like Christ. And he loved our children and always played with them.[14]

No unrealistic superspirituality that ignores the truth

We should still retain our objectivity and our critical faculties: we can't pretend there are no native characteristics which are difficult to accept. Paul wrote to Titus about the Cretans, 'One of their own prophets has said: "Cretans are always liars, evil brutes, lazy gluttons." This testimony is true' (Titus 1:12–13)! In 1822 the Scottish missionary Robert Moffatt wrote about Africans he had met: 'Only satiate their mendicant spirits by perpetually giving, and you are all that is good; but refuse to meet their endless demands and their theme of praise is turned to ridicule and abuse.'[15]

So we should not shut our eyes to real problems and we must face the realities of longstanding pagan environments. No nation is perfect and not all national characteristics are lovable. People often show their worst face to foreigners.

Discriminatory attitudes to avoid

1. Avoid foolish national caricatures: all English are reserved and proud; all Americans are loud and brash; all Australians are crude and simple minded; all Chinese are

superstitious and greedy for money; all Japanese are polite and deceitful; all natives are dirty, dishonest, incompetent, stupid, etc. If we think of other people like that, how can we ever relate to them?

2. Avoid any suggestion of lack of trust or confidence in a fellow Christian: he may be expecting us to distrust him or her. Hospitable welcome is important.

3. Avoid making unfavourable comparisons with your own country, even when invited to do so. The glories and excellence of your own country are not part of the gospel! Jerusalem was not built in England's green and pleasant land, nor will God bless America above the rest.

4. Avoid appearing to prefer the company of fellow expatriates to fellowship with national Christians.

5. Avoid any hint of pride, arrogance or despising others.

6. Make it clear you have not come to work *on* people or even *for* people, but *with* people, alongside them as equals in God's service. In the series *The Jewel in the Crown* a British officer says to the Indian soldier, 'I am your father and your mother . . .' We must shun the slightest whiff of such paternalism. While we might say, 'I am your brother and your sister,' it might be better to say, 'I am your younger brother or younger sister.'

7. Avoid a merely professional interest in people, such that we are only interested in them to get them converted, or while they fit into some programme with which we are involved.

Bonding actions to make

1. Determine prayerfully before God to seek to establish friendships with national Christians which are as deep or deeper than those enjoyed previously with Christians in your own country. Such friendships are the most reward-

ing part of missionary work, and the best missionaries are those who establish many real and deep friendships. Pray for such relationships.

2. Be as welcoming and hospitable to national Christians as to missionaries.

3. Always esteem others better than yourself (Philippians 2:3) and remember you have the opportunity to treat people as though they were the Lord (Matthew 25).

4. Show your pleasure and appreciation at meeting, parting and being with national brethren. Use all appropriate cultural means of showing respect and affection.

5. Be more eager to give opportunities for others to minister than to take those opportunities for yourself. A highly qualified mission surgeon in South Thailand heard that the teenage child of a colleague had fractured his skull in an accident, and travelled to the hospital to find only a young Thai house surgeon on duty, and immediate surgery imperative. The Thai doctor asked the surgeon to operate, but he replied, 'Oh no. You will operate and I will assist you.' In speaking like this he gave great face to the young doctor. Our missionary task requires the attitude of John the Baptist: 'He must increase: I must decrease.'

Making friends can be the most rewarding aspect of cross-cultural missionary service; the building of real relationships across cultural barriers. If there is one secret of successful Christian work, this is it.

What role should a missionary try to fulfil?

Our role is important if we are to gain credibility for ourselves, and for the gospel. I am not talking here about functional roles like doctor, minister, literature worker, but of roles which can apply to any foreigner seeking to penetrate a new culture. While these were mentioned briefly in chapter 2 it seems important, even at the risk of repetition, to underline them and elaborate them further.

1. *Guest*. Hospitality is an important aspect of courtesy, highly valued in many cultures. Just as hospitality goes beyond our expectations, so does the host's kindly tolerance of our ignorance. In the west one does not remain a guest for very long, but in the two-thirds world it can last much longer, especially if some obligation is felt.

My most vivid memory of being a guest is being welcomed to a Kayan longhouse at Long Atip on the Upper Baram River. We came in on the MAF plane, were met by a crowd and escorted to a large room in the longhouse, where everybody gazed at us for almost half an hour (some people find this quite unsettling) almost in silence with occasional whisperings. At the end of that time they reckoned they 'knew us' well enough to recognise us again! Later they adopted us into adjacent families in the longhouse and gave us names. In their kindness and courtesy, these former head-hunters made us feel more than just visitors.

Being treated as a guest may be all right when you are on a short visit, and you can feel honoured to be welcomed and feasted in this way, but to be treated like a guest on a semi-permanent basis is almost insulting. We may begin like tourists, fascinated by all that goes on but still outsiders. Among Australians, you know you are making progress when they feel they know you well enough to be rude to you and tease you.

2. *Learner*. This role is not assigned, but deliberately chosen by the guest, and clearly expressed to his or her hosts: I need to confess that I am an ignoramus in this culture and society, and ask for induction and instruction. It pays the host respect and paves the way for a deeper relationship. Expressing such voluntary dependence is non-threatening, and shows humility and vulnerability. We make it clear that we want to understand, not to criticise or ridicule. Learners are often tested by asking them to compare their own culture with the newly-encountered host culture. It may seem like an invitation to be very honest, but they will be disappointed if you take it that way. You are a learner in this new culture for the present, and not a critic of it! It is a time for asking, and not telling; for requesting, not commanding. The foreign tourist in the hotel pays for help and expects attention as part of the service, but the pupil-learner-novice cannot do this. Genuineness and trust in your teachers is essential. Coming as a student-learner is absolutely basic to effective cross-cultural integration. It might even be said that the Lord Jesus came as a learner for the first thirty years before he began his ministry.

3. *Friend.* We may remain avid listeners, always ready to glean new information or to understand new behaviour patterns, but we cannot remain as children for ever, any more than we can remain guests. Africans are very shrewd in assessing how genuine people are. Some foreigners are self-deceived in thinking they are well liked simply because they have been kindly received. Values like courtesy and saving face mean that even strangers are friendly and obliging. We found Canada one of the most friendly countries in which we have been privileged to live.

Empathy and sensitivity, rapport and reality are essential to genuine friendships. 'Unconditional positive regard' is a positive gesture: you feel safe with the person. This matter of friendships is basic to being a fruitful missionary. Good missionaries are the ones who can make friends, while bad missionaries are those who cannot make friends.

In chapter 1 we mentioned the Brewsters' article on Bonding.[16] The idea is based on the way human and animal babies bond with their mothers provided they are close together in the first few weeks. If they are separated immediately after birth then the infant may attach to a surrogate. These studies on infant bonding are seen to parallel an adult's entrance into a foreign culture. In both situations there is increased adrenaline and an enhanced alertness to new things. The new missionary is ready to bond, unless snatched away by the expatriate missionary community and isolated from the new language community. The danger is that new missionaries may bond with other expatriates instead of with nationals. This can wreck the whole future ministry of the wrongly bonded person. Subsequently and consequently, evangelism and church planting are carried out by a 'foray' method. Missionaries live in isolation from the local people, making forays out each week to evangelise, but always returning to the perceived safety of the missionary ghetto. They do not pursue significant relationships as a way of life, and always distance themselves from the people they are supposed to be working with. They stand off and criticise: 'Oh these people! Why do they always do things this way!' The sense of belonging is basic. The proper attitude is: 'I belong to Jesus and I want to belong to you, so that through me God can invite you to belong to him.'

The first few weeks are crucial. Is your desire first to get settled? Then you can only get settled in a western way, locking yourself into a pattern foreign to local people. The missionary whose first priority is to discover how the local people cope with their environment – how they organise their lives and get their food, do their shopping and travel around – will belong so much more easily. Looking back I realise that we related much better in Japan, where we lived in a Japanese house surrounded by Japanese families, than we ever did later in Singapore living in our mission's international headquarters. We had local friends in Singapore, but they tended to treat us as distinguished guests! Many new missionaries are carefully cushioned from the full impact of the culture by their senior expatriate colleagues. The Brewsters feel this is a disservice and urge that from the very first day relationships should be established with the local people. I remember now that on our first night in Japan we went to a Japanese home and had a meal with Japanese friends, the ones who had urged us to come to Japan in the first place. Culturally-cushioned people do not have the opportunity to engage with local people: in trying to grasp the situation of local people, they get other outsiders' answers to insiders' situations, and so perpetuate the gap between themselves and the locals.

Bonding then is the factor that enables people to belong and build many friendships with national acquaintances. Needless to say they usually have excellent language learning experiences as well. Language acquisition is a social activity rather than an academic one. It may be better to keep newcomers in isolation from other missionaries as far as possible! The biggest menace are senior, unbonded missionaries. The Brewsters suggest four helpful guidelines:

1. Be willing to live with a local family.
2. Limit personal belongings to 20kgs (what you can carry on an airplane!).
3. Use only local transportation.
4. Learn language in the context of relationships with local people.

Notice the implication that foreign lifestyle (masses of baggage, cars, etc.) are a hindrance to, perhaps even a deterrent to bonding. The birth bonding analogy is not entirely satisfactory.

Marriage bonding might be seen as an alternative model. An established but so far non-bonded missionary might set themselves right by deciding to 'marry' the new culture. They announce a date after which their life patterns will change, probably by moving in with a local family and accepting a learner role. Needless to say such steps will be seen as threatening by other non-bonded missionaries. The total involvement lifestyle model contrasts with the 'foray' lifestyle of non-bonded missionaries. People who bond well may be regarded as maverick oddballs, even traitors who are accused of having 'gone native'. (When John Dunbar in *Dances with Wolves* has identified with Comanche culture, he is attacked and totally misunderstood by his former 'foray' type foreign colleagues.)

Becoming bicultural is different from rejecting our own culture. It is a new kind of Christian maturity to become a bicultural person. Bonding may be established in those first few critical weeks: the host culture realises that we are biased in their favour. This sense of commitment, feeling safe and at home lessens culture stress and shock. We feel safe and at home with people we have become familiar with. We may have had a similar experience as children with an uncle and aunt perhaps. Initially cautious, we soon realised they were on our side and we identified with them. This is well illustrated in the film and even more the book *Dances with Wolves*. At first the cavalryman and the Indians are extremely wary of each other. But this gradually gives way to mutual respect. This progress may be hindered because many westerners have an unconscious sense of racial superiority. They regard others as 'primitive' or 'savage'. Even when we know how absurd this is, for example, with Chinese or Japanese, we feel ill at ease because we do not understand, we feel strange, and the signals are different.

Many cultures are much more people-orientated than

western ones. We are always looking at our watches, thinking of the next task to be performed. True friends never look at their watches, for they value friendship more than time. Much of the time the foreigner is afraid of being taken advantage of. But if you display trust in the other person, then you can trust them.

In Asian cultures Chinese, Filipinos and Koreans may be superficially friendly, but real friendships are much harder to establish. The essential factor is time: duration over a considerable period; quantity in actual time spent sharing ideas; and quality – when we laugh or cry together. Sharing a crisis with someone else is always significant, when we are able to show that we care by responding to someone's need. Great care needs to be taken in using touch, always liable to misunderstanding, but facial expression of affection and concern is rarely a problem. Vulnerability in voluntary self-disclosure can help greatly.

Ailish Eve S. Hasabuan, a British missionary in Indonesia, was adopted into a Batak clan by a retired major general. At first it was nominal and informal, but in Batak culture unmarried women had low status unless they belonged to a senior clan. One night sharing a *betchak* (jeepney), two drunken men were being very objectionable. When they asked her name, she replied that her name was Hasabuan and that her adopted father was General Hasabuan. The men paled and apologised, positively grovelled in fact, saying, 'Your clan is senior to ours.' When Ailish reported this to General Hasabuan he adopted her more formally and she added the clan name to her own. Few missionaries can have achieved such acceptance that they are formally adopted into an extended family in their country of service. Bonding really matters.

Notes

1. Phyllis Thompson, *D.E. Hoste 'A Prince with God'* (London: CIM/Lutterworth, 1947), p.47.
2. *Ibid.*, p.62.
3. *Ibid.*, p.66.
4. Stephen Hayes, *Turbulence and Toeholds: The Life and Work of Dr Christopher Maddox* (Bangkok: Kanok Bannasan [OMF Publishers], 1991).
5. *Ibid.*, p.119.
6. Roland Allen, *Missionary Methods: St Paul's or Ours?* (Grand Rapids: Eerdmans, 1962), p.152.
7. 1 Corinthians 13:1ff.
8. Dorothy Parker, *The Best of Dorothy Parker* (Methuen 1952).
9. Richard T. France, 'Henry Martyn' in *Five Pioneer Missionaries* (London: Banner of Truth, 1965), p.271.
10. Stuart Piggin, *Evangelical Christianity in Australia: Spirit, Word and World* (Oxford University Press, 1996), p.22.
11. Davidson and Lineham, *Transplanted Christianity: Documents illustrating aspects of New Zealand Church History* (Auckland: College Communications, 1987), p.53.
12. Richard T. France in 'Henry Martyn', *Five Pioneer Missionaries* (London: Banner of Truth, 1965), p.274.
13. *Ibid.*, p.282.
14. Constance Padwick, *Temple Gairdner of Cairo* (London: SPCK, 1929), p.142.
15. Quoted in Geoffrey Moorhouse, *The Missionaries* (London: Eyre Methuen, 1973), p.65.
16. Thomas and Elisabeth Brewster, 'Bonding and the Missionary Task: Establishing a sense of Belonging' in

Winter and Hawthorne, eds, *Perspectives on the World Christian Movement* (Pasadena: William Carey, 1981), p.452 and published separately.

CHAPTER SIX

LAMBS LEARN TO APPRECIATE WOLF CULTURE

We have looked at what happens when the heralds of Christ enter a foreign country, learn a new language and seek to bond with human beings of a different culture. But we have not attempted to define what 'culture' means. During the course of history, Christians have attempted a variety of approaches to culture, often without thinking very deeply about it. In terms of our inherent prejudices we all assume that our own culture is essentially good, and tend to judge other cultures as in varying degrees less than the best. While some early missionaries *did* think deeply about culture and contextualisation (the Serampore Covenant produced by the first English Baptists in India, and Church Missionary Society work among Maoris in New Zealand are good examples), it may be true that others found it very difficult to disentangle biblical Christianity from their own cultural expressions of it. Charles Abel of the London Missionary Society started mission work on Kwato Island at the eastern end of Papua New Guinea in 1891. Being a keen cricketer he thought he could teach team spirit and sportsmanship. Today, though the total population is only 550, there are five cricket teams in which eighty adult men are involved. The women go to the gardens, while the men play and watch cricket.[1]

Culture is all-pervasive; we are all immersed in our own culture like a fish in water. Just as goldfish presumably are unconscious of their wetness until they jump out of the bowl, we may not even realise that we have a culture until we jump out into another and experience 'culture shock'.

Culture is not just verbal, of course. Suppose I sit down quietly in an airport departure lounge and say nothing. The observer could still make some general observations about me: a Caucasian male, married (the ring on the left hand), early seventies (greying hair), probably European (from clothes) and Sherlock Holmes might even identify a British old school tie. And the moment we open our mouths we can be identified as Americans, Canadians, Australians, New Zealanders, South Africans; then of course we have our own national regional accents. But even if we keep our mouths buttoned up, the moment we begin to move we start communicating.

Cultures vary to the extent that certain recognisable gestures mean different things in different countries. Unconsciously I decide to finger my earlobe because it itches from a mosquito bite, but in southern Europe this conveys various threatening messages. Scratching my lower eyelid instead, a Saudi Arab may think I am calling him stupid, while a Latin American woman might think I am being forward. One of the most confusing is the circular 'O' signed with the fingers. This means OK in the United States, 'zero' to the French, 'money' to the Japanese, 'I'll kill you' in Tunis, while in some countries it has bawdy implications! Even the 'thumbs up' sign can be misinterpreted as obscene.

In other words the moment we begin to move, even if we speak no words at all, we start to communicate cross culturally! I might decide to avoid saying anything or making any signs which might get me into trouble. So I just hand someone a tract instead, but unfortunately use my left hand, which is the toilet hand, and suggest that this paper cannot be worth very much! Even the way some westerners walk conveys a message in Asia: Look how arrogant foreigners are! All this means that even before we get to language and thought patterns, we are forced to recognise that different human beings have very different cultures.

Defining culture

There is one verse that speaks of 'culture' in an aesthetic sense in the New Testament, namely 'Finally, brothers, whatever is true, whatever is noble, whatever is right, whatever is pure, whatever is lovely, whatever is admirable – if anything is excellent or praiseworthy – think about such things' (Philippians 4:8). But please recognise that 'culture' refers just to music, art and good manners as in 'he is a very cultured person'! The word is used by missionaries in a much more technical sense.

When each of us are born (apart from any alleged learning experiences in the womb) we are culturally a white sheet, an unprogrammed disc, on which a great deal will get written from the earliest years of our lives. Some things are genetic and instinctive: puppies brought up in isolation from other dogs will still whine, growl, yap in the manner typical of their breed, just as birds build nests typical of their species, and all human babies cry and yell in the same way irrespective of their race. Because these things are typical of all human beings the genetic inherited characteristics are not usually regarded as part of human culture, but only what may be learned and transmitted. It could be said that having 'culture' is what actually distinguishes human societies from other created species, although it would be possible to speak of the 'culture' of a troupe of gorillas, a pod of orcas, a pride of lions or even of an ant or social bee colony.

Textbooks supply a large number of complicated, technical definitions of what 'a culture' is, but we need to suggest a simple, general definition of culture. Louis Luzbetak called it 'the total lifeway and mentality of a people'.[2] This includes all the traditions and learned behaviour acquired from one's social group, namely knowledge, beliefs, attitudes, moral values, customs and all that is passed on from one generation to another. Culture describes the totality of all the accumulated experience common to a specific social group, transmitted to all of its members both formally and informally. That process begins from birth in the way we as babies are dressed, suckled, talked to and cared for. We may all be virtually identical members of the same species, like blank floppy discs, when we are born, but the process of differentiation begins at once, as file upon file, indeed whole new directories of information are opened up in rapid succession. These contain all the specific properties of our tribe, nation or linguistic group.

Defining societies and people groups

Many of these definitions refer to social groupings, which may vary in size from 'the people of China' to much smaller groups, so that a 'society' may refer to any group of mutually interacting individuals, regardless of size. Smaller social units or sub-cultures may be recognised, showing a variety of behaviour patterns distinguishable from the main culture.

Cultures clearly relate to specific societies or groups, which have developed the particular culture, so that definitions are inevitably circular, because a culture describes those properties, which define the society. Thus a society may be said to be 'a social organisation made up of a group of people, who share a geographical area and culture'.

We should notice, in passing, the definition of the phrase 'a people group' that forms the basis of a lot of contemporary church growth thinking about breaking down larger communities into smaller unreached ones. Donald McGavran sought to derive this from the use of '$\pi\alpha\nu\tau\alpha$ $\tau\alpha$ $\epsilon\theta\nu\eta$' in the New Testament (but this has been effectively challenged by Bosch and others).[3] Thus a so-called 'people group' may be defined as a significantly large grouping of individuals who perceive themselves to have a common affinity for one another because of their shared language, religion, ethnicity, residence, occupation, class or caste, situation or combinations of these. From the standpoint of communicating the message of Christ, it is the largest group within which the gospel can flow along natural lines without encountering barriers of understanding or acceptance due to culture, language, geography, etc. [4]

1. God's relationship with human cultures

While God's common grace is poured upon human beings in general, we need to think about how God as our creator relates to differing nations and cultures. Christian attitudes towards culture have varied throughout history, some even trying to escape from society and its culture without realising how all-pervading human culture is. Richard Niebuhr[5] and Charles Kraft[6] both discuss at length how God regards human cultures, and are worth reading. Here is an abbreviated summary.

1. 'God is against culture' position
God is against 'culture', if we choose (wrongly) to identify it solely as the world in the power of the evil one (1 John 2:15–17). In the past, some Christian groups have tried to separate themselves from human society, because they perceived it to be evil and corrupt. The

monastic revulsion against corrupt Graeco-Roman culture, and Exclusive Brethren hostility to 'this wilderness scene' are two examples. Some missionaries (like the 'Judaisers' of the New Testament period) have required their converts to abandon their native cultural system and to isolate themselves from it. This response results from focusing upon the occasional negative use of 'world' ($\kappa o\sigma\mu o\varsigma$) in the New Testament (eg 1 John above), and ignoring other uses of that word, and disregarding synonyms like 'this age', 'earth' and 'inhabited earth' which are uniformly positive (or neutral) about the creator's attitude towards the human race in general and the environment in which we live. This 'world denying' ascetic tendency appears in branches of most religious traditions, within Hinduism and Buddhism, and notably in Jainism. Its adoption by Christian groups has almost always hindered evangelisation.

2. 'God is in culture' position (relativist)

In this view 'God' is seen as merely a product of a particular cultural world view, thus creating God in their own cultural image and thus essentially relativist. It is true that members of different cultures *do* have differing concepts of deity. It is also true that such differences correlate with their world views, and at perceptual level, people do 'create' their own view of God. This is partly a translation problem, because the translator has to look for a roughly equivalent word already existing in the language. 'God' was the best available existing word in Anglo-Saxon that could be used to translate the Hebrew and Greek words used in the Bible. Korean had an existing word for the supreme creator of everything, *hananim*, which was much closer to the biblical words than either the Japanese *kami-sama* (a common noun rather than a proper name!) or the various Chinese constructs using characters for heavenly Lord, the emperor in heaven, etc. It is suggested that this partially explains the greater progress of the gospel in Korea compared with either China or Japan. In every case the existing native word has to be redeemed, transformed and filled with new biblical meaning to avoid the existing cultural presuppositions.

But to say that 'God' is no more than a cultural construct is a reductionist and relativist dogma.

3. 'God is in our culture' position (restrictive)

As with Israel in the Old Testament, the Lord is absolutised as relating only to one's own culture, an attitude adopted by many tribal groups regarding their own deities. Stephen was martyred for insisting that the Lord was not limited to the holy land, the holy city or the holy place, but that he called Abraham in Mesopotamia, was present with Joseph in Egypt, allowed patriarchs to be buried in Samaria, and gave the Law on Mount Sinai in Arab territory.[7] Some Christian primitivist groups have alleged that there is a *biblical culture*, eg Christian Brethren and some house churches claim to be 'the New Testament church'. All primitivist movements commonly identify their own sub-culture with 'the New Testament church'. Liberal Judaism seems to adopt this position in eschewing proselytism and insisting that everyone is saved through their own beliefs. Jewish beliefs are only seen as salvific for Jews!

4. 'God is above all culture' position (deist)

God is seen as above and unconcerned with our human culture, a view held by many African ethnic groups, many of which believe in a benevolent, albeit somewhat irrelevant, supreme deity. This provides appropriate words in various languages that can be used to describe the God revealed in the Law and prophets, and supremely in Christ, but the whole concept has to be reinterpreted to show that this God is indeed deeply concerned for and committed to human beings of every tribe, and that there is no other God beside him.

5. 'God above culture' position

Justin Martyr, Clement of Alexandria and Thomas Aquinas taught a spiritual dichotomy, in which the Christian is accountable both to Christ and to culture, to render to God what is his and to Caesar what is his, serving both in their own separate spheres. While many Christians have adopted this kind of compartmentalisation during the course of history, a more holistic approach both to God's sovereignty and to our relationship with society is spiritually and intellectually more satisfying. At its most extreme this produces a dualism, in which we see human culture as depraved and corrupt and Christians are spiritual amphibians forced to live in two different realms. Humans are all evil and God is all-good. He redeems us for a future world which is all good.

6. 'God above culture' position (conversionist)
St Augustine, John Calvin and John Wesley see Christ more as redeemer than as law-giver, seeing culture as under God's judgement as well as under God's sovereign rule. Culture is corrupted but convertible, usable and perhaps even redeemable by God's grace and power. This is essentially the position adopted by the Lausanne Covenant (see below).

7. 'God above but through culture' position
Many of the earlier positions were adopted before our modern understanding of the total pervasiveness of culture, as the general human condition. God is above, and exists totally outside of all cultures. Humans exist totally inside of their cultures. God uses culture as a vehicle for interaction with human beings, the milieu in which all encounters with or between human beings take place. Language is part of culture, and God has used human language with all its finitude, relativity and misperceptions of eternity.[8] The task of mission involves communicating the biblically-revealed truths about the one God in all the available human languages, and in terms which each individual culture can understand.

2. The cultures of the Bible
The Bible is not a textbook of anthropology, but it does say some important things about human cultures and society. In the book of Genesis, man and woman are placed in the garden to cultivate it (the word culture derives from Latin *colere* meaning to 'till' or to 'cultivate'). Both male and female are to

'rule' and 'subdue' (Genesis 1:26, 28) and are 'to work it and take care of it' (Genesis 2:15). However, fallen man and woman are driven out of the garden, but 'Abel kept flocks and Cain worked the soil' (Genesis 4:2). After the flood Noah is told: 'Everything that lives and moves will be food for you. Just as I gave you the green plants, I now give you everything' (9:3). Then we read: 'Noah, a man of the soil, proceeded to plant a vineyard' (9:20), to get drunk and embarrass his sons. In Genesis 10 we have seventy (Hebrew) or seventy-two (LXX) Gentile nations, and in the following chapter they are building Babylon in the plain of Shinar.

In Genesis 12 God establishes a relationship with Abraham, and promises that in him shall 'all the families of the earth' be blessed. God also establishes relationships with Isaac and Jacob, and their descendants, culminating in the covenant with Moses and all the children of Israel: that is he builds a relationship with one particular culture and communicates with them through one Semitic language (or two, if we include Aramaic along with Hebrew). However he does not abandon Hagar or her son Ishmael either, but is with the boy and promises his blessing (Genesis 16:7–15; 21:11–21). In spite of this apparent narrow focus upon the Jewish people, God's continuing interest in other nations is constantly revealed: look, for example, at Psalm 33:13–15 and Psalm 96 (all the earth, nations, peoples). Amos addresses Israel's neighbours (Amos 1 and 2), and speaks of the Lord overruling other major ethnic migrations (Amos 9:7).

In verses which were to become significant for the church later, the Lord speaks of 'all the nations that bear my name' (Amos 9:12; Acts 15:17). Major prophets all address the nations as well as Israel (Isaiah 13–23; Jeremiah 46–51; Ezekiel 25–32). Malachi looks forward to a future day when as the Lord says, 'My name will be great among the nations, from the rising to the setting of the sun. *In every place* incense and pure offerings will be brought to my name, because my name will be great among the nations' (Malachi 1:11, my italics). These words of Malachi (εν παντι τοπο) keep on cropping up in the New Testament (1 Corinthians 1:2; 2 Corinthians 2:14; 1 Thessalonians 1:8; 1 Timothy 2:8). Malachi's prophecy is being fulfilled through Paul's evangelism and church planting.

Jesus himself restricted his own immediate ministry to the lost sheep of the house of Israel, and, as far as we know, never entered the Gentile cities of Tiberias with its hot springs and the garrison city of Caesarea. Nonetheless, he spoke of the blessing to come to the Gentile nations. 'Many will come from the east and the west, and will take their places at the feast with Abraham, Isaac and Jacob' (Matthew 8:10); 'I have other sheep who are not of this sheep pen. I must bring them also' (John 10:16); this gospel of the kingdom is to 'be preached in the whole world . . . and then the end will come' (Matthew 24:14); as well as the great commission (Matthew 28:18ff).

All humankind has a common origin; human beings as we know them today are all of the one species *homo sapiens,* but belong to diverse races and diverse cultures. Paul proclaimed this on Mars Hill: 'From one man he made every nation of men, that they should inhabit the whole earth; and he determined the times set for them and exact places where they should live' (Acts 17:26). Acts tells the great story of the spread of the gospel to those other nations: the first Gentile, Nicholas, a proselyte of Antioch (Acts 6:5); the conversion of the first Ethiopian (Acts 8:26ff) and then the Petrine precedent, the first Italians, Cornelius and his friends in Caesarea (Acts 10:1–11:18) and the great turning in Antioch (Acts 11:19–26). This also marks the significant shift in language from Aramaic to Greek (though both languages must have been used in the Jerusalem church [Acts 6:1]). Paul wrote his letters in Greek, and while Jesus may have spoken in Aramaic, and Peter taught in it in Rome, the Gospel writers all write in Greek, even when like Matthew they are apparently writing for Jews.

We thus have to face the fact that God's communication came to us in the first place through two cultures and languages – Hebrew and Greek. Hebrew culture was constantly influenced by its contact with neighbouring cultures, for good or ill. They were impacted by the Egyptians during the years in Goshen; by the Canaanites still occupying the land; by the encroaching Philistines driving them up into the hills; by contact with the Babylonians and Persians while in captivity; and then by forced enculturation under the Greek Empire. Greek became the common trade language of the whole Mediterranean world at that time. We cannot ignore the cultural media that God used to communicate with humankind. One great problem of interpretation is distinguishing between the cultural and supracultural in both Old and New Testaments. This matters to all of us in the hermeneutics we adopt in relation to our own native cultures, but becomes even more acute for the missionary teaching the Scriptures in other languages and in relation to other cultures. As missionaries we cannot avoid having to relate the cultures of the Bible to the cultures in which we are working.

Howard Marshall in his article on 'Culture and the New Testament'[9] supplies some interesting examples. The phrase 'son of man' used repeatedly by Jesus of himself had a Jewish background (Daniel 7:13), but would have communicated little to Greeks, so that it disappears apart from tradition about the teaching of Jesus preserved in the Gospels. The Hellenistic missionaries working in the Graeco-Roman world found alternative useful words like 'Lord' and 'Saviour' used as titles of dignity by Roman emperors and other rulers, which could be transferred across to describe Jesus. The word 'redemption' which originally derived from the deliverance of God's people from Egypt, now develops against the background of the freeing of slaves by paying a ransom price. Marshall points out that the two quotations Paul uses in Acts 17:28, namely 'In him we live and move and have our being' and 'For we are indeed his offspring' both come from pagan poets, and both originally refer to Zeus, the supreme deity of the Greek pantheon. Many other beliefs about Zeus would in no way fit Yahweh, but in these two respects at least, Paul could borrow them.

He also shows that Jesus himself questioned some Jewish cultural traditions, like keeping the Sabbath and ceremonial washing. Jews would have insisted these were scriptural, yet Jesus questioned them because they had sunk into legalism. The decisions of the early church (Acts 15:16–21) were confirmed by the Amos 9:11–12 quotation about 'nations called by his name'. From that time onwards, Gentile Christians did not have to adopt the whole Jewish cultural package, nor need they abandon all their Gentile culture in order to become Christians. They did not need to be circumcised or keep the food laws: they had been cleansed by the Holy Spirit, and were unclean no longer. Both the temple and the synagogue were ultimately abandoned by all Christians, whether Jew or Gentile by race.

One of the tragic facts of Christian history is that having escaped from Jewish culture, Christian thinking was then imprisoned by Greek philosophy and Latin theologians. This has given rise to the great contextualisation debate and consequent cry for fresh, contemporary expressions of biblically revealed truth in terms of other cultures. Just one example: Brahmabandhab Upadhyaya (1861–1907) argued that:

> Indian thought can be made just as useful to Christianity as Greek thought has been to Europe. The truths of the Hindu philosopher must be 'baptised' and used as stepping stones to the Catholic

Faith. . . . The European clothes of the Catholic religion should be laid aside as soon as possible. It must assume the Hindu garment, which will make it acceptable to the people of India.[10]

Here he is again:

The Hindu mind is extremely subtle and penetrative, but is opposed to the Greco-Scholastic method of thinking. We must fall back on the vedantic method, in formulating the Catholic religion to our countrymen. In fact the Vedanta must be made to do the same service to the Catholic faith in India as was done by the Greek philosophy in Europe.

(Animananda, p.74)[11]

He argued that Hellenistic culture became detached from Greek religion, which died, and that therefore it ought to be possible to accept cultural Hinduism while rejecting Hindu religion. He wrote a magnificent devotional hymn worshipping the Trinity as Sat-cit-ananda (Being, Intelligence and Joy), in which he expresses Christian orthodoxy using Hindu terminology.

3. Culture and mission

The anthropologist Bronislaw Malinowski outlined 'seven basic human needs'. Different cultures manifest, experience and pass on traditions that vary enormously from each other, but these seven areas of human existence are absolutely fundamental:

1. Metabolism – oxygen, food and drink.
2. Reproduction – replenishing of society, perpetuating species.
3. Bodily comforts – shelter, housing, clothing.
4. Safety – protection, weapons, organisation of police.
5. Movement – play, games, travel.

6. Growth – babies, childhood, adolescence, maturity, old age.
7. Health – maintenance and repair of the organism, hygiene.

Of course different societies with different cultures are going to differ in every one of these basic areas. People will have different eating habits and staple food, differing marriage customs, different housing, weapons, games and transport, rites of passage, approaches to health and healing. They will also differ significantly in their world-view and religious presuppositions: such things as fatalism, transmigration (*samsara*), our present life influenced by previous existences (*karma*), freedom of the will, destiny, what constitutes holiness and so on. The missionary adventure involves identifying with the basic needs, while seeking to understand all these cultural norms and presuppositions. Then the unchanging, revealed gospel of the Lord Jesus must be related to the particularities of each specific set of beliefs. This provides an enormous intellectual stimulus. Manifestly gospel communication involves much more than language learning, although learning the words is a necessary step to understanding the ideas. The language student is a culture explorer. It is impossible to do one without at the same time doing the other.

The Lausanne Covenant definition was an especially helpful corrective in helping missions and missionaries think about their response to culture.

The Lausanne Covenant definition (*Clause 10. Evangelism and Culture*)

The development of strategies for world evangelisation calls for imaginative pioneering methods. Under God, the result will be the rise of churches deeply rooted in Christ and closely related to their *culture*. *Culture* must always be tested and judged by Scripture. Because man is God's creature, some of his *culture* is rich in beauty and goodness. Because he is fallen, all of it is tainted with sin and some of it is demonic. The Gospel does not presuppose the superiority of any *culture* to another, but evaluates all *cultures* according to its own criteria of truth and righteousness, and insists on moral absolutes in every *culture*. Missions have all too frequently exported with the Gospel an alien *culture*, and churches have sometimes been in bondage to *culture* rather than to the Scripture. Christ's evangelists must humbly seek to empty themselves of all but their personal authenticity in order to become the servant of others, and churches must seek to transform and enrich culture for the glory of God.[12]

This clause of the Covenant is so well stated that perhaps we would do well to memorise these words, so significant for mission.

Some summary propositions

1. *Culture is constructed by humanity*

It is therefore part good and part evil. All that is beautiful in it will be preserved and brought into the heavenly city as the 'glory and honour of the nations' and the 'splendour' of the kings of the earth (Revelation 21:24, 26), while all that is evil will be excluded from it (Revelation 21:27). This being so, it is a part of the missionary adventure to revel in all the good things that we discover in our adopted cultures. This is not only in order that we better proclaim the gospel and communicate God's truth, but also because it is good and properly human to do so: in fact both things go hand in hand.

2. *Culture is related to the created order*

Animals, crops, soil, climate and humankind itself are all created by God. So the material upon which human culture has to work is all given by God the creator. We should therefore worship God because of it, as the Psalmist does in Psalm 104 and Job does in Job 38–42. In many cultures there is a profound appreciation of the beauty of the seasons and of natural beauty (Japanese Christian worship services always begin with some reference to it!), and we need to direct that appreciative wonder towards the blessed God who is the source of it all, as many of the Psalms do.

3. Both anthropology (the study of human cultures and societies) and theology are human-made disciplines

While insisting that the authors of Scripture were inspired by the Holy Spirit, and that we who read what they wrote also need to be illuminated by the Holy Spirit, we hesitate to claim that all theologians without exception are necessarily either permanently inspired or inevitably illuminated! Our human theologies are man-made and culture-bound too. It is fashionable in the west to talk about African theology or Asian theology, while arrogantly regarding what we teach in Europe or America as simply 'theology', without realising that our theologies may be just as much culturally-determined as those stemming from Christian thinkers in other continents.

To give a concrete illustration of this: the Bible teaches that churches need leadership. New Testament cities all have political leaders, but call them by a variety of different names: Asiarchs in Ephesus (Acts 19:31), politarchs in Thessalonica (Acts 17:6, 8), ethnarchs in Damascus (2 Corinthians 11:32); Areopagites in Athens (Acts 17:34), etc. But they also have a variety of terms for Christian leaders: 'elders' (a Jewish concept), 'overseers' (a Gentile concept), *prohistamenoi* in Romans and Thessalonians, *hegemenoi* in Hebrews, *kuberneseis* in Corinth, and so on. Reading these biblical references through our cultural glasses, we find lord bishops (if we have a feudal culture), presbyters or elders if we have a more oli-garchic kind of government (as they had in the Swiss city states where Calvin came from) or something like the Independent Bible Church if we are individualistic Americans. We all have the same Bible, but inevitably we all read it in the light of our own cultural presuppositions.

That churches must be governed is clear. The function is essential, but the form that government should take seems to vary in the New Testament churches, and certainly varies in our churches today. However much denominations argue that their way is the only proper New Testament way, it does not really matter at all what names we give to our leaders. What matters is that we have leaders, and that they function accord-ing to biblical rather than secular leadership principles. The biblical function must be fulfilled: the cultural form it takes is much less significant.

4. God has adapted his approach to us human beings

Our creator has adjusted to all the linguistic, cultural, sociolog-ical and psychological levels on which we humans must live, each of us within our own time and culture. We are time-bound, people of our own time, as well as culture-bound. God has consistently adapted his approach to our cultural contexts. He is not culture-bound any more than he is time-bound! There are therefore absolutes that are supracultural truths about God's character and nature. But how about our perceptions of these absolutes? Are we so culture-bound, seeing everything from our own ethnocentric viewpoint, that we are left in a quagmire of relativism? Part of the stimulus of cross-cultural mission is that one is forced to look at Scripture and Christian truth from the standpoint of another culture and that is a mind-blowing experience. It is a privilege and we should thank the chief harvester for assigning such responsible duties to us.

5. *Cultures are not fixed but in a constant state of change*

It is sometimes said of cultures that they 'have not changed since the Stone Age' – and that is frankly rubbish. Change may occur relatively slowly or may come rapidly. For example, television causes greatly accelerated change in languages: a new word used on a popular TV programme will be incorporated overnight. Japanese does not contain a single native word beginning with 'p', but has assimilated many such words over the years: eg *pan* for bread introduced from Portuguese in the sixteenth century, and many, many more from English in the twentieth century: *pai, painappuru, paipu, pajama, panchi, paamanento* (a perm), *panku* (a puncture), *panti* and *pantsu* (following European rather than US, meaning underpants); *parashuto; paasenteeji; pasupooto; penishirin; peshimisuto; piano; pitcha; poozu; poniteeru; purankuton; purutonium; puuru; puropaganda; purimadonna; purotestanto*, etc.

So cultural change comes in Borneo from Shell Oil; in Nigeria from British Petroleum; in Malaysia from Islam; and so on. Meet a lady called Freda Kadung – the first female member of her Kelabit tribe to go away to secondary school. She became personal assistant to the managing director of Shell in Sarawak; she uses an IBM word processor and entertains missionaries at the yacht club. That is cultural change! Some of her male counterparts, whose grandfathers were head-hunters, drive Mercedes, others are members of Parliament and gynaecologists!

We could remark on the vast, traumatic cultural changes in China throughout the twentieth century – the Manchu dynasty losing the mandate of heaven, leading to the Republic of 1910; warlords ravaging the country in the 1920s; the Guomindang putting their struggle with the Communists on hold while they beat off the Japanese invasion; the communist revolution of 1950, leading to what was actually called 'the cultural revolution'. Later there is more openness to the west, followed by the repression of Tiananmen Square. And the theories of collective communes are quietly replaced by capitalistic competition.

When I first visited Hong Kong in 1958 it had quite a different skyline. Shatin was still rural – cocks crowing, cows lowing and dogs barking. Today it is all high-rise apartments. And the changes in Hong Kong will continue. All of this involves cultural change and not merely historical or political change. Reducing population pressure and high-rise living has changed the whole pattern from huge extended families living in vast compounds of several hundred related people to small nuclear families with only one or two children. The influx of refugees needing to be housed and integrated created fresh problems. There is increased prosperity: bus queues are full of people using mobile phones! But there are much more subtle changes in thinking and expectations: how we think about life, success, what our dreams are for the future – each generation is different from the one before it.

Every long-term missionary in his or her lifetime lives through huge cultural and social changes, and needs to perceive what is happening and adapt to it. But this is a great privilege and adventure. So far we have been talking about the fact of cultural difference and cultural change on a large canvas. But we may also see the mind-blowing possibilities, the intellectual challenge of grappling with different world-views, differing attitudes to so many fundamental areas of human life. How does all this impact upon the daily life of the cross-cultural missionary, learning the language and seeking to bond with people whose thought patterns, customs and whole culture are new and unfamiliar?

The great cross-cultural adventure

Those of us who engage in cross-cultural mission are offered a great privilege and stand before a great adventure, the greatest of our lives. If we enjoy space fiction – finding ourselves in a new world, *Star Trek* adventures, with different people and different cultures to explore, then we may indeed boldly go where no one has ever been before. Or if we enjoy spy fiction and the idea of moving into an alien country and being able to speak the language so well that nobody realises we are foreigners, then here is a similar great adventure. What I want to convey is the joy and privilege of being able to share the cultural heritage of another family of human beings than the one we were born into. God promised Abraham that 'through you shall all nations of the earth be blessed'. So this is not just a great adventure, but a mission to the nations intended by the Lord from the beginning. It would be bad theology to compare the thrill and the privilege of this experience unfavourably with the relatively dull life of remaining in our own familiar cultural surroundings, because if the Lord himself calls us to remain within our own culture, then we must obey. A life with the Lord is an adventure, in familiar surroundings just as much as in new and strange ones.

Some are apprehensive about leaving the familiar society in which they were born and growing up to live in an alien environment among strangers. Christ's strong challenge to us as disciples 'If anyone comes to me and does not hate his father and mother, his wife and children, his brothers and sisters – yes, even his own life – he cannot be my disciple' (Luke 14:26ff) must always be read alongside 'No one who has left home or wife or brothers or parents or children for the sake of the kingdom of God, will fail to receive many times as much in this age, and in the age to come eternal life' (Luke 18:29).

In other words, we may fear the possibility of sacrifice, but the Lord does not want to impoverish us but rather to enrich us immeasurably by our cross-cultural experience: they who are willing to lose their life for Christ's sake, will find it. That is his promise and he keeps it. We may be understandably apprehensive, but none of us will ever regret trusting Christ with our future. What then are some of the abounding blessings of the cross-cultural adventure?

1. A new understanding of Scripture and theology

Going into another culture can be a mind-blowing experience. We begin to realise that the way we have so far explained the gospel in our own language and culture will not always make the same sense or seem equally relevant in another one. The whole of our theology and our way of explaining the Christian faith has to be completely rethought, and a totally new set of words and images and illustrations developed. The issues that hold people back from faith in our original culture and what holds people back from faith now will be different. This provides a huge intellectual and spiritual stimulus, and can deepen our own understanding of theology and the gospel.

Many things in Scripture come alive in our new situation: for example, when Abraham is purchasing the cave of Machpelah (Genesis 23:4–16) he is told he can have it for nothing, but he recognises this as politeness, and naturally pays a fair price for it. Or when Moses says, 'Send by the hand which Thou sendest' (NASB margin) in response to the Lord's command that he go to Pharoah, he is actually saying, 'No. I won't go!' but very indirectly and obliquely (Exodus 4:13). This is much more the polite way things are done in Asia, and many westerners would make little sense of it. When the resurrected Christ says, 'See my feet', this has much more relevance in cultures where ghosts are supposed to have no feet.

For us western evangelicals, the key issues of the mid-twentieth century in the churches were the doctrine of Scripture and the doctrine of the atonement. In other parts of the world, the central issues may have been different. For example, the doctrines of creation and providence may not be at issue in the west, but in confronting animism, Shintoism and Buddhism may prove critical.

Scripture itself provides different ways of explaining Christ's atonement (see chapter 9). It seems that the Holy Spirit has built this flexibility into Scripture so that it will always have particular relevance in particular cultures. Bible verses which did not seem significant in our own culture now become much more significant, eg Luke 1:78 – 'The rising sun will come to us from heaven.' To call the incarnate Son Jesus Christ 'the rising sun' may not seem to mean much in Europe, but it means a lot in Japan. That Jesus says, 'I am the true and living Tao' (John 14:6) develops new significance in the Chinese world, where the Tao is a similar concept to the Greek *logos* as the underlying creative principle of the whole universe.

So trying to evangelise, developing new apologetic approaches, looking for relevant explanations of the truth, develops your theological thinking. In the Asian context, explaining the cross in terms of terrible loss of face, so that Jesus who claimed power and glory died in weakness and shame helps us to grasp the impact of the resurrection. The Lord Jesus was publicly humiliated and discredited: how could such a person ever be believed to be the Messiah or the Son of God? Only a real physical resurrection would reinstate someone who had been so publicly shamed, or convince disciples so disillusioned about their earlier conviction that he was the promised Messiah.

2. Understanding different ways of thinking

Consider the way different peoples think about death. In Thailand, for example, those who die, even loved family members, become hostile evil spirits. Much as in the Chinese world, if there is nobody to comfort certain ancestors and perform the right ceremonies, such spirits return as ghosts and ghouls to haunt the living.

In Thailand a smile is the solution to everything; if there is any problem, smile. In Japan a smile does not necessarily reveal that I am happy and joyful, but serves to conceal rather than reveal true feelings. 'My dear mother died yesterday' (smile). Here a smile conceals tragedy or embarrassment rather than revealing pleasure. A classic example of cross-cultural cross-purposes in Cambodia was when an American evangelist appealed for those who wanted to turn to Christ to raise their hands – many people started to smile and laugh and raised their hands. He was appalled, thinking that these people could not understand, they were making fun of him! Now listen: if you want to become a Christian, please stand up. The same people stood up, laughing and giggling. Then he tried to get them to come up to the front, and again they laughed and came up. It was perfectly genuine: they did want to believe, and the laughter was not mocking, but only an expression of their embarrassment.

In the west it is often considered rude to make any kind of noise when eating; in some other cultures, if we eat in silence it may seem that we are not enjoying our meal. It is necessary to belch and burp and make approving noises. Sometimes cultures misunderstand each other. Mr Shinada had been the principal of a Bible college in Hokkaido for ten years, and missionaries wanted to show appreciation by giving him a sabbatical and sending him on a tour of other ministerial training colleges all over Asia. But the rumour went round that the missionaries were scheming to get Mr Shinada out of the church of which he was a part-time pastor, for how could he continue as pastor if he was away for three months? Needless to say there was no such hidden agenda, for it would never have occurred to the foreigners with a different view of the role of pastor, that being away for three months was any kind of problem.

A committee trying to arrange evangelism for the Tokyo Olympic Games kept minutes in both English and Japanese. After the first planning, several significant Japanese evangelical church leaders were invited to attend, in an attempt to get them on board. The English minutes said they were all very enthusiastic, but the Japanese minutes said that none of them were interested! The Canadian taking the minutes heard all the politeness and missed the real message: we appreciate all the hard work you people have done thinking about this, and clearly you anticipate it will be useful. Please get on with it if you want to, but please don't bother to enlist us in trying to evangelise non-Japanese speaking spectators whose minds are full of sports events!

3. Identifying with different ways of living

Different countries eat different foods. The Japanese are not excited about Europeans eating kidneys and liver, while Europeans are not used to eating raw egg, raw fish, seaweed, bamboo shoots or chrysanthemum petals. My first experience of chewing raw Beluga whale on Baffin Island lost me a dental filling! In the Philippines where tribal people were very short of protein, a short-term medical missionary learned to catch, skin, cook and eat rats, though in his home country people would be horrified at the idea. The whole aesthetics of food is different. The Japanese theory is that colour, pattern and texture are as important as taste. The natural flavours of the raw vegetable or meat must be preserved. Chinese food is different again. As a Japanese person said, 'Who but the Chinese would have learned to make money by selling the skin of a duck?'

There are different approaches to privacy, a concept which may not exist in more crowded parts of the globe. Attitudes to clothing oneself also vary. On the OM ship *Logos* a Chinese girl was very offended when it was said that she never washed, (she was so discreet that others never saw her undress), whereas Scandinavian girls would walk around the women's quarters wearing nothing. Some Japanese mothers were horrified that a western child was wearing nothing under his pyjamas in Singapore. Their children would all wear vest and underpants under pyjamas, while western ones would not, especially in such a hot country. In Mindoro some of the mountain tribes wear hardly any clothes at all: in the jungle it is so humid that clothes can never be properly dried and wet clothes encourage various respiratory infections. But the lowland Filipino tell them it is uncivilised to go without clothes. In some cultures only young women wear bright colours and older people wear very quiet subdued colours.

4. *Learning to appreciate different fauna and flora*

There are new insects to experience: fleas and bedbugs, mosquitoes by the million, and leeches that climb between our toes in the jungle. Staying in a missionary home in South Thailand, I was told not to worry if I met a big snake on the stairs – it lives here and kills off the rats! An army chaplain related how while a man was away, his female household noticed a hissing cistern and asked him to repair it when he returned. He lifted the toilet seat and found a snake coiled around beneath it. After that everybody gingerly raised the seat first! One night, sleeping in a small bedroom half way down the stairs in Central Thailand, I found my pillow had a horrible stench, but slept on it none the less. The second night I smelled the stink again, and this time noticed two tails hanging down beneath the pillow: a couple of water lizards (two feet long) had found refuge there during recent floods, and I had slept the previous night on top of them! In the Cameron Highlands of Malaysia, occasionally a hungry tiger may carry off large guard dogs from more remote bungalows, while bears scavenge dustbins even in North Vancouver.

It's not all horror stories: there are the beauties of the thousand and more species of butterflies in the Cameron Highlands of Malaysia. There is a wonderful variety of tasty fruit in the tropics. In Japan the spring brings out the most gorgeous flowering trees and shrubs. In North Thailand, beautiful orchids grow as epiphytes on trees along the trail. Four of us were once lost in the Cameron jungle and found water to drink by squeezing it out of sphagnum moss. Visiting a group of young missionaries pioneering among mountain tribes in Mindanao, Philippines, we went for a walk at dusk and found a tree lit up with fireflies like a huge Christmas tree. We collected a jam jar full, took them back to our bamboo hut, and after getting into our sleeping bags, released the fireflies which glittered upwards to the roof while we chuckled with delight like children at the spectacle.

5. Learning to appreciate new art and music

I was very impressed by artists in Java experimenting in landscape, portraits and impressionism, as well as the characteristic art of Bali. There are batik paintings and cloth designs. There are Eskimo carvings in soapstone. In Japan there is flower arrangement, calligraphy, ceramics, lacquer, wood prints – so many things we would never have appreciated in our own country. We may enjoy the simple Japanese lifestyle, sleeping on *tatami* matting, enjoying the grain of natural wood not obscured by paint; light, airy rooms not heaped with western bric-a-brac, but with a simple focus on the *tokonoma* (alcove), with perhaps a hanging scroll illustrating the season, and a flower arrangement. We used to experience the pleasure of sitting with friends with our feet in a pit under the table warmed by a charcoal pot (a fire hazard now replaced by electric warmers!). There is an attractive tradition of gracious and courteous living and hospitality.

Pentatonic music may sound weird and unfamiliar initially, but once our ears are tuned to the music of the koto, the samisen or the peepaw, it is beautiful. On arriving at an airstrip in the interior of Sarawak, my wife and I were greeted by a tribal band. The girls were all playing flutes made out of bamboo, and the young men other bamboo instruments of wider diameter that made an unusual 'oompah oompah' noise reminiscent of a tuba. Tribal singing, even of western hymns, carries a distinctive sound. At the end of the weekend they handed us a cassette recording of all the music we had heard over the visit!

The Koreans are most gifted musically. At a Korean memorial service celebrating the centenary of the Welshman Robert Thomas who distributed Bibles for the Scottish Bible Society and travelled on an ill-fated American ship where all on board were clubbed to death, I heard a woman with a most beautiful voice singing arias from Handel's *Messiah*. As a child her grandfather had thrown stones at the first missionaries, but later became the first moderator of the Presbyterian Church! They have a wonderful patriotic hymn about the beautiful land of 200 Li sung to the only cheerful chorus in Donizetti's *Lucia Di Lammermoor*: and I have to admit that even their ordinary congregations sing as well as Welsh choirs do!

While we were living in Singapore we were privileged to listen to Ravi Shankar and the Indian sitar – most sophisticated and enthralling music. The world is full of gifted musical performers in many styles on many different instruments, and they all enrich our human experience. Biblical culture involved many different instruments, the word 'psalm' comes from a verb meaning 'to pluck', so that a musical accompaniment was expected, and King David excelled at it.

6. The joy of new literature

Learning a new language suddenly opens to us a new literature as rich and varied as our own. Ayako Miura's autobiography *Michiariki*[13] shows how weather may reflect and influence human moods, so that frost and blizzard, howling wind, and warm spring sunshine all illuminate human feeling. A similar shorthand exists in poetry – cherry blossom means transient and short-lived, while evergreen pine trees speak of long life. Today people can remember vivid experiences by recording them with a single-lens reflex camera. In the past, the seventeen-syllable poem was a very pithy, concentrated way of doing the same thing.

There is a wonderful short story written by Kikuchi Kan, speaking of the frustration of a feudal Lord Tadanao because nobody speaks their mind or treats him like a human being. It illustrates well that God our maker does not want us to be puppets, only relating to him because we must, and only good because we must be. Neither love nor obedience has any meaning unless it is possible not to love and not to obey: it is only when we *choose* to love and to obey God that we may please him. I was able to tell this story once at a meeting made memorable by the presence of the present Crown Prince when he was studying at Oxford.

Niwa Fumio has an iconoclastic story called *Hideous Old*

Age in which two young women discuss their grandmothers and all that makes them a burden, in defiance of classical Confucian respect for the aged. Kabuki opera is beautiful and multi-dimensional: quite apart from the storyline, it sounds extraordinary, and has special effects of snow, fire and rain. We could freeze the visual scene as though it were a Japanese print. Good literature will always provide cultural traditions that help in explaining the gospel. For example, the transformation of the beguilingly beautiful woman into a hideous demon. Or the way the Shoogun departs from Edo (*Shoogun wa Edo o saru*) showing the significance of parting words spoken by your liege lord (compare the great commission of Matthew 28:19–20).[14]

It is also true that few words have exact equivalents in another culture: and such words provide keys to understanding that culture. While *Sayonara* is a farewell word like 'Goodbye', both words represent very different world-views. The Japanese means literally: 'If that's the way it is, that's the way it's gonna be!' It is an expression of fatalistic resignation: 'We have had the illusion of meeting and now we have the illusion of parting.' The other person has no more permanent reality than an attractive character in a television play, whom we may never meet again. The etymology of 'Goodbye' or 'God be with you' implies that God exists, that you exist, and that this God is determined to bless you. None of those things have any meaning in the Buddhist world of illusion, where the sadness of farewell is deepened by the transience and unreality of both parties. Do you see how language relates to culture, and illuminates its inner secrets?

7. *Art forms and evangelism*

In Indonesia the *wajang* is an indigenous form of dramatic evening that combines scenes from classic Hindu epics with droll contemporary political comment. This has been used by some creative Christians as a way of communicating Christian truth. In Thailand drama often invites audience participation. When Christians produced their version of 'The prodigal daughter' (they were short of male actors, and daughters leaving home and ending up in prostitution in Bangkok is a common problem), the audience were so sympathetic with the penniless daughter that they threw money onto the stage. Some of these productions later appeared on television in Thailand.

In South Africa a converted Jewish artist created an art exhibition of his work that explained his conversion to faith in Jesus the Messiah. I heard of it through a converted Jewish student who was president of the Christian Union in the Witswatersrand University.

The cross-cultural missionary may face a couple of years of struggle with learning the language, but stands on the threshold of a new world, a great adventure, a significant privilege. Before us a great cultural door is swinging slowly open to invite us in. We shall certainly be affected and changed by it, and by the grace of God the message he has entrusted to us will also have an impact in terms of that culture. There can be few real life adventures to compare with this.

Notes

1. Yasuko Nagai, *Being Indigenous as well as Christian* in *Missiology*, Vol.xxvii, No.3, July 1999.
2. Louis J. Luzbetak, *The Church and Cultures* (Illinois: Divine Word, 1963), p.4.
3. David Bosch, 'The Structure of Mission: An Exposition of Matthew 28:16–20' in Wilbert Shenk, *Exploring Church Growth* (Grand Rapids: Eerdmans, 1983), pp.235–240.

4. Edward Dayton, *That everyone may hear* (MARC, 1983).

5. Richard Niebuhr, *Christ and Culture* (New York: Harper Row, 1951).

6. Charles Kraft, *Christianity and Culture* (New York: Orbis, 1979), p.103ff.

7. Acts 7:2, 9, 16, 33.

8. Kraft, *op. cit.*, p.113.

9. Stott and Coote, *Down to Earth* (London: Hodder and Stoughton, 1980), p.25.

10. Robin Boyd, *Indian Christian Theology* (Madras: CLS, 1969), p.65.

11. *Ibid.*, p.68.

12. J.D. Douglas, ed., *Let the Earth hear His Voice* (Minneapolis: World Wide Publications, 1975), p.6.

13. The English translation of *The Wind is Howling* was translated by my wife Valerie.

14. Not the whole story – see the concluding chapter.

CHAPTER SEVEN

LAMBS TRY TO EXPLAIN GOD TO WOLVES

The Contextualising of Theology and the Gospel

In the previous chapter we thought of missionary lambs seeking to understand, appreciate and adapt to the indigenous culture of the Gentile wolves. It is self-evident that this is not a one-way process. The whole purpose of these lambs being among the wolves is to explain their super-cultural belief system, as far as is humanly possible, without contaminating it with the presuppositions of their own national form of enculturated Christianity. This is a far from simple task. The hardest adjustments we missionaries have to make relate not to the outward aspects of church music, architecture and organisation, but in thinking out fresh concepts and new ideas. We have all grown up in a particular society using a particular language related to a particular world-view. Other societies will differ from our own in a variety of ways and to different degrees. We have to make necessary adjustments if we are to communicate effectively, and these may be lumped together as 'contextualisation'.

In this section we look at the problem of Bible translation, contextualisation of the word of God, and at the related issue of contextualising the gospel. How may the unchanging gospel be presented in changing language understandable to the changing receptor culture? Traditionally home churches have regarded their church ministers as a higher order of beings needing longer training when compared with their undervalued missionaries. People seem to think any muscular Christian will be able to reach the illiterate heathen. Actually, presenting the gospel in our own language, and in terms of the culture in which we have grown up is a relatively simple matter compared with the intellectual challenge of presenting it in a totally alien culture. This requires a fairly sophisticated grasp of biblical language and ingenuity in presenting biblical truths in ways which will attract the interest of the hearers in a very different receptor culture.

In the earliest days of the London Missionary Society (founded 1795) it was cheerfully resolved that it was 'not necessary that every Missionary should be a learned Man' and 'Godly men who understand Mechanic Arts' might best meet their requirements.[1] Some considered that ill-educated men unsuited to the home ministry were 'quite adequate instructors of the ignorant heathen'.[2] When William Ward the Baptist printer wrote from Serampore to Andrew Fuller of the Baptist Missionary Society asking him to send men 'thoroughly qualified for the work of translation', Fuller remarked that 'scholars' were 'as rarely willing to be missionaries as noblemen!' When Ward asked for men acquainted with Latin, Greek and Hebrew, Fuller said irritably, 'They write as if Latin, Greek and Hebrew grew in our hedges.'[3] The gifted linguist Henry Martyn was not impressed with the quality of Serampore translation, and took on the Islamic languages of Urdu, Arabic and Persian himself. So this chapter aims to remind us that the lambs who intend to explain the good news to wolves face a stimulating intellectual challenge, and need to be spiritually thoughtful and intelligently perceptive.

Contextualisation of the word: translation

As I write I have in front of me the *Alkitab* (meaning 'holy book' published 1987 by the Bible Society of Singapore, Malaysia and Brunei) in the Malay language, and a *Seisho* (also 'holy book') in the Japanese language, and several English versions of the Bible. So how did we get from the original Hebrew and Greek texts to these 'Bibles'? Many of the early missionary Bible translators worked from English, Dutch or German translations of the original biblical text. Only today are they endeavouring to translate the Thai Bible directly from Hebrew and Greek for the first time. It is 180 years since Anne Judson first attempted to translate Matthew's Gospel into Thai in 1819.

Problems of names for God

Problems arise the moment we want to find an equivalent word to use for 'God'. We recognise that 'God' was originally an Anglo-Saxon word used to translate *elohim* in Hebrew, and θεος in Greek. Herein lies our greatest problem in explaining the person we want to speak about. The Lord God revealed himself to Moses and the prophets in the Hebrew language, and though Jesus seems to have taught in a related Semitic language (Aramaic), all the New Testament documents are written in Greek. The early church mainly read Moses and the prophets in the Good News for Modern Mediterranean Man, more properly known as the Septuagint. This translation of Moses' Law and the prophets into Greek made Yahweh's revelation of himself available for the first time to people unable to read Hebrew. This is why we keep on meeting Gentiles in the New Testament who are described as 'devout' or 'god-fearers' or 'proselytes'. These were non-Jews who having read the Law and prophets in the Septuagint had come to believe in the one creator God of Abraham, Isaac and Jacob. There they would have come across words originally used as titles of Greek and Roman emperors like *kurios* (Lord) and *soter* (Saviour) and the marvellous word *pantokrator* (Almighty or Lord of hosts).

When we move to another language with no Jewish or Christian history, we have either to look for an existing word which approximates to the Christian understanding, and redefine it in order to use it in a fully biblical way, or invent a totally new word into which biblical meaning may be inserted. If I turn to the Malay translation I find the words 'Allah' for God, and 'Tuhan' for Lord. Islam came to the Malays in Arabic language. Arabic also being a Semitic language related to Hebrew, 'Allah' is a cognate word to the Hebrew 'El' or 'Elohim' used in our Bible. There have been recent difficulties for Christians in Malaysia since under Islamic pressure, they have endeavoured to ban Christians from using *Allah* for God, *nabi* for prophet and *rasul* for apostle (the book of Acts in Malay is called *Kisah Rasul-Rasul*). These are all good Christian words used before Mohammed was born or the Koran written. So even translating from closely related languages like Hebrew into Arabic there are problems.

If I now pick up my Japanese Bible the difficulties are much greater. The Chinese character for 'god (s)' is pronounced in Mandarin as '*shun*' and by the Japanese as '*shin*' (as in Shinto meaning 'the way of the gods'). When it occurs alone rather than linked to a second character alongside, Japanese pronounce it '*kami*' (usually with the high level honorific '*sama*' added to it). The word '*kami*' means literally 'above' and can be used for the emperor, high government officials, mountains and trees worshipped in folk Shinto, and for brave soldiers who die in battle for Japan. For want of anything better, the Japanese Christian has to use '*kamisama*' for the God of the

Bible when actually it means 'honourable god(s)'. To most Japanese this is a common noun describing a whole class of objects. So whenever Christians use it, we have to explain that we are using it as a proper name for the one and only true God, the creator of heaven and earth. We can pick up the Chinese character for 'Lord', pronounced '*syuu*' and qualify the vague word '*kami*' by speaking of 'the god who is Lord' ('*syuu-naru kami*').

If we were looking at a Chinese Bible it would get even more confusing, because Chinese characters allow us to make up new words and speak of God as the 'heavenly lord' or the 'emperor above'. Problems arose when Roman Catholics had settled on the first and then Protestants settled on the second, and subsequently liberals and evangelicals disagreed among themselves. Small wonder that if the missionaries could not agree among themselves on the name of the God they wanted to recommend to the Chinese, then the Chinese were hesitant about accepting him! The Koreans, by contrast, had a clear existing word '*hananim*' for the supreme creator God that could be used without the need for much qualification and redefinition. This may partially explain why the Koreans have responded to the gospel more rapidly (thirty per cent in 100 years) than either the Chinese or Japanese.

Am I suggesting that evangelism may depend upon the clarity of our translation? Well, it certainly is not the only factor, and we have to think carefully about the sovereignty of God and the work of the Holy Spirit, but manifestly the clarity and lucidity of our proclamation matters greatly. The apostle Paul asked for prayer that God would enable him to make the good news clear (Colossians 4:4).

The doctrine of the Trinity as defined in the Athanasian Creed is complicated enough in English, but how shall we translate it? The Japanese took over from Chinese an attempted translation of 'Trinity' which means literally 'three court ranks, one body' and which fails to communicate. More recently a contextualised alternative has been suggested that means 'three relationships, one harmony (or one concord)'.[4]

This may seem involved, but it is important to show that no word in one language is exactly equivalent in meaning to one word in another. On top of this, words are constantly changing in meaning. For example, consider Authorised Version words like 'charity', 'conversation' or 'prevent' (then meaning doing something before somebody else, and only subsequently coming to mean to stop somebody doing something). It is easy to pick up a dictionary and think that words there are exactly equivalent in meaning. Think of the difference lying behind *Sayonara* and 'Goodbye' as outlined above. We are beginning to understand that the problem of which word to use to convey what we want to say is a major problem for Bible translators. Actually the same problem arises every time missionaries open their mouths. We know what we want to say, and know what meaning we think we are expressing, but what our hearers understand may be entirely different!

Problems of cultural differences

Take a familiar verse like 'Behold, I stand at the door and knock.' In tribal North Thailand it may need to read: 'Behold, I stand at the door and cough' because only thieves hammer on the door, to warn those inside to run out of the back if they wish to avoid harm. Friends cough gently to announce their presence and desire for admission.

The tax collector standing afar off may 'beat his breast' in Palestine, but in Central Africa this would mean that he 'patted himself on the back'! In that part of the world 'beat your head' expresses the idea. Eugene Nida gives a wealth of examples.[5] The sources of emotion may be heart, stomach, bowels, abdomen or liver. 'Our mouth is open to you' (2 Corinthians 6:11) could mean the person is raving mad in some West African languages. Where English says, 'Hold your tongue', Gourma says, 'Hold your gallbladder.' Forgiveness in Nilotic Shillok is expressed as 'God spits on the ground' in front of us.

Problems of definition

Sometimes the necessary word or concept may not exist at all in the target language, or alternatively there are too many words. Arabic is said to have more than seven hundred words describing camels, while some jungle tribal languages may have hundreds of words for 'palm tree'. Thus descriptions of Palm Sunday seem imprecise. Which of the many, many varieties of palm branches did they wave?

In one Philippine Mindoro tribal language there is no word for lion. They did believe in a spirit-lion that ate human beings. So how to translate Psalm 34:10 in the absence of large carnivores? 'If we trust in the Lord, the spirit-lion will go hungry' is scarcely what the text means. Fortunately it was realised that the cognate word in Arabic meant not 'lion' but 'unbeliever' (*kaffir*!). The verse shows perfect Hebrew parallelism if we read 'Unbelievers lack and suffer hunger, but believers shall lack no good thing' (which is how NEB translates that verse in English!). In view of the title of this book, it is worth noting that in cultures where there are no wolves, we could speak of hyenas or jackals instead, though leopards would be the true equivalent. Thus some African languages translate 'I am sending you out like sheep among leopards' (Matthew 10:16), and 'they come as hungry leopards disguised in the pelts of sheep' (Matthew 7:15).[6]

Problems of linguistic diversity

How should we translate the future tense? In some languages, by definition the future is uncertain, so how can we describe the sure promises of God? The Bible Society's post-war Kogotai version in Japanese was much criticised for its use of the indefinite future. Culturally how can anything in the future be certain? Puebla Aztek has no passive tense at all, so all passives must become active. Or take those generic singulars often used in the New Testament: 'If anybody desires the office of a bishop', 'the widow must be', 'the disciple is not greater than his teacher', or even 'love your neighbour'. This last would prompt the question, which particular neighbour must I love? So they had to translate in the plural 'love your neighbours'. Nida subdivides the problems as follows:[7]

1. Non-existent in source language: but obligatory in receptor language

A dialect of Zatopek requires the speaker to indicate whether an event is the first time or a revisit, eg, Matthew 4:13 – 'Leaving Nazareth, he went and lived in Capernaum.' Japanese has a causative tense, so the house help politely requests at the end of the day, 'Please cause me to go home.' This is a marvellous tense for God who 'works in you to will and to act according to his good purpose' (Philippians 2:13). So if Japanese lose out on the future tense, they gain on the causative. Some things may be hard to express in the target language; other things may be better expressed than they are in the missionaries' mother tongue. We are often helped and blessed by using foreign language versions, because the different translation throws fresh light on the meaning of Scripture.

2. Obscure in source language but obligatory in receptor language

Some languages abound in honorific nouns, pronouns and even verbs that express the relative status of the parties and respect. The respectful words for your wife and your house will be different from the humble words for my wife and my house. Words for brother and sister may be too vague and obscure for the words available refer either to older or younger brother, and older or younger sister. This may be important in translating a respect language, like Thai. Did the Pharisees address Jesus as a rabbi? And how did Jesus address the Pharisees? How polite were they to each other?

3. *Ambiguous in source language but obligatory in receptor language*

Some languages distinguish between inclusive and exclusive first person plural. John 4:12, 'Are you greater than our father Jacob who gave us this well?' Did she include Jacob as father of both Samaritans and Jews? Yet we know that the well was given specifically to the Samaritans, so perhaps she meant 'our (Samaritan) father'. This is a helpful question to ask in John 3 also for in the west we tend to assume that Jesus and Nicodemus spoke one to one, as they might in some western cultures, but respected rabbis would always travel with their disciples. So John 3:2, '*we* know', and John 3:11, '*we* speak of what *we* know' are actually plural statements made on behalf of a group.

4. *Implicit in source language but obligatory in receptor language*

Melchizedek 'without father or mother, without genealogy' (Hebrews 7:3) has to be translated 'there is no record of his father or mother or family line', because it is biologically impossible not to have parents or ancestors. The words 'there is no record' seem to be an addition, but are really implicit in the text. How should we translate reverential passive tenses in Greek: 'they shall be comforted' and 'they shall be filled'? Jews avoided using the name of God wherever possible, and the passive tense actually implies 'God will comfort them' and 'God will fill them', which is how they are translated in the Good News Bible.

5. *Explicit in source language, requiring different treatment in receptor language*

Many languages include classifiers along with numbers, so that 'five long things', 'five birds', 'five boats', 'five fish', 'five flat things' all require different words. In the days of silent films a Japanese commentator was endeavouring to explain the passionate succession of kisses the hero was giving to the heroine. How does one count kisses in a culture where public demonstrations used to be non-existent? The best he could find was a word meaning 'salvos of artillery': fire one, fire two, fire three. Similarly, using languages unfamiliar with Palestinian geography, it may be helpful to classify as River Jordan, City Jerusalem, Province Galilee.

Problems of cultural bias

The English translation of Ephesians 4:11 is ' he . . . *gave* some to be apostles, some to be prophets', etc., and is clearly picking up the concept of giving from 'grace has been *given*' (v7) and '*gave* gifts to men' (v8). The Japanese Shinkaiyaku evangelical translation says they have been 'elevated to be apostles', etc., omitting entirely the concept of 'given' required by the context, and reflecting Confucian respect for ministers, even though in the context they are slaves given to serve the people of God, and not teachers to lord it over them!

Problems of gender bias occur in English translation, and have caused a major row in the United States over the inclusive language NIV. In 1 Timothy 3:1–7 the NIV inserts 'he' or 'man' into the text eleven times, even though the Greek could equally refer to men or women, until 'husband of one wife' seems to settle the matter. Or does it mean if the overseer is a male, and could it equally include wife of one husband if the overseer is a woman? In 1 Thessalonians 4:4 we all tend to assume that 'each one of you' refers only to men. In Acts 4:4 'the number of men' almost certainly means 'males' so the actual number was much greater, but in 1 Timothy 1:3 almost certainly means 'certain persons' because women were also involved in false teaching as emerges in 2:12. But in 2 Timothy

2:2 'entrust to reliable men' (NIV) almost certainly means 'reliable persons' without any distinctions of gender. Two other gender issues arise in relation to Phoebe and to Junia (Romans 16:2, 7): Phoebe is described by three nouns – sister, deacon and a word probably to be translated 'patroness', that is the citizen who acted as sponsor and whose home would be a meeting place for the church. In the masculine the same word is used for Christ as guardian of the church, but translators are uncertain because of prejudice against female leadership and so use the word 'helper' or 'succourer'.[8]

The person paired with Andronicus is called Junia or Junias, which according to Sanday and Headlam is 'less usual as a man's name' though Cranfield points out that this is misleading since 'apart from the present verse, no evidence of its having existed has so far come to light'. Cranfield goes on to say, 'It is surely right to assume that the person referred to was a woman.[9] Originally no accents were printed in Greek New Testament translations, then for several hundred years the acute accent has defined Junia as female, though in quite recent years some interference with the Greek text has resulted in the addition of a circumflex accent to ensure that she appears as a male! If even our English versions are not free from cultural gender bias, and powerful commercial interests are opposed to inclusive language versions, we need to be scrupulous and objective in translating biblical text. [10]

The stimulus and illumination from fresh translation

The Melanesian pidgin translation of justification as 'God 'e say "im alright" ' conveys in simple, basic language what Latin-based words like 'justification' somehow fail to put across. Eugene Nida comments with enthusiasm on J.B. Phillips' equivalent translation, which though it 'often departs from the so-called "wording of the original" nevertheless communicates the equivalent concepts in a brilliant manner'.[11] He goes on to quote from the Phillips' version of Romans 8:

> The whole creation is on tiptoe to see the wonderful sight of the sons of God coming in to their own . . . it is plain to anyone with eyes to see that at the present time all created life groans in a sort of universal travail. And it is plain, too, that we who have a fore-taste of the Spirit are in a state of painful tension.

Many of us who have had the privilege of studying, teaching and preaching from translations of Scripture in languages other than our own can bear testimony to the mind-blowing insights into the meaning of familiar passages that are handed to us. Just one example: 'If God is for us, who can be against us?' is enriched when we read: 'If God is our ally, on our side, who . . .'

Contextualisation and inculturation of the gospel

We turn now from contextualisation of the word itself in Bible translation, to the whole way in which the gospel is presented in resonance with the receiving culture. It is possible to hear worthy presentations of the gospel translated literally into the words of the target language, but differing not one whit from the way it might be presented in Australia or Scotland. The language has changed, but the evangelist makes no concessions whatever to differing ways of thought or cultural difficulties in comprehending what he or she is saying. This can be excused in the visitor, as when Billy Graham in Hong Kong told the story of the child who asked his parents where he came from and was told the stork brought him; and then checked with his grandparents to discover where his parents came from only to be told that the stork brought them. The child began his essay: 'There have been no natural births in our family for two generations . . .' Unfortunately the Chinese have no stork tradition even though cranes bring good luck. Asking the interpreter how he handled it, he said smiling: 'I just said that a bird brought them!' The long-term integrated and bonded missionary, however, has much less excuse – the gospel has to be contextualised in order to be understood in the new cultural situation. As Sadhu Sundar Singh put it – we must give people the water of life in an Indian cup![12]

1. Use of parables and illustrations

The old illustrations and expressions have to go. I remember with embarrassment the puzzled looks of some Southern Baptist missionary friends when I inadvertently spoke of some idea being 'hit for six'. Cricket is a mystery in many parts of the world. I derived many new illustrations from *sumoo* wrestling. Martin Goldsmith would islamicise some parables – so two Muslims went up to the mosque to pray (more acceptable than a story about two Jews!), and the question of who was putting their trust in whom comes out just as strongly, even if one was an imam and the other a moneylender.

Sadhu Sundar Singh followed his own advice in the wealth of word pictures and parables from everyday Indian life. A person bathing in deep water does not feel the weight of the water, but on the bank lifting the heavy pot full of water is difficult. A sinner does not feel he is a sinner as long as he lives in sin. Or again: Christ is like a king going incognito among his people in order to help them. Hinduism has been digging channels; Christ is the water to flow through those channels.[13]

2. Use of cultural 'keys'

(a) Concept ideas. Don Richardson popularised the notion of appropriate cultural keys in his book *Peace Child*, where the surrender of a child as an act of trust by one tribe to a hostile neighbour secured peace, while that child lived. This provided a way of explaining God giving his only Son in order to bring a peace, which lasts for ever. A Catholic missionary to the Cree Indians discovered they had a myth about a bear ancestor who told the starving tribe to kill and eat him so that the whole tribe might survive the killing cold and famine of winter: he proclaimed instead one who gave his life that we all might live. As I suggested earlier, to some of us in Japan reference to the 'rising sun from on high' (Luke 1:78) may prove to be a key to unlocking the door to the the Japanese heart. The sun that the Japanese have ignorantly worshipped, we now declare to you as the true sunrise enlightening the land of the rising sun.

(b) Character impact. We were all astonished when an English nurse teaching a group of Japanese nurses saw an unparalleled seventy-five per cent response rate among young women wanting to become Christians. What on earth had she said and taught? Could we learn from her experience? She said it was just the Christian doctrine of mankind, that was all. We finally came to the conclusion that it was not the content of her message so much as her own experience and character. She was very weak and ill at the time, and she was admired for her gutsy courage in carrying on with the course even when she was so obviously anaemic and unfit. This is paralleled by other evidence of the Japanese psyche, which admires courage in the face of adversity. Thirty-eight per cent of Japanese converts cited Mrs Ayako Miura's books as a major influence in their conversion. What was so remarkable about her? Most Japanese Christian books would have a 3–5,000 copy print

run. Her book on the Old Testament for laypeople had a first run of 70,000 copies. This spirited woman had spent seven years of her life in a plastercast fighting against tuberculosis.[14] That battle won, in later life she faced a long battle with cancer. Japanese people were deeply moved by her courage.

The Brethren evangelist Mitsuhashi was so disabled that his wife had to carry him on the meeting platform on her back, but he was remarkably effective, the more so perhaps because of his disability. Tamura Yoneko had lost portions of both legs and an arm in a suicide attempt before she came to Christ: people came to listen to her because she had suffered and had triumphed over it all. Meeting this exceptionally beautiful young woman it was hard to believe that she was so disabled. The combination of suffering, courage in enduring it and radiant Christian faith seems an unbeatable mixture of 'cultural keys'!

3. Problem of people's own cultural assumptions

In the 1950s and 1960s the Moody *Fact and Faith* films were a valuable evangelistic tool in the west with their combination of showing the wonders of the created world and the preaching of a simple gospel message. The presenter, Dr Irwin K. Moon would appear with his big Bible and red tie to proclaim, 'You must be born again', and the films circulated around the world with appropriately translated or dubbed sound tracks. As a young missionary, I had the temerity to write and suggest that they might be even more effective if they were to produce versions using Chinese and Indian presenters. The reply pointed out that because of American movies everybody was used to American voices and accents. The real problem was the lack of contextualisation: the message of the need to be born again was incomprehensible to Hindus, who kept on being reborn again and again. For them the good news of salvation was knowing how to stop being born again!

The first time Bill Bright of Campus Crusade came to Japan, he reported several thousand converts after one week of meetings. Why had everyone said it was so difficult to get conversions in Japan? He had failed to appreciate that courtesy and politeness would ensure that everyone appeared to comply with the evangelist's request for decisions, names and addresses. At a similar meeting at the closing appeal a student friend asked, 'Is it all right if I don't go forward?' After all, if people have taken all this trouble to lay on a meeting it would be discourteous to disappoint the guest speaker and cause him to lose face. In the event the evangelist was pleased with the encouraging response until it became clear that many of the names and addresses given were of non-existent people from non-existent addresses. It was a problem of untransferable methodology: that a time-honoured way of doing things in the west was culturally inappropriate in Japan. People will do the polite thing, go up to the front, put up their hands, take a booklet in order not to disappoint the organisers. If the evangelist recasts the appeal, and calls people to lifelong commitment to the Lord Jesus, just as a *samurai* once promised his lord obedience to the death, vowing to obey all his commands without question, and serving him with our lives while we have breath, we will get a much smaller response, but people will know what we mean!

4. Problems of contextualisation and syncretism

The question must occur, how much liberty and licence do we have to change the way the gospel is presented? Eager to explain it in terms meaningful to the new culture, might one unintentionally change and misrepresent it? The missionary to the Cree unfortunately took his illustration too far and drew pictures of a crucified bear upon the cross! This was an un-biblical syncretism with one aspect of national culture. We are faced with a spectrum with contextualisation at one end and syncretism at the other. In contextualisation the biblical content is unchanged, but the cultural envelope is changed. Syncretism alters the content as well as the envelope. Somewhere between them one crosses over from what is wise and acceptable to what becomes wrong and heretical.

5. Contextualisation and syncretism

The Bible actually gives us a great deal of flexibility in contextualising without being guilty of syncretism. Take the doctrine of the cross and atonement, for example. Scripture uses several different illustrations or ways of explaining the significance of the death of the Lord Jesus Christ.

1. *Sacerdotal* – the language of priest and sacrifice in the temple (notably in Hebrews).
2. *Forensic* – the language of crime and punishment, judgement and justification (Romans).
3. *Victory* – the language of defeat of evil spiritual forces (Colossians 2:15).
4. *Redemption* – the language of emancipating slaves by paying ransom (Matthew 20:28, etc.).
5. *Relational* – the language of human estrangement and reconciliation (2 Corinthians 5:18–21).

All of these sets of language may be found in the New Testament, but not all of them are equally appropriate in every culture. The language of Hebrews and animal sacrifice may not naturally communicate with cultures like twenty-first century Europe. The language of defeat of spiritual forces, often called Christus Victor (after a book by Gustav Aulen), is extremely appropriate in animistic cultures where people live in constant fear of evil spirits. The language of estrangement and costly reconciliation is almost universal and understandable. This is the weakness incidentally of some A,B,C approaches to evangelism in our own culture, which rely exclusively upon the forensic metaphor. Because the Bible contains several sets of ideas to explain the meaning of Christ's death, in order to contextualise, we are free to select the biblical explanations that prove most helpful in a particular culture. Contextualisation is not compromising, but common-sense determination to communicate!

Cross-cultural preaching

1. Language different?

People who have prepared a message in English using alliteration discover, sometimes too late, that it will not translate into another language. There is the famous story about the dimwit who preached on the 'ships' of Scripture – worship, fellowship, etc., without realising that for his interpreter this was quite untranslatable! The one-word headings used by those who alliterate prove very difficult in languages where there are words which sound the same when spoken but are written in different ideographs with different meanings.

The advice to those who have to use interpreters is to assume nothing, however busy you may be, and insist on going through the message with the interpreter beforehand. A good translator will explain when you will not make sense, and thus avoid the translation: 'He is telling an untranslatable joke – please all laugh politely!'

A good approach is to listen carefully to good native preachers, asking yourself how do they communicate? Why do people listen to them and enjoy listening to them? Find some successful models and note their style. Later on you may feel free to modify and use your own style more. It was a matter of amusement in our church in Tokyo that the pastor always illustrated from Wesley or General Booth, while the missionary illustrated from Japanese literature, *kabuki* opera and *sumoo* wrestling!

2. World-view different?

We have already seen how difficult it is to find a good word for 'God' in some languages. Translating Bill Bright's 'four spiritual laws' can be very hard because our western assumptions may not carry through into other languages. In western culture even an atheist declaring that he doesn't believe in God will use a capital letter G meaning the creator of the world and Father of the Lord Jesus Christ. Even what he denies still carries a Christian meaning! If a Muslim says God, he means Allah. If a Hindu says God, he may mean Brahma (total impersonal reality); or Vishnu or one of his avatars like Rama or Krishna; or Shiva or many other things. If a Japanese person tells me that they are an atheist (literally, 'a no-god-theory-person') I usually claim to agree with them in their denial, for I cannot believe in the gods they cannot believe in either!

(a) *Reality*. Because we are Christians we assume that other people have objective existence; that they really exist and are not illusory. In western countries for the most part we believe that other people exist. In Monist (Hindu and Buddhist) philosophical thinking other people have no objective reference, they are illusions. There is the famous story of a rajah being taught by a guru the truths of *maya* or the illusory nature of human experience. He arranged for an enraged elephant to be let loose in his palace grounds as his guru was arriving. He was most gratified to see the alarmed guru take off at high speed and climb a tree to escape. After the elephant had been called off, the rajah, rubbing his hands said to the guru, 'I notice that you did not think the elephant to be an illusion!' The guru looked at him pityingly and said, 'I am sorry that you are still lost in the mists of ignorance: what you thought you saw was an illusory guru, climbing an illusory tree in order to escape from an illusory elephant!'

The Monist sees this present visible world like an image on a television screen. We have the illusion of meeting actors on television and then the illusion of saying farewell to them. This makes nonsense of 'I think, therefore I am' which becomes 'I have the illusion of thinking, and so I have the illusion of being.' Such systems are deterministic: what I experience is like a dream over which I have no control. Good and evil alike are part of the illusory world, and 'sin' is what happens to me, and for which I am not responsible. The good evangelist must know where people are coming from and how they perceive the world. Many of our western assumptions about objective and subjective distinctions break down in the Monist world.

(b) *Illness.* David Burnett, who describes a rain-making ritual in Africa, also tells the amusing story of the African explaining that somebody died because a witch-doctor put a curse upon him. The western missionary corrects him by saying that the man died of malaria contracted when he was bitten by a mosquito. Maybe, replies the African, but who sent the mosquito?[15]

(c) *New birth.* This is an important biblical concept in which natural birth as breath enters the body is paralleled by spiritual rebirth in which the Spirit of God enters the soul. Difficulty arises in Hindu and Buddhist countries where the concept of *samsara* is widely believed: namely that in one year of Brahma (six million human years) a human soul may be reborn 200,000 times. Salvation (*mukti*) means release and deliverance from this endless round of births and deaths. The individual's caste and levels of blessing and suffering are determined by previous lives (*karma*). The matter is oversimplified here, because it is not necessarily the same person who is reborn, rather that one has inherited the debts and credits of past existences, a set of eternal baggage that will be passed on through a whole series of existences. The concept is utterly different from Christian teaching, yet the mention of 'rebirth' is likely to cause confusion. In this situation it may help to explain that Christian liberation is indeed emancipation from everything from the past, whether inherited or sins committed by the individual.

(d) *Death and ancestors*. Many cultures both in Africa and Asia believe that their ancestors continue to influence their present lives, and that ancestors need to be assisted and comforted after death or they may wreak vengeance on the living. It is a double benefit system, for the prayers and worship of the living, both benefit the deceased delivering them from posthumous suffering, and are a blessing to their filial descendants still living in this world. How can we be so unfilial as to cease caring for loved relatives after they have died? Should we Christian missionaries just disregard such notions or even pour scorn on them, because they differ from our contemporary European notions? Traces of similar views can be found in fears of ghosts, graveyards and the 'wake' in some regions of the British Isles. To my knowledge, there are no courses of systematic theology which give much attention to a biblical doctrine of ancestors.

There is actually much more material in the Bible than one might imagine. God is the God of Abraham, Isaac and Jacob (Acts 7:32). David slept with his fathers (1 Kings 2:10). The following description of exactly which Ezra is being referred to is impressive (and fun to read in public!):

Ezra son of Seraiah, the son of Azariah, the son of Hilkiah, the son of Shallum, the son of Zadok, the son of Ahitub, the son of Amariah, the son of Azariah, the son of Meraioth, the son of

Zerahiah, the son of Uzzi, the son of Bukki, the son of Abishua, the son of Phinehas, the son of Eleazar, the son of Aaron the chief priest – *this* Ezra . . .   (Ezra 7:1–6, my italics).

If we translate every reference to 'fathers' in Stephen's speech to 'ancestors', we discover the concept appears again and again (Acts 7:2, 11, 12, 15, 19, 32, 38, 39, 44, 45, 51, 52). The parable of Dives and Lazarus shows that the dead 'ancestor' wants the surviving members of his family to repent so that they do not share the same torment (Luke 16:19–31), a parable which carries enormous force in any ancestor-caring community. The Christian emissary in Africa and Asia needs to have a well thought-out biblical doctrine of ancestors.

3. Daily life different?

The detailed circumstances of daily life vary in different communities. Christ uses agricultural and rural metaphors in the Gospels, while Paul tends to use urban metaphors in the epistles – the games, triumph processions, soldiers and so on.

I once found myself trying to expound 'treasure on earth' in a tribal long house in Sarawak. I assumed that I couldn't go wrong if I expounded the Bible. But how should I apply 'not storing up treasure on earth' in a non-cash culture? What are riches on earth to tribal people? I discovered later that it is water buffalo, and ancient glass beads stored in Chinese jars.

At the Lausanne Congress in 1974 Dr Edward Hill, a black American preacher, spoke of first base as the new birth, and second base as forming a visible brotherhood, and third base as embracing the social aspects of the gospel. It was an excellent illustration for Americans, Japanese, Filipinos and other baseball-playing nations, but almost incomprehensible to most of the rest of us. Preaching has to be adapted to the needs and understanding of the hearers – it has to be contextualised.

4. Teaching approach different?

We know that even in our own countries congregations vary in the teaching styles with which they are comfortable: some are more cerebral and are used to longer preaching sessions, while others get restless after twenty minutes or even less. Some are used to presentations made with an overhead projector: in the Outer Hebrides this would be an innovation, as unwelcome in worship as new-fangled things like modern songs! It should come as little surprise to realise that whatever we may have been used to in our home churches, we may have to make considerable adjustments in other cultures.

Some of these adjustments may add a new dimension to our teaching style. Western tradition tends to pack cerebral content into preaching. A Japanese Christian said to me, 'You people pack a huge amount of information into your messages, but we Japanese do not wish only to know what a doctrine is, we want to feel it and experience its truth.' The Japanese sermon may have less objective content, but it contains more subjective feeling and application than a corresponding British message.

Black American preaching is very effective both in congregational participation and in the repetition of significant phrases like the 'I have a dream' of Martin Luther King. Some cultures are much more anecdotal than ours: Hinduism explains a great deal with stories and parables. Sadhu Sundar Singh was an outstanding Christian example of such contextualised teaching. Audiences vary too in their listening style: Cambodian congregations listen with great intentness. In the Outer Hebrides they never laugh or even smile inside the church building (though they do chew sweets during sermons). The apparent lack of response means that it feels like preaching into a pillow, but it does not mean they are not listening!

The cross-cultural adventure can be intellectually challenging, but it is extremely worthwhile. It is an enormous privilege to feel at home in a different culture from our own, and to preach Christ as Lord and Saviour, and to see churches being planted which are not foreign and alien, but deeply rooted in their own culture, crowns which may be laid at the feet of Christ our king when he comes (1 Thessalonians 2:19).

Notes

1. LMS Board Minutes, September 1795.
2. W.N. Gunson, *Evangelical Missionaries in the South Seas 1797–1860.*
3. BMS Letter quoted by Piggin, *Making Evangelical Missionaries 1789–1858* (Sutton Courtenay Press, 1984), p.160.
4. Nozomu Miyahara, 'A Japanese Perspective on the Trinity' in *Themelios* Vol. 22, 2 January 1997.
5. Eugene Nida, *Message and Mission* (Pasadena: William Carey, 1960), p.139.
6. *Ibid.*, p.138.
7. *Ibid.*, pp.144–149.
8. In 1 Clement 61:3; 64:1 of Christ as our 'guardian'(προστατης) in the masculine, while here of Phoebe in the feminine (προστατις) equivalent Cranfield says to *patronus* and *patrona* in Latin. C.E.B. Cranfield, *Romans* (Edinburgh: T and T Clark, 1979), p.627.
9. *Ibid.*, p. 788 where Cranfield points out that Chrysostom came to the same conclusion.
10. See discussion in C. Powell, 'A stalemate of genders? Some hermeneutical reflections' in *Themelios,* Vol. 17, No. 3.
11. Nida, *op. cit.*, p.142.

12. Robin Boyd, *An Introduction to Indian Christian Theology* (Madras: CLS, 1969), pp.86–109.
13. *Ibid.*, pp.97, 98, 102, 107, etc.
14. See the English translation of her biographical *The Wind is Howling* (OMF, 1977).
15. David Burnett, *Unearthly Powers* (Eastbourne: MARC, 1988), pp.13f, 109.

CHAPTER EIGHT

LAMBS BOND WITH WOLVES IN A NEW FLOCK

Contextualisation of Churches and their Leadership

The missionary lamb settling among the wolves must not only learn to dance with them, and seek to bond with individuals, but with the whole pack. Those won for Christ need to bond with one another in the truly biblical 'body-life' of indigenous churches. J.B. Phillips translated Ephesians 4:25 – 'For we are not separate units, but intimately related to each other in Christ.'[1] The aim of the Christian worker is not vaguely to do good, or even solely to preach the gospel, but to make disciples, baptise them and bind them together into warm living congregations.

The missionary commitment to 'bonding' is not merely some effective technique for making friends and influencing people, but rather a model or prototype of what is meant to happen between all Christians in the fellowship of Christ's church, as we all relate first to him and then to one another. If we are obsessed with buildings, pastors, church music and all the accoutrements of a western institutionalised Christian cultus, then we shall evolve a ghastly mutant that is called 'church' but which lacks its fundamental biblical elements. We are not there to produce a clone of the church we belonged to back home, but to start afresh with a group of new eager disciples, Bible in hand, to seek to reproduce what we find in the New Testament in terms of their culture. And we ourselves are the chief problem, a cultural bottleneck, because though we will have a concept of 'church' in our heads, that may or may not conform closely to biblical expectations, and the new Christians initially may have no concept at all.

As missionaries we will encounter differing church situations along a broad spectrum. The two possible extremes are (1) pioneer situations where no national church yet exists, and where the missionary contributes to the development of a national ecclesiology, and (2) places where a national church already exists and where the missionary has to accept the existing church, as it is, cultural warts and all. It seems logical to look at pioneer situations first, though some of the aspects covered in this section may apply equally in longer established groups of churches.

The missionary in pioneer situations

Paul could write to the Corinthians: 'Are you not the result of my work in the Lord? Even though I may not be an apostle to others, surely I am to you! For you are the seal of my apostleship in the Lord' (1 Corinthians 9:1–2). The pioneer church planter is a founding apostle. If there are not yet any authoritative Scriptures translated, the missionary is the only channel of apostolic teaching. This means therefore that they enjoy the unique privilege of influencing the church polity as it emerges, in a way that none of those who follow in a supporting role may do. Just because the missionary exercised a parental or midwife role in starting the local witness, his advice and her suggestions must carry more weight than those of any successor however excellent. If the individual belongs to a confessional or denominational group that expects the founding of a specifically Lutheran, Reformed, Anglican, Methodist, Baptist or Pentecostal church, cloned in the image of the denomination with all its historical accretions, there will be much less freedom to influence patterns.

1. Some problems arising from cultural assumptions

There is a Ganda proverb which says: 'He who has never travelled thinks his mother is the only cook.' All of us are limited by our experience, and not least in our experience of what we think of as 'church'. Individual missionaries may have been part of only one or two congregations, in just one country. Certainly we are committed to 'church planting', but what content will we put into the word 'church'? It is so easy to assume (without realising that one is making any assumptions) that the church which we go to plant will be a clone of the church in which we have grown up.

I once dropped a throwaway remark at a missionary conference in Thailand that if we were Americans a 'church' requires lots of real estate and a large professional staff; that if we were Germans we thought of large gothic buildings, slow ponderous hymns and loud tolling bells. I was rewarded by sustained and embarrassed mirth from German missionaries of another mission. They had just imported three large bells into Thailand!

The mental image of 'church' held by a Scottish Presbyterian used to the godly minister of the word exercising a solo monologue in prayer, reading and preaching from a central pulpit is poles apart from the expectations of Christian Brethren assemblies seated around the Lord's table. The two mental concepts of 'church' are scarcely compatible, though both would be equally convinced that they were being 'biblical'. Others might feel that an overhead projector was indispensable to Christian worship, and wondered how it had survived nineteen hundred years without! Every denomination from every nation has to wrestle with the problem of our ecclesiastical contact lenses that are so difficult to remove. It cannot be denied that Germans, Scots, English and American missionaries have all tried to produce replicas of their own national variants of 'church'. In recent years the encouraging influx of hard-working, committed missionaries from Korea has sometimes been less than enthusiastically received because they are seeking to reproduce their own cultural Christianity and ecclesiastical patterns across the globe.

One sad obverse reflection of this problem is that Japanese who have professed conversion overseas, and have been drawn into English-speaking congregations, have huge problems in adjusting to Japanese church style when they return home. Some even fall away from any profession of Christian faith at all. Those who have belonged to Japanese-speaking congregations generally fit in easily and are readily incorporated into churches back at home.

We have to recognise that we are all entrenched in ecclesiastical subcultures. The culturally insensitive, denominational or sectarian missionary with a rigid package to impose is very different from the more thoughtful missionary who sees something of the complications of moving across cultural boundaries.

Descriptions of Spanish colonisation of native South America are quite horrifying. The invaders came from a feudal society, used to lording it over the serfs who worked on their estates in Spain. The indigenous Indians were invited to submit, and become serfs, and were slaughtered when they failed to do so. Stephen Neill[2] reports an eyewitness account of the procedure. The *Requerimiento* or demand for obedience was publicly read aloud to them in Latin. It gives a brief account of the history of the world, explains the sovereignty of the Pope, that he has given authority to the king of Spain, and they now have the opportunity to submit to the Christian king who is their lawful sovereign. They must accept their role as vassals, receive the missionaries and be converted to the Christian faith. If they refuse to submit they will be forcibly enslaved, and made to surrender to superior force of arms. These extraordinary European presuppositions must have seemed utterly appalling to the unfortunate native peoples. The first Jesuits in China and Japan were intelligent enough to realise that such an approach could never be acceptable in those countries.[3] But if we are horrified by such imposition of European Catholic ecclesiastical presuppositions in Latin America, we need to recognise that we are all in danger of imposing our own ecclesiologies even if to a lesser degree.

The account of the heroic Anglican missionaries in the Yukon and Western Arctic territories is deeply impressive. Their commitment and readiness to accept the frightful rigours of the Arctic winter in order to bring people to Christ deserve the highest praise. At the same time many of them seem to have been extraordinarily insensitive in cultural matters. Stained-glass windows were imported from Britain for St Pauls, Gitwandak, surrounded as it is by Indian totem poles. Mrs Bompas, whose husband became bishop of a diocese 3,000 miles long (London to Istanbul!), introduced Christmas puddings (though knives and forks provided were rapidly abandoned) and a Christmas tree (which involved making improvised moulds in order to make candles for the tree). Thus were elements from Europe's pagan past introduced to North American Indians, as somehow part of celebrating Christmas. They were more to comfort missionaries hungry for their own cultural traditions than of intrinsic value as Christian teaching.[4]

2. 'Church' – what does it mean? What does it look like?

If we have our own preconceived concept of 'church', new national Christians will have no such experience to fall back on, but may readily look to apparently similar structures like temple, shrine and mosque, and their minders and ministers as models. The very word presents its own translation problems. William Tyndale always translated *ekklesia* as 'congregation', and used the word 'church' only once when he translated Romans 2:22 as 'robbers of heathen churches'! His translation would have helped us to focus more upon the human members of the congregation rather than upon the buildings. Perhaps the complexity of translating apparently simple words like 'God' and 'church' will alert us to the difficulty of finding words that approximate to biblical meanings. The Chinese characters for 'teaching association' used by Japanese and Koreans, as well as Chinese, inevitably give a Confucian flavour to what a 'church' is, the more so if the church members are seen as the pupils or disciples of their Bible teacher, as they so often are. Ministers or missionaries who see themselves as apart from or even above the 'ordinary' lay believers perpetuate hierarchical church patterns, rather than following Jesus who taught his followers to abominate both secular Gentile (Matthew 20:25–28) or Jewish religious (Matthew 23:8–12) patterns of leadership and to follow his example of humility.

The 'bonding' model of relationship requires that the missionary lamb sets a pattern of human relationship, as a member of the emerging group, and not a teacher lording over it. The way the first missionary relates often becomes a model for how subsequent national church leaders will relate to other congregational members in future. We see what a heavy responsibility this is. Both those of us who may be shy and diffident, as well as extroverts with a tendency to autocratic bossiness, will need to spend time on our knees asking for help, and to be conscious always of Christ's presence alongside us, enabling us to relate to our fellow believers and body-members as we should.

3. Seating and architectural layout

This problem hit me forcibly when studying a series of church building layouts with a group of Chinese students in Hong Kong. Most of our western church models (but not all) tend to be bilaterally symmetrical, with one end as the focus of attention. Whether traditional Anglican cross-shaped buildings with transepts or traditional 'chapel' oblong boxes, there is always a 'holy end' with a focus upon the table for communion, a lectern for reading and a pulpit for preaching. Clearly prayers have to be led from somewhere, and teaching given from some position where all can see and hear clearly. If leaders at the 'holy end' dress up in cultic clothes on a raised platform this adds to the lack of symmetry. In modern western churches where so often screen and overhead projector have displaced the pulpit and the lectern, the impression that members are sitting in a bus all facing the same direction is further reinforced. Piano, organ and worship bands also tend to be placed in the 'holy end'. In the Baptist tradition a prominent baptistry may also be a focus at the end where all the action happens.

Fortunately in Hong Kong we also looked at the pattern favoured by Quakers and Christian Brethren. They used a circular arrangement with the table central and the believers ranged around it. This alignment had much to commend it in expressing visually and non-verbally the egalitarian and non-hierarchical form of church organisation. I realised more forcibly than before that even the spatial layout of a church

building may have doctrinal implications. Many cultures seg-
regate men and women on opposite sides of the church
meeting-place for sound cultural reasons: the synagogue certainly did the same; in many things the synagogue provided a
background model for the early church as, for example, in
reading the Law and the prophets, and teaching from them (cf
Acts 13:15; 1 Timothy 4:13).

I have said enough to show that we have all inherited shapes
or arrangements within church buildings, and that all of them
say something about the centrality of Christ's table, the
reading and preaching of the word, the place of singing in
worship, and perhaps the ecclesiology. The question is
whether we will unthinkingly export these, and start everybody off on a basis of western church history, building design,
furniture and so on. Or do we do some fresh thinking to
diminish our being perceived as a foreign import as much as
we can?

This has to be thought about and prayed about from the
initial stage of planting a new church. Men wrestling with
some new mechanical gizmo for home or garden, tend only to
read instructions if all else fails! When building churches it is
both wise and spiritual to consult the biblical instructions in
cultural context rather than slavishly copying foreign models.
The Inuit cathedral in Iqaluit, Frobisher Bay, Baffin Island uses
a vertical sledge as a pulpit and horizontal sledges as communion rails; there is imaginative use of narwhal tusks and seal-
skin banners. The building outside looks circular shaped like
an igloo, but inside it is still a 'holy end' pattern with a font
near the entrance and a holy table at the east end, and
Anglican clergy wearing traditional English clerical robes. (It
was refreshing to see the bishop was wearing trainers under-
neath!) A story of the pioneer E.J. Peck concerns an early 'contextualised' church in the Arctic: 'They had built a little

"church" twenty feet long, of whale bones and sealskins and called it their "tabernacle in the wilderness"; but, unfortunately one night the hungry dogs seized the "tabernacle" and devoured it![5]

The simplest church building I have ever worshipped in was a leprosy sala church in Thailand with large fronds and leaves forming the roof of a bamboo structure with no sides at all. The benches were horizontal bamboo poles, sufficient to support gluteus muscles, but impossible to fall asleep safely upon! The entire congregation consisted of leprosy sufferers. The building was the simplest and the crudest one could imagine – but the presence of the Lord was among us. It seems foolish to import western architectural forms – too many Presbyterian churches in Korea look as though they might equally well have been built in Aberdeen or Philadelphia. Diliman Bible church in Manila was determined to use Filipino architecture, and many Indonesian churches are pleasingly ethnic in style. We may think the famous dome-shaped Catholic Igloo cathedral in Inuvik, North West Territories, is a bit over the top, but it is a great advance on St Paul's, Iqaluit mentioned above.

Even small items of church furniture may be significant in some cultures. The Koran is a holy book and it would be unthinkable to lay it on the floor or to treat it disrespectfully. For this reason new churches in Bangladesh provided book-stands so that Bibles (unmarked, for defacing God's word would seem sacrilege to Muslims) could be reverently placed, and facilities for washing hands and feet before services also provided.[6] In Sikh *gurdwaras* the central place is occupied by a copy of the Guru Granth Sahib, the Holy Book, which replaced the ten Gurus, reverently placed upon a large cushion (like a very large lectern or pulpit Bible). In the one Christian *gurdwara* of converted Sikhs that I know of, near Vancouver, it seems culturally proper that the central place should be occupied correspondingly by an equally large Christian Bible, and they maintain a restaurant downstairs also just as they do in a *gurdwara*. This seems a wise and proper contextualisation in church layout, familiar rather than foreign to Sikh converts.

Our forebears seemed to have little problem in taking over earlier religious buildings for Christian worship. Pope Gregory's advice to Augustine's missionaries in Anglo-Saxon Britain seems to have been generally followed:

> If those temples are well built, it is requisite that they be converted from the worship of devils to the service of the true God; that the nation seeing their temples are not destroyed, may remove error from their heart, and knowing and adoring the true God, may the more familiarly resort to the places to which they have been accustomed.[7]

The synagogue in Pisidian Antioch became a Christian basilica. There is a mosque in Ankara which began as a temple of Cybele, then became a temple for the state cult of Caesar Augustus and then a Christian basilica, before it was taken over as part of a mosque. In the South Pacific, the Raiatean pioneer missionary Papehia, co-worker of John Williams of the London Missionary Society, channelled their initial exuberance into a permanent memorial of their change of loyalties by enlisting the whole community in building a huge new place of worship.[8]

The theory here was that the new Christian building dwarfed previous idolatrous temples and because the community built it themselves, was valued by them as their own. The Korean church also lays great store by the expensive, prestigious church buildings in which the Christian community invests sacrificially.

4. Church music

Someone has commented that Africans all sang in the minor key until Christian missionaries arrived and taught them to sing in the major! In East Asia most music is pentatonic (scale of five) rather than diatonic (in octaves like western music). The problem for the western missionary in the past has been that whether musical or not, the only hymns he or she knew were diatonic. It was possible to translate the words (often very badly!), but not to produce new tunes. It is possible to sing 'Yes, Jesus loves me, the Bible tells me so' in the Japanese aboriginal Ainu language ('*Iesu en omap, Iesu en omap*') to William Bradbury's familiar tune. If people had only sung pentatonic music up to that point, the resulting cacophony jarred as weirdly on the foreign as the indigenous ear. Over the course of time Christians became familiar with diatonic music in church. Christians in Japan and Korea will sing melodies from Weber, Beethoven, Handel, Stainer and even Donizetti. Some Japanese evangelical leaders once admitted to me that it was a pity Christians were now so used to diatonic music that it was too late to change!

In some more recently pioneered fields it has been possible to declare a moratorium on merely translating western hymns. In South Thailand they sing the New Testament in the Pattani dialect of Malay in the same style in which the Koran is sung from the minaret: the music is familiar to them, but the words are biblical rather than koranic. In both Laos and Cambodia, a musically gifted female missionary produced hymn books using indigenous melodies. More recently it has been good when Japanese have created their own modern choruses first for children and then for adults like '*Iesu wa ichiban*' (Jesus is Number 1), though translations of nineteenth-century English and American hymns still tend to dominate. Again this is something that needs to be thought about from the beginning when singing is first introduced to new Christians. We need to pray that God will raise up new Davids and Charles Wesleys, indigenous Frances Havergals and Graham Kendricks so that such congregations may have their own Christian music from the outset instead of mediocre translations of western hymns and choruses sung to diatonic music, and expressing foreign rather than indigenous sentiments. Singing about the apostles in Galilee walking 'beside the Syrian Sea' does not go down too well in Israel!

5. Church services and meetings

There are simple decisions to be made in the process of contextualisation. We naturally assume that Sunday morning (and perhaps evening too) may be the appropriate time to hold Christian worship services. The early church may early have settled on the 'first day of the week' (Luke 24:1; John 20:19, 26; Acts 20:7; 1 Corinthians 16:2; Revelation 1:10), but it seems probable that so many being slaves (half the population of Greek cities) they met late at night or early in the morning as they did in Acts 20:8–11. We need similar flexibility today, for in Israel the Jewish Sabbath begins on Friday evening, while in Islamic countries, Friday is the public day for going to the mosque, and in both situations Sunday is a working day. In such circumstances Christians may wish to hold their main gatherings on Fridays or Saturdays rather than keeping to a weekly celebration of the resurrection, as they can still in European countries and in North and South America. But at what time of day?

In the Philippines, some of the earliest Protestant morning services were held at eleven o'clock in the morning. This was the time of day when it was hottest, and people were beginning to feel sleepy and possibly hungry for a mid-day meal. It would have been difficult (before air-conditioned church buildings) to imagine a less suitable time of day. It was not that missionaries determined that Filipinos must be compelled to follow western church-going habits, for it seems they did not think at all. Churches always meet on Sunday mornings, so let's do it! Significantly, Brethren churches in Singapore have tended to meet at eight o'clock in the morning while it is still cool and people are fresh.

It is possible for western missionaries to be more time bound than the people they work with. Philip Parshall has a story from Africa of a time-orientated missionary so infuriated that a service was continuing past midnight that he switched off the power supply to the church, plunging the worshippers into darkness.[9] In Indonesia, David Bentley-Taylor relates how night after night the best time for evangelistic preaching in *kampongs* (villages) in Java was in the early hours of the morning, and the missionary had to adjust to the timetable of his Indonesian colleagues using the relaxed cool time after midnight.[10] This meant that his sleep patterns had to be adjusted so that he slept through the later mornings, but it was worth it to have a relaxed audience at the quiet reflective time of day.

In rural communities, villagers may opt for a different pattern of meeting than in our commuter cities. A Chinese church in a South Thailand village (a recreation area for communist terrorists making a nuisance of themselves over the border in Malaysia at the time) met informally in one another's homes every night for a time of prayer and singing, and the consequent fellowship and bonding was rich.

6. Art and illustration

The Roman Catholic 'Igloo cathedral' in Inuvik is decorated with paintings of the stations of the cross done by a local artist. The Anglican cathedral in Iqaluit is decorated with a series of banners illustrating Inuit life. North American Indian pictures of the nativity differ markedly from Thai pictures of divinity, but both are culture friendly.[11] In western culture, Italianesque pictures of Jesus and his disciples have tended to predominate; though the icons of the Orthodox tradition are different again. This raises the whole issue of different mental pictures of the Lord and of his disciples. Is it accepted that Jesus of Nazareth was ethnically Jewish and recognisable as such? The Bible actually forbids making images of God: 'You saw no form of any kind the day the Lord spoke to you at Horeb out of the fire. Therefore watch yourselves very carefully, so that you do not . . . make for yourselves an idol, an image of any shape, whether formed like a man or a woman or like any animal on earth' (Deuteronomy 4:15–17).

In recent years Christians seem to have overcome objections to actors representing Christ and his disciples on film and television, although at the Reformation there was widespread destruction of Catholic images by zealous Protestants. Jews and Muslims alike regard all such images as blasphemous. The bearded actors who play Jesus in Christian evangelistic films inevitably seem less than satisfactory; often our earliest mental images may be shaped by what appears in books for children. When Dorothy Sayers was writing *The Man Born to be King* for Children's Hour on BBC Radio in 1941 there was enormous indignation that any actor might 'impersonate' Christ.[12] We need to be careful what we introduce, to obey Scripture and to be sensitive to culture.

7. Ministers and church leaders

The aim of the good missionary is always to hand over to native leadership as soon as possible. The first Christian missionaries in Japan, Jesuits under the Italian Alissandro

Valignano, actually created a new order of Japanese workers known as *dojuku* who were a kind of apprentice clergy who shaved their heads and wore cassocks. As early as 1580, Valignano was looking forward to a genuinely Japanese church under a Japanese bishop.[13] One difficulty is that while people may have experience of priests, witch-doctors, imams, shamans and their leadership role in earlier local religions, they have no Christian precedents, except possibly the foreign missionary. The danger is to assume those church officers and leaders are the equivalent of priests, druids, imams, etc. It is natural to find those in a similar niche in society. Sometimes the Christian minister is seen to have taken over the functions of the shaman or Confucian mentor.

At the same time there is often great reluctance on the part of some missionaries to accept that local people are not ready yet to assume leadership. Thus C.C. Fenn wrote in 1878 that: 'in all Missions without exception the tendency acting irresistibly in almost every Missionary is to undervalue the strength and the worth of Native Christian activity.'[14] Roland Allen much later did a great deal to persuade others that the Holy Spirit could prepare, shape and use national Christians just as much as missionaries.

How far should we go along with the notion of ministers being financially supported for their work, something we often assume from our church traditions? The Independent Methodist (so called Quaker-Methodists, who date back to the early nineteenth-century) ministers were always virtually self-supporting from the beginning. In the early years of the Korean Presbyterian Church the missionaries, after conference input from John Livingston Nevius, an experienced missionary from China, had agreed not to use overseas money to support national ministers or church building projects. This meant that all their early ministers were either self-supporting, or only partially supported by their fellow believers. It seems a pity merely to perpetuate our own current system without first rethinking it from our biblical roots. Paul disavowed church support as a matter of principle (cf 1 Corinthians 9:6, 12, 15, 18; 1 Thessalonians 2:9; 2 Thessalonians 3:7–9; Acts 20:33–35). Karl Gutzlaff's pioneer work in China collapsed because he was paying out money to native 'evangelists' who took his money but did no evangelism![15] It is interesting that it was China missionaries of very different traditions like Nevius and Roland Allen who came to similar conclusions on the dangers of foreign missionaries paying church workers.

8. Lifestyle

Many of us have inherited a Christian subcultural lifestyle. The Christian Brethren in Italy began with the conversions of a Florentine nobleman Piero Guicciardini (1808–1886), who was influential in the conversion of a cousin of Christina Rossetti. However, the Italians never seem to have had problems over drinking Chianti, even though a succession of British and American missionaries sought to bring them round to their own cultural shibboleths.

I well remember my own culture shock when my hosts of the Danish Covenant Mission said, 'Now let's all have a glass of sherry to help us sleep, pray, read our Bibles and go to bed.' (!) But the matter needs to be settled with regard both to Scripture and the indigenous situation. Wesleyan teetotalism arose at a time when drinking was a social evil; and Japanese churches have largely taken the same route for the same reason – *sake* drinking is a social evil. Sarawak tribes like the Lunbawang (Muruts) were almost destroyed by alcohol. The *Sarawak Gazette* reported that villages of this tribe were drunk on average a hundred days a year, and whole communities would be in an alcoholic stupor for days at a time, so much so that babies died because their mothers were too drunk to succour them. The Brooke government left them in quarantine to die out, until the gospel reached them across the Indonesian border. Understandably, having been delivered from extinction by alcohol, total abstention has been the church rule. So whether we come from a permissive or restrictive subculture, we do well to rethink the new situation from biblical principles, and in terms of our new Christian social context.

An interesting sidelight on cultural attitudes comes from the same area, where churches asked the Missionary Aviation Fellowship to withdraw their pilot because he lost his temper, behaviour unacceptable among Christians. The Australian in question, a fine Christian with very long fuses, finally blew his top when a tribesman smuggled a hundredweight bag of rice onto a small plane without his knowledge, thus endangering the lives of all on board! We may all have the same Scriptures, but our differing subcultures tend to be selective on the issues we think ethically significant.

Even among missionaries there can be substantial differences between Scottish sabbatarians and Swiss or Norwegian believers, who having been to church (or even organised one on the ski-slopes) have no problem in enjoying the rest of the day in recreation. Way back in 1800 in the Cape, the newly arrived William Anderson of the London Missionary Society was distressed to find that William Edwards and John Kircherer did not get on well. Edwards (who was English) was critical of Kircherer (who was Dutch) because he was slack in 'sabbath-keeping': they came from different cultures![16] In whatever part of the world we may be working, such issues have a habit of reappearing, whatever the Colossian epistle may have to say on the subject. Philip Parshall gives a list of ten 'culturally relevant' commandments devised by early European missionaries in Indonesia:

1. Thou shalt have thy hair cut short.
2. Thou shalt not take off thy head kerchief in church.
3. Thou shalt not listen to *gamelan* music.
4. Thou shalt not attend a *wayang* performance.
5. Thou shalt not be circumcised.
6. Thou shalt not attend a *slametan*.
7. Thou shalt not read Javanese verse.
8. Thou shalt not care for the graves of thy ancestors.
9. Thou shalt not decorate thy cemeteries with flowers and trees.
10. Thou shalt forbid thy children to play idle games.

The ethnocentric missionaries seemed to have banned everything in the local culture which they could not understand. Whatever their reasons for these attempts to cut Indonesians away from their cultural roots, it should serve as a warning to us to be cautious to aspects of local culture which seem foreign and threatening to us. We are wise if we wait to see how emerging church leaders taught by the Holy Spirit apply the Scriptures to their cultural situation.

9. *Creeds and statements of faith*

When we start asking contextual questions like those in this chapter, we realise that the creeds of the church and even our great Protestant statements of faith are both historically and linguistically conditioned, dealing with some issue significant at that particular time in history in a particular subculture. Neither the Nicene Creed in Greek nor the Apostles' Creed in Latin are in the Bible. There is much more here than a mere translation problem. If we look at sections of African and Thai statements, we quickly appreciate that they are dealing with immediate issues significant for their cultures, but not necessarily so for others. Indeed all doctrinal statements tend to date as the flow of discussion and debate within the church moves forward. A tribal catechism based on Bible stories had much to commend it in cultures where oral tradition and narratives learned by heart are familiar patterns.

The doctrinal statement of London Bible College (prior to its replacement in 1998) was very clearly written to contend against a neo-orthodox, Barthian view of Scripture, perceived as a problem when it was written. Since that time new dangers and problems have arisen.

The danger here, as has often been pointed out, is that in suggesting to new Christians they need to have a written church constitution (an idea which comes more from western cultures than theirs), the final result may reflect more the denominational background and doctrinal orientation of the missionary rather than the Bible or the immediate needs of the emerging native church. How easily we claim to see the Bible as our only rule in all matters of faith and conduct, and then produce man-made traditions of our own, much as the Pharisees did. It is clear from the Gospels what the Lord Jesus himself thought of those human constructions; see especially the woes of Matthew 23 and the rebuke of human traditions in Mark 7:1–23.

Working with already established churches

The missionary's situation is now entirely different because, for good or ill, the structure and discipline of the national churches have already been established. Some mission agencies specifically instruct their members not to interfere with established church patterns (recognising that situations may well arise when they may be tempted to do so).

The established orthodoxy that the national church is right and the alien missionary wrong bars the newcomer ignorant of culture from exercising any prophetic role. In fact, we are aware that outsiders, uninfluenced by our own cultural presuppositions, often see us more clearly and objectively than we can see ourselves. But in missionary situations that can be seen as unacceptable foreign arrogance. Missionaries seconded to work with existing denominations or groups of churches have the status of invited guests, even if they are not employees. The fact they are not financially supported in some situations may be their chief attraction: they cost nothing, whereas a national person would have to be paid to do the same work. There may even be exploitation of the seconded missionary as a cheap way of getting English teachers without having to pay for them!

The plain, unvarnished truth is that long-established churches in any continent can be just as much stuck in a rut of denominational institutionalism as the oldest European churches. Even when the mother church has repented, and has enjoyed revival and the reforming breath of the Holy Spirit, the daughter churches may have become fossilised in the traditions of the past, having the form of godliness and denominational ecclesiology to be sure, but denying its power. Denominational pride and nominal Christianity in the third world can be worse even than anything known in the old world. The tendency to bureaucracy and institutionalism knows no national or ethnic boundaries, indeed some two-thirds world traditions are more hidebound in their observance of established precedents than their founding denominations ever were.

The problem of bonding into such churches may be more difficult. The authority of the national church and its leadership must be respected and its dictates submitted to, and the seconded missionary may be left feeling powerless, frustrated and even angry when he or she discovers the real situation of the church they have been invited to work with. There may even be a hidden agenda, so that what the missionary is actually asked to do after arrival is quite different from the job description that came with the original invitation, which was accepted in good faith. One American Methodist gifted in evangelism was utterly frustrated when the inviting church wanted to siphon him off into English teaching: he refused to do it for this was not his gift or training, or calling.

Supporting existing church leadership

Some missionaries working with established churches may be tempted to build their own spiritual clique or faction enshrining their own personal enthusiasms, perhaps in opposition even to duly appointed church leadership. There is then the danger of division and schism, with men and women of Christian integrity torn both ways between their loyalty to established leadership and their recognition that such leadership is inevitably imperfect in some degree. However frustrating, the missionary must be faithful to established leadership, unspiritual or misguided though it may be, and seek to have influence through their friendship and bonding. Suggestions can be made and hints dropped – these can then be taken up by leadership and presented as their own: such plagiarism is to be encouraged! In this role, women missionaries are often highly successful for they are usually perceived as less threatening than their male counterparts.

In pre-revolution China many women missionaries served under national pastors with great acceptance and effectiveness. In some cultures pastors are easily threatened even by junior assistant ministers, who may appear to be more gifted and acceptable to the congregation than they are. The overseas missionary can appear even more threatening. There is need therefore for great tact, and truly biblical servant leadership. The person who remains detached and aloof from the people he has been sent to work with has little hope of being effective, compared with those determined to establish a heart relationship, and bond in genuine sacrificial friendship.

Biblical teaching is clear on the responsibility to honour, respect and obey church leaders and I know of no scriptures excusing missionaries from this. Consider passages like: 'respect those who work hard among you, who are over you in the Lord and who admonish you. Hold them in the highest regard in love because of their work' (1 Thessalonians 5:12–13). And

> Remember your leaders, who spoke the word of God to you. Consider the outcome of their way of life and imitate their faith . . . Obey your leaders and submit to their authority. They keep watch over you as those who must give account. Obey them so that their work may be a joy, not a burden, for that would be of no advantage to you.
>
> (Hebrews 13:7, 17)

If the leaders in question fail to speak the word of God, seem to lack faith, and fail to keep watch, we may be tempted to forgo the obedience which Scripture commands. We have to live with the paradox that the same body of people who are the church of God, the body of Christ and the temple of the Spirit, may at the same time be childish and carnal (1 Corinthians 3:1–17). The church is at one and the same time God's church, and a fallible, sinful human organisation led by fallible, sinful and sometimes even stupid leaders. This is as true overseas as it is in our churches at home! And we cannot give up, or wash our hands of the situation, until we have prayed long and faithfully, and obeyed and loved beyond the call of mere duty.

Encouraging the next generation

The new generation may seem to offer greatest hope for the future, not least because they themselves are often justifiably critical of existing adult leadership. On the other hand, the missionary must not foster rebellion. Once I was approached by a group of rebellious young people in Singapore – understandably rebellious, for the elders of their church were very conservative, repressive and almost paranoid in their fear of new ideas. I reminded them of biblical commands to obey leaders, and I urged patience and suggested that they might well be in leadership within ten or fifteen years, and please to remember then how they felt now! It was most satisfying to see that this in fact happened. The mother assembly continued, regrettably, determined to stick with King James English and addressing God as 'Thou' at a time when Singaporean English was developing grammar of its own. The young brethren in question became youthful leaders of spiritual caves of Adullam in the satellite towns.

We need to be aware of the danger of what is sometimes called 'my boys-ism'. The missionary feels gratified to have protégés (it would be unbiblical to call them 'disciples' for only the Lord has disciples now, apostles never do) who may be encouraged in wholehearted commitment. The difficulty arises at a point when they discover that we are not infallible as mentors, and start asking awkward questions like rebellious teenagers. This is an especial danger for single missionaries (male or female) in being reluctant to allow such protégés to break free of our apron strings. In other words, 'bonding' between people of widely disparate age has its own problems.

Our greatest opportunity as new missionaries is bonding with our peers, people of our own age who befriend us or whom we befriend. With these we may share dreams for the future church as equals, and grow up together. Those whom the long-term missionary knows first as students or young graduates will probably be senior church leaders by the time the long-term missionary retires or returns to their home country. Even when the churches are locked into religious institutionalism and antiquarian ritualism of the worst type, the younger generation who share our vision for a glorious church without spot or blemish may be the best hope for the future. They can achieve reforms for the church which we may never attain to. A young Korean scholar once grumbled to me: 'What our churches need is a Korean Martin Luther!' We would do well to pray for such fresh reformation according to the word of God in every country. It may be that those with whom we ourselves have bonded will, under God, be instruments in his hand to achieve such goals. The apostle John expresses this as: 'It gave me great joy to have some brothers come and tell me about your faithfulness to the truth and how you continue to walk in the truth' (3 John 5). We may not be old enough to repeat him without sounding paternalistic, but among the greatest pleasurable privileges of missionary service is vicarious joy in the spiritual triumphs of those we have known in the earlier years of their Christian commitment.

Notes

1. J.B. Phillips, *The New Testament in Modern English* (London: Bles, 1960).
2. Stephen Neill, *Colonialism and Christian Missions* (London: Lutterworth, 1966), pp.43–45.
3. Andrew Ross, *A Vision Betrayed: The Jesuits in Japan and China, 1542–1742* (New York: Orbis, 1994), p.xii.
4. *Five Pioneer Women of the Anglican Church* (Whitehorse: Anglican Church Women, 1964).

5. Eugene Stock, *History of the Church Missionary Society,* Vol. III (London, 1899), p.628.
6. Philip Parshall, *New Paths in Muslim Evangelism* (Grand Rapids: Baker, 1980), p.25.
7. Bede, *Ecclesiastical History of the English Nation* (1:30).
8. John Hitchen, 'Our South Pacific Missionary Heritage – the Forgotten Central Strand' (Paper given at South Pacific Conference).
9. Philip Parshall, *Op. cit.*, p.40.
10. David Bentley-Taylor, *The Great Volcano* (London: CIM-OMF, 1965), and see also the same author's *The Prisoner Leaps.*
11. John Davis, *Poles Apart: Contextualising the Gospel* (Bangkok, OMF Publishers, 1993).
12. David Coomes, *Dorothy L. Sayers: A careless rage for life* (Oxford: Lion, 1992), p.17ff.
13. Andrew Ross, *op. cit.*, p.60.
14. Peter Williams, *The Ideal of the Self-governing Church* (Leyden: Brill, 1990), p.66.
15. A.J. Broomhall, *J. Hudson Taylor and China's Open Century*, Vol. 2, *Over the Treaty Wall* (London: Hodder and Stoughton, 1982), p.394. Or see 2001 new edition under the title *The Shaping of Modern China* (OMF / William Carey Library / Paternoster).
16. Peter Anderson, *Weapons of Peace: The Story of William and Johanna Anderson* (Hong Kong: Logos, 1995), p.17.

CHAPTER NINE

LAMBS RELATE WITH THEIR FLOCK LEADERS

It has always been wise for missionaries to work together with other like-minded people. Human beings learn from experience, and there is no point in all of us starting from scratch and repeating each other's mistakes. We all claim to be working for the same Lord with the same ends in view so it is much better to co-operate rather than to compete. This book has warned against the dangers of bonding with other expatriates rather than national Christians, but once bonding with national fellow-believers is developing, then belonging to a team of like-minded people within one's own missionary group and beyond it in the same area would seem to be a Christian duty. This will also provide a natural support group. In Central Asia, for example, the widely-scattered members of several different Christian organisations may well find close fellowship with like-minded people, whether self-supporting or church-supported in the same town or city. In countries like Nepal and Mongolia these have been formalised as loosely formed umbrella groups, co-operating together in helping governments with development projects in medicine, engineering, and education. This kind of fellowship and mutual help has a long history – the East India Chaplains, all Anglican, had good fellowship with the Baptists arriving in Calcutta. Hudson Taylor met the American Presbyterian John Livingston Nevius as he arrived off the ship in Ningpo.

The Roman Catholic monastic orders exercised very tight discipline. The Jesuits who began work in Asia were possibly even more disciplined. Roberto de Nobili was doing an excellent work among Brahmins in Mathurai, but when he was ordered to move to Jaffna, even though he was seventy years old, he obeyed.[1] Protestants, who had no established tradition of obedience, began with religious societies – the Halle Mission (1706), the Moravians (1732), and then the several British missions founded at the end of the eighteenth century. These began with groups of concerned ministers and laymen of different denominations. Two Anglican ministers, John Eyre and Thomas Haweis, and the Congregational David Bogue of Gosport together helped found 'The Missionary Society' whose first official meeting took place on 8 September 1795.[2] The word 'London' was added later after the foundation of societies in Scotland. The foundation principles were superb:

> As the union of Christians of various denominations in carrying on this great work is a most desirable object, so to prevent, if possible any cause of future dissension, it is declared to be a fundamental principle of the Missionary Society, that its design is not to send Presbyterianism, Independency, Episcopacy, or any other form of church order and government (about which there may be differences of opinion among serious persons), but the glorious Gospel of the blessed God, to the heathen; and that it shall be left (as it ought to be left) to the minds of the persons whom God may call into the fellowship of His Son from among them, to assume for themselves such form of church government as to them shall appear most agreeable to the Word of God.[3]

On 12 April 1799 sixteen clergymen and nine laymen, 'largely at the instigation and through the persistent persuasion of Charles Simeon' founded 'The Society for Missions to Africa and the East' (later known as the Church Missionary Society).[4]

In the nature of the case such missions were ruled by committees in the sending country, served by strong-minded and gifted general secretaries like Rufus Anderson of the American Board of Commissioners for Foreign Missions (ABCFM) and his contemporary opposite number in Britain, Henry Venn of the CMS. When distances were great and communications slow it soon became increasingly clear that more immediate leadership on the field was important. CMS work in New Zealand was originally the vision of Samuel Marsden (another of Simeon's protégés) based in Sydney. He bought his own ship, landed livestock, dismissed missionaries, and took charge each time he visited. The first so-called 'godly mechanics' were artisans lacking wide experience. The mission did not really take off until Henry Williams, a former naval captain, took hold and provided strong leadership on the spot in New Zealand.

Hudson Taylor's early experience working for the Chinese Evangelisation Society, waiting for months for funds to arrive, and frustrated by the time taken for letters to be answered, convinced him that leadership on the field within China was the answer. The mission he founded based its international head office in Shanghai, rather than London, until Japanese invasion forced them to move to Chungking and the 1950 Maoist revolution compelled evacuation to Singapore. In spite of this precedent, even today many Protestant missions, denominational and interdenominational alike, for the most part are given instructions from offices based in London, Sydney, New York, Illinois or the Black Forest.

However, missionaries tend to be independent-minded people who do not always agree with their leaders or even with the majority. The lambs and sheep analogy really breaks down at this point. When we talk of people behaving like sheep, we may think of the way a whole line will jump over an invisible obstacle one after the other. However, New Zealand sheep-farming friends tell me that Merino breeds can be very independent minded. And the Bible does say that sheep go astray.

The very first party of LMS missionaries on the ship *Duff* actually excommunicated two of their party (for a week!) because they had doubts about limited atonement. It was this strong Calvinistic bias that convinced both Anglicans and Methodists that however high the original ideals of LMS were for a single, united and non-denominational society, it was so strongly Calvinistic that they would be impossible to work with, and so now they should start their own societies.

There were some sensational early breakaways. Adoniram and Ann Judson went out in 1812 in the first ABCFM contingent from the United States, but withdrew having been convinced by the English Baptists in Serampore of the truth of believers' baptism. This resulted in their adoption by a hastily formed American Baptist Foreign Missionary Society in 1814. Around the same time a German missionary Gottlob Bruckner, who went out with the LMS to Java in 1814, was baptised by immersion in 1816 by Thomas Trowt and transferred to the Baptist Missionary Society. Five years later he completed the Javanese New Testament.

Single women missionaries were few and far between. Maria Newell was appointed by the LMS to Malacca in 1827 and left after only two years to marry Karl Gutzlaff, who was working for the Nederlands Missionary Society in Bangkok. Apparently in consequence, LMS stopped recruiting single women for the next thirty years! Not all of the missionaries Hudson Taylor took with him to China settled happily under his leadership. For example, some were especially restive over his insistence that all must wear Chinese dress.[5] Though we often think of Hudson Taylor as an individualist, China missions co-operated with each other, gave hospitality to each other, and were not exclusive in relating only to members of their own society.

There have always been individualists. Benjamin Broomhall in London was more enthusiastic than Hudson Taylor about the 'Cambridge Seven' who sailed in 1885. Of that group, D.E. Hoste, a former army officer, became Taylor's successor in 1900, and W.W. Cassels became an Anglican bishop in China from 1895. However, Stanley-Smith, gifted linguist and evangelist, sadly resigned because of his heterodox doctrinal opinions. The former England cricketer C.T. Studd was something of a maverick throughout his time in China, until asthma finally forced his return home (1885–1894)[6]. He then served in India (1900–1906), and joined the Africa Inland Mission in 1910 but after two or three years moved out to form his own Heart of Africa Mission in North East Congo. He parted company with his home board after a famous confrontation in Africa, resulting in the formation of the World Evangelisation Crusade (1913).

Some countries were so vast and communication so difficult that individualists could usually manage to do their own thing with a minimum of interference. It was said of the shy, dour Scot, George Hunter, based in Urumchi in Xinjiang, that he placed the Gobi Desert between himself and the CIM directors in Shanghai. After his first eleven years, he took his only home leave in 1900, returning to China in 1902 where he remained until his death in 1946. His biographer writes: 'He soon broke away from the exasperating toils of community life to breathe the freer air of a trek which was to know no limits.' He visited Shanghai for a Conference in 1907, and again in 1931. Later he was imprisoned by the Russians for thirteen months, and deported to Lanchow in China proper, dying in 1946.[7]

Several newer mission agencies have been founded by people who started with existing societies and then hived off to start their own. We may properly question whether this has always been the result of direct divine guidance, or of more or less sanctified impatience with existing leadership, but God in his merciful overruling has been pleased to use many of them to achieve fruitful work. We have to recognise that all our splendid societies are temporary, voluntary human associations with no permanent biblical sanction for our eternal existence. Some fine groups like the Algiers Mission Band, the Borneo Evangelical Mission and the Central Japan Pioneer Mission have merged into other societies and disappeared from view.

New Testament missionaries display independence and flexibility

Luke's account in Acts suggests that even the apostle Paul's missionary teams were fairly shortlived. Paul worked with Barnabas (and John Mark until he deserted them in Pamphylia [Acts 13:13]) until they parted company after a couple of years together (Acts 15:39). Barnabas then teamed up with Mark and went to Cyprus, where tradition has it that he was martyred and buried near Salamis. Paul then teamed up with Silas (Acts 15:40), and recruited Timothy (Acts 16:3), but Silas disappears from the narrative in Corinth (Acts 18:5) before the end of the second journey. There were those whom Paul had the authority to 'send' like Timothy and Erastus

(Acts 19:22) and Tychichus (2 Timothy 4:12), but other more independent workers like Titus can only be 'urged' (2 Corinthians 12:18), and while Apollos can be 'urged' to go, he can and did refuse (1 Corinthians 16:12). Thus while the apostolic bands may be regarded as mission society proto-types, making their own decisions rather than referring them back to the churches in Antioch or Jerusalem, they seem to have been rather loose associations whose members did not stay permanently working together.

It seems useful to have this historical perspective upon our mission societies, their existence, and the impermanence of their membership. Demands for 'loyalty', insistence on guid-ance 'that you are called to us' and a proper desire for *esprit de corps* can sometimes fog our true voluntary status and cause unnecessary agony in individualists who find corporate discipline and regulations irksome. We sometimes talk as though in 'the good old days' missionaries were all sanctified, submissive and obedient, whereas the nature of modern edu-cation means that 'these modern young missionaries' have been trained to do nothing without asking questions and dis-covering reasons for regulations before they feel bound to obey them. The truth of the matter is that from New Testament times and throughout Protestant mission history some individuals have always been prepared to disagree with the leadership and even with the collective democratic will.

Personally I believe that a proper biblical doctrine of the church and a love for fellow Christians requires us to pray and work together with others, rather than being independent, self-promoting mavericks determined to run our own show and be answerable to nobody. A high biblical doctrine of the church should be the death of individualism! I believe that we all should as far as possible co-operate and work together with fellow Christians in the mutual submission commanded in

Scripture (Ephesians 5:21). Some people learn this the hard way, and others see their need to find people to work with, rather than people who can manage to work with them! I heard it said recently of one strong leader (who was also a workaholic) that he didn't want colleagues, only disciples! Paul's teaching about the church as a body deplores those who claim to be self-sufficient without the body, and those who claim they have no contribution to make to the body.

Objectively, however, we have to accept that individualists find submitting to a fellowship an irksome discipline, and that the Lord in his mercy is still pleased to use them. Many missionary societies were started by exactly such kinds of people, provided they could persuade others to follow them. But such leaders subjected themselves to huge pressures.

> Hudson Taylor did not allow any trial to deflect his eyes from the goal. He was tireless in his devotion to his fellow workers. He travelled incessantly, visiting each station in turn, encouraging, exhorting, advising, preaching and caring for the health of all. He once made a journey of five hundred miles to attend a sick colleague. This was in addition to the heavy administrative work for which he was solely responsible. No one was surprised when he suffered a breakdown.[8]

A few years ago, George Verwer, founder of Operation Mobilisation, personally interviewed 2,500 volunteers for short-term mission before finally recognising that he had to delegate!

Allen Gardiner entered the navy at the age of fourteen in 1808, three years after Trafalgar. His naval experience seems to have given him a larger global view than many. He offered to join the LMS if only they would send him to Patagonia, but they refused. So he set off to evangelise the Zulu, and persuaded Dingaan, the Zulu chief, to lease him huge areas of territory, now Natal, and laid out the city of Durban! However, when war broke out between the Afrikaners and the Zulu, he set sail for Rio de Janeiro in 1838. He then embarked on a 1,000-mile trek across Patagonia and the Andes! He experienced considerable opposition from Roman Catholic authorities, and so decided to try New Guinea next. He had problems with pirates and volcanic eruptions, and finally the Dutch refused him a residence permit. Next, taking a holiday in Capetown on the way, he attempted entry to Chile once again. All of this took place before aeroplanes or even motor vehicles. One begins to wonder what this man needed: better information, more pastoral support or firm oversight![9] The fact remains that he was a pioneer of Protestant missions in South America, and that his example and tragic death in Tierra del Fuego inspired many. His persistent determination to establish mission work in South America was very significant. His Patagonian Missionary Society became the Anglican South American Missionary Society (SAMS).

A missionary society is a society of consent

Missionary society members serve on a voluntary basis and are free to opt out at any time. Some agencies insist on signed contracts, but it is quite different from being employed by a secular employer. The China Inland Mission guaranteed its members nothing: they were to put their trust in God and not in human beings, or human organised societies. Hudson Taylor insisted, 'The mission may cease to exist' but God will go on providing your needs in answer to prayer. A missionary society provides a symbiotic relationship, which is advantageous to all its members: pooling information, experience, resources and energies, and giving each other all the help they can. And yet any of them may terminate their membership at any time.

In the past they were held together by mutual sharing and pooling of their common funds, although missionaries with a private income (like Lawrence of Arabia's older brother Dr Montague Lawrence with the CIM in China) had more freedom to come and go when they wished. Others had to wait for the availability of funds to take home-leave. Today when increasingly missionaries are expected to 'raise their own support', mission agencies are becoming little more than a loose federation of independently supported individuals. This is bound to weaken the sense of mutual belonging. They bring their money with them when they come and take it away again when they go. The donor's sense of spiritual commitment to a task, a work and to a society bound together with a sense of purpose is being downgraded to financial commitment to individual Christian workers who may be only loosely bonded to those they work with.

Missionary societies vary enormously in structure

Small societies may be very simple in structure, though that can have its problems. A gifted young engineer I knew joined a mission of only twenty members all working in one small country, and within a few days was tactless enough to say: 'The trouble with this mission is that it is run by the field leader's wife!' At the other end of the scale a huge mega-mission like Wycliffe Bible Translators, with three or four thousand members working in many different countries, needs a very sophisticated organisational structure. There are several different types of mission, and even within such groupings there are wide differences in ethos and tradition.

Denominational (mono-national) eg the Free Church of Scotland in Peru, the Liebenzeller Mission from Black Forest, Conservative Baptists from the States, Korean Presbyterian Missions, Southern Baptists and so on. The greatest dangers exist of promoting poorly contextualised versions of national and denominational models.

Denominational (multinational) eg Salvation Army, Lutheran, CMS where the denominational ties cross national boundaries, but are committed to propagate the distinctives of their historical traditions.

Interdenominational (mononational) like the Indian Evangelical Mission where many denominations are involved, but all from one country. Many American missions fall into this bracket, while some of them focus upon one or two target countries only.

Interdenominational (international) eg WEC, SIM, Interserve, OMF, etc., where Christians of many nations and denominations co-operate. Interserve and OMF tend to limit themselves to East Asia or West Asia. SIM used to work only in Africa, but has now diversified its operations.

These different kinds of missions vary in size and ethos. The Christian Brethren have a minimum of structure, though they are linked by a common church polity. Others have a very complex hierarchy. Some are under Home Board control, in others field leadership controls and the home boards serve their aims. They vary in ethos – some are very poor, some very rich. Some are cheerfully chaotic and disorganised, while others like to do everything by the book (usually a very thick one!).

How an individual approaches a missionary society

Please remember that, humanly speaking, a mission is only as good as those it recruits who will become its leaders in ten or fifteen years' time! Home staffs are often made up of more senior people who, for one reason or another, have returned to their home countries. Reading books and magazines about a work and meeting returned missionaries seem two main factors in attracting recruits.

When the widowed Robert Morrison returned to Britain in 1824 he appealed for single women willing to work among Chinese women, and to this end started a Chinese language course for them in his own home in Hackney three days a week. Among those who came was Maria Newall, the first woman member of the LMS working in Malacca; Maria Tarn who worked in Penang until she married Samuel Dyer, and Mary Ann Aldersey, the first single woman missionary to enter China. He was also instrumental in starting a language institute in London, where he taught the other three days a week. This was attended by thirteen students, including Samuel Dyer (father of Mrs Maria Hudson Taylor) and Jacob Tomlin (LMS) who was the first Protestant missionary in Thailand with Karl Gutzlaff in 1828. Morrison married Eliza Armstrong and returned to China in 1825.[10] It is a remarkable illustration of the influence one person may have during a home leave.

A responsible voice among one's colleagues

Some older missions were autocracies; some are bureaucracies (it would be invidious to name them); while some are more democratic. My advice is to keep a low posture in your first term. After all, the people there before you may not be entirely stupid and will certainly have learned a great deal by experience, which they will share with you if asked (or even if you don't!). When a newcomer raises an issue at a field conference in all innocence, there is an almost audible groan because it has all been discussed before! One needs to be well through culture shock and language study before saying much! There are a number of levels at which people may make a contribution.

(1) Field conferences of missionaries working together in an area provide a forum where most issues can be raised for discussion. Much can be learned privately, off the floor, by getting veterans to talk about their own experiences and methods. Unfortunately not everybody is able to analyse and reflect in a way that is helpful to younger workers. Many just fly by the seat of their pants, as it were. Such conferences can deepen the friendships and bonding between missionaries. But as increasingly national fellow-workers are invited to attend, bonding across cultures becomes more and more important.

(2) Field councils or committees elected by their fellow-missionaries ensure that the individual is not at the mercy of a single leader should they not get on well with him (or her). Such elected councils provide a useful think tank of experienced missionaries appreciated by their fellows, and able to influence the policy and direction of the field. Men and women who are new arrivals may not feel that they have much voice to start with, but often second term missionaries may be elected to such committees.

(3) Field directors and superintendents are usually elected at intervals, and therefore need to be re-elected. In the past people were appointed because they had proved able in the work, and were sometimes given little training in leadership or administration. Today the opposite tendency may lead to bureaucracy.

(4) Area directors (in missions working in several countries) who also are nominated and renominated. The tendency of the majority female vote can be to go for older father figures who will not rock the boat, but when the elected leaders go on home assignment, there is sometimes a chance to put in a young stirrer with acting powers as a deputy while they are away. People may then come to appreciate and later appoint someone younger.

If for any reason you become disgruntled, it is always possible to appeal to one or more of these leadership levels. However, remember that people tend to get sensitive if they feel that others have gone over their heads to get a favourable decision.

(5) The inevitability of increasing responsibility. When we are newly arrived we may feel we have little voice. But people like to share out leadership and it is surprising how quickly good people are given responsibility. Retirements, illness and resignations all create vacancies, and there is plenty of work for all.

(6) The women's voice. In the nineteenth century, women had little voice. At one conference in China there was consternation when the gifted but maverick Southern Baptist trainer of Bible Women, Adele Field, dared to voice a question publicly. In 1933 D.E. Hoste of the CIM wanted to co-opt women onto the China Council, but met opposition from some home countries. Today good missions will insist that women's voices be heard on all councils and committees. It is not merely that the 2:1 majority of women missionaries needs to be represented, but that women make a contribution in their own right, because they think more practically than men do. A Brethren Assembly in Canada was so impressed with its first woman elder that they appointed two more. 'Before we had women

elders, we discussed things, but often got no further. The women urge us to make decisions!' Sometimes culture is a problem, and it was some while before I could persuade mission councils in Germany and Japan that they ought to include women.

(7) In-house journal articles and letters to the editor. Larger missions will have some kind of in-house journal where ideas can be aired and discussed. Sometimes editors are scratching around to find copy and your comments may find a responsive chord in others.

Conflicts between individual and missionary society

1. Guidance

Perhaps the group to which you belong wants you to go somewhere and do something and you yourself demur, because your guidance is to do something else. Sometimes people are reluctant to move, especially unmarried men and women, who tend to paternalism and maternalism, building a substitute family. There are several possible courses of action open to you. You could:

a) argue your case and persuade your leaders
b) accept provisionally and see whether it works out
c) (as a very last resort) withdraw.

Some on occasion claim strong subjective guidance – 'The Lord has told me' – but unfortunately he does not seem to have told others! The same three possibilities are still open to both parties.

Leadership must beware of the false spirituality of the kind that says 'Surely you are willing to put up with this for the

Lord's sake?' But that is no excuse for bad administration or lack of organisation. Nor should we claim a more direct line to heaven than our fellow missionaries. Remember that 'submitting to one another' is a biblical virtue.

2. Resignation

I have always enjoyed the somewhat archaic words of the 1662 marriage service, which says that matrimony is 'not by any to be enterprized, nor taken in hand, unadvisedly, lightly or wantonly . . . but reverently, discreetly, advisedly, soberly, and in the fear of God'. The same might be said of anyone joining others in a missionary fellowship, and by the same token, of resigning from it on impulse or the heat of the moment. Resignation and withdrawal is a last resort – very painful to family, friends, colleagues and supporters. Judge for yourself. When you discover a famous missionary switched between three different continents, and in the third of them served in three different societies, does not the nagging thought enter your head that this man seems a mite unstable and not altogether reliable?

People who set their hands to the plough and then pull out inevitably make others wonder what lies behind their action. Reasons for resignation are often quite complex and rarely straightforward. It may seem to clear the air immediately, but others may see it, perhaps wrongly, as a rejection of them, and that is hurtful to all parties. For Christians repentance and reconciliation are much happier states than separation and estrangement. So when the harvest is great and the workers are few, losing even one is grievous. For one reason or another, the average length of missionary service has been dropping in recent years. There may be times when resignation may be seen as mutually acceptable, but when those to whom you are bonded plead with you to stay, you need to be absolutely certain that you are in the centre of God's will and your guidance is clear. An interesting book on missionary attrition and reasons for it is William Taylor's *Too Valuable to Lose* (Pasadena: William Carey Library, 1997). The title says it all.

3. Evaluation

Most missions have some mechanism for feedback, appreciation and affirmation, or correction and reproof. How am I doing at language study? We all need to know we are making progress. There may well be official evaluation of our first term of service, with important and probing questions like: 'Is there a welcome back after home assignment? From the superintendent (pastorally responsible)? From national Christians? From fellow-missionaries?' If two or more of these are negative, people must ask themselves whether they are making an effective contribution. If there are likely to be some negative responses to these questions, given sufficient notice, there should be 'time for amendment of life', and opportunity to turn the situation around.

4. Discipline

We may need to have our attention directed to areas which are hindering our ministries. Is there perhaps a failure to control one's temper and to blow one's top? Or insensitivity in the way we relate to national Christians? What about your marriage relationship – are you neglecting your partner? Or your children? What about your attitude to fellow-missionaries? Misdemeanours of a more serious nature might mean your being asked to leave.

5. Policy

The machinery usually exists for initiating change. What about field manuals and books of regulations? Regulations and rulings usually have some reason behind them, although none can be framed that meet every possible exception. If you meet conflicts, try to talk it over dispassionately with fellow missionaries, with your leaders, and then get it put on agendas for field council or field conference.

Leadership structures

Some kind of organisational chart may help you to see the various checks and balances (see diagram below). Except in the most sudden crisis, no one person ought to be able to make decisions without first having to consult with others. Leadership needs to provide both oversight and pastoral care of missionaries on the one hand, and coherent policies for maximum usefulness from deploying the gifts and energies of its members. This is sometimes quite difficult. Should someone be retained in his or her field ministry, or field leadership or home leadership, for example? Yet leaders are all chosen by their peers, so we have to accept responsibility for those we have elected.

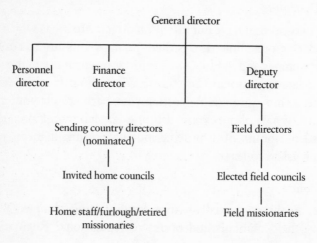

There are clearly a variety of organisational possibilities, depending upon the number of personnel involved, or the diversity of fields or countries in which work is being carried out. Councils in sending countries tend to be staffed by deeply committed and interested men and women who vary greatly in their degree of knowledge or experience of the overseas situations. By contrast, field councils are made up of professionals and veterans who know the grass roots well. Hudson Taylor opted to give the authority to the field rather than to home councils, and history suggests this is the wisest course.

Clearly all manner of variations are possible, and as the national churches develop more and more will the field councils invite national leaders to join them. The bonding of the individual leaders and missionaries with national friends make this a natural development.

Notes

1. Stephen Neill, *History of Christianity in India*: Vol. 1, *The beginnings to 1707* (Cambridge University Press, 1985), p.297.

2. A. Skevington Wood, *Thomas Haweis 1734–1820* (London: SPCK, 1957), pp.193–195.

3. Richard Lovett, *The History of the LMS 1795–1895* (London: Frowde, 1899).

4. Hugh Evan Hopkins, *Charles Simeon of Cambridge* (London: Hodder and Stoughton, 1977), p.151.

5. A.J. Broomhall, *J. Hudson Taylor and China's Open Century* (London: Hodder and Stoughton, 1988), Vol. 4, *Survivor's Pact* contains much detail on this. Or see 2001 new edition under the title *The Shaping of Modern China* (OMF / William Carey Library / Paternoster).

6. *Ibid.*, Vol. 7 *It is not death to die,* pp.41, 58, 200, 310 (pages relate to 1988 edition).
7. Mildred Cable and Francesca French, *George Hunter: Apostle of Turkestan* (London: CIM, 1948).
8. Leslie Lyall, *A Passion for the Impossible* (London: Hodder and Stoughton, 1965), p.42.
9. Phyllis Thompson, *An Unquenchable Flame* (London: Hodder and Stoughton, 1972), p.72.
10. Eliza Morrison, *Memoirs of the Life and Labours of Robert Morrison* (London:Longmans, 1839), Vol. II, pp.301–302.

CHAPTER TEN

LAMBS STAY SINGLE

We have already considered problems arising because missionaries come from different nations and races. However, even more fundamental adjustments are needed, because missionaries come in two different genders. While many missionaries are married, many of them are not. The married need to understand the unmarried and the unmarried need to understand the married. Thus the importance of this chapter!

One of the biggest barriers to effective bonding with a host culture is the pre-existence of bonding with a fellow human being. The single person, like John Dunbar, will find it easier to bond than will a married couple, already bonded to each other. An unmarried person may dive straight into the new culture and begin to work almost entirely in the new host language. Married couples spend a lot of time talking with each other and to children (if they have them already), in their own mother tongue for much of the day. So they use the second language only when not talking to each other. As a general observation, unmarried missionaries tend to learn language faster and better than married people do. A couple, for the sake of their children, endeavour to maintain their own native culture within their home. Visit British, American, Swiss or Japanese missionary homes in any country, and they will retain the distinctive flavours of their home countries. This is not a bad thing, but it may slow down or even hinder the development of bonding to the new adopted culture.

Whether we are married or single, we need to have some understanding of those who are in a different state from our own. Some time or another, we may be asked for counsel, and need to be able to give intelligent, informed and sympathetic advice. At other times nothing needs to be said at all, but we always need to behave with empathy and understanding. I will have to write generally, but use specific examples. What may be generally true is not necessarily true of all, and any particularly horrifying examples should be regarded more as unusual cautionary tales.

Unmarried missionaries

Readers will have to excuse my earthy biological background when I say that all missionaries, whether married or unmarried, are sexual beings. They are not clothed in emotional asbestos but subject to all normal human passions, like Elijah who was 'a man of like passions as we are' (James 5:17, AV). We are sexual beings because it was God's own idea in the first place to make us male and female. This means that our normal, human emotional and physical desires are God given. Statistically it might be argued that anybody who leaves his or her own country to live in another may, in consequence, have less chance of getting married. On the other hand, we are perhaps more likely to meet a feisty kindred spirit with the same high motivation as ourselves, and, in the sovereignty of God, may well do so.

Until Protestants began to engage in mission, all missionaries were celibate single men. Protestants faced a whole range of problems that Jesuits and Franciscans had not, because in the absence of birth control babies arrived with remarkable frequency and there was a high mortality rate in childbirth. In the nineteenth century, life expectancy was short, terms of service were long and some missionaries never returned home at all. Widows and widowers were often reluctant to make the long perilous journey back to their homeland to search for a new like-minded spouse.

Unmarried expatriate women were in short supply, and ran a high risk of being proposed to. Maria Dyer had received proposals of marriage from Joseph Edkins and Robert Hart before she was twenty.[1] She married Hudson Taylor just after her twenty-first birthday. In the remaining eleven years of her life she had no fewer than eight pregnancies. William Carey never returned to Britain, and found his second and third wives in Serampore. His colleague William Ward travelled out single and married Mary Fountain (née Tidd),[2] the widow of a young Serampore colleague John Fountain, who died before his first wedding anniversary. In 1815 the widowed Mrs Charlotte White was travelling out to Burma under the American Baptist Board of Foreign Missions to join Mr and Mrs George Hough. However, en route she had to pass through Calcutta and was there persuaded to marry Joshua Rowe, an English Baptist in Serampore. The next Baptist Conference in the US was informed: 'her expectations, by a controlling Providence, had been disappointed'.[3] Adoniram Judson was practical even if he seemed less charitable.

Mrs White very fortunately disposed of herself in Bengal. Fortunately I say, for I know not how we would have disposed of her in this place. We do not apprehend that the mission of single females to such a country as Burmah, is at all advisable… had she resided in the same house with us, it would have been impossible to have prevented the impression on the minds of the Burmans that our preaching and practice on the subject of polygamy were directly the reverse.[4]

Today, because of the enormous speeding up of communications and transport, advances in medicine allowing family planning, safer childbirth and better health, married missionaries are much less at risk than they once were.

Missionaries are normal human beings

While it is true that 'No temptation has seized you except what is common to man' (1 Corinthians 10:13), it follows that it is not unlikely that missionaries will be subject to most of the temptations which are common to both men and women. Missionaries are tempted daily just like everybody else, perhaps more so because they are in the forefront of the spiritual battle. There may be times when we want to pray that the Lord will remove from us some of our basic drives and desires, and yet these are what help to make us human. We have to accept and live with our own personalities. Certainly we want to be as spiritual as possible, but we also want to be as human as possible, in the way our creator first intended and for which Christ has now redeemed us.

It follows that it is not at all unlikely that missionaries will be attracted sometimes to members of the opposite gender, not only among their fellow-missionaries, but also by inhabitants of the countries to which they go. The opposite is also significantly true, namely that national believers (and unbelievers) may be attracted to missionaries. It is a feature of the *Rough Guide* travel books that they give advice to travellers on how to fend off unwelcome attentions. A large number of sheep were offered for one of our youngest students on a London Bible College tour in the Middle East. This naturally poses problems for the unmarried person. Unmarried missionaries of both sexes may receive both honourable and dishonourable proposals from both Christians and non-Christians. In Laos it was almost a daily occurrence for people to make passes at missionary ladies, though in most other countries they were always treated with great courtesy. In the Philippines where people graduate from university much younger, and men marry younger, it is very difficult for single male missionaries who will not only have to fend off attractive girls, but also approaches from male homosexuals.

The unmarried state is not always generally understood in the two-thirds world, especially in countries where loving parents arrange marriages for all of their children. In rural Japan it is assumed that women missionaries have either had a husband and lost him, or have someone stashed away somewhere. People may be asked highly personal, biological questions about their singleness. It is embarrassing when people do not believe we are unmarried, and a thick skin is a missionary necessity. A female missionary in Korea commented that either people want to put you on a pedestal as a special kind of saint, or alternatively suspect you had a less common sexual orientation. Embarrassing questions are not restricted to the unmarried. Newly-wed missionaries in the Philippines were greeted in the market place by people calling out, quite loudly, 'What, not pregnant yet? What's wrong with your man?' They were not to know that the couple was under doctor's orders to delay starting a family till fully recovered from hepatitis. Childless couples can face most hurtful comments being made to their faces. If a woman is pregnant, polite Japanese enquiries about the honourable date of expectation in the early months, may become 'Wow you are enormous, aren't you?' In the Philippines admiring young people may even ask to feel the baby kicking!

Mentioning these difficulties and being so blunt should embarrass nobody. In many parts of the world there may not even be a word for 'privacy', because the concept may be non-existent. It's better to be embarrassed reading a book than in some of the situations which may be faced in the years ahead.

Three wonderful things

1. God in his providence keeps us and protects us in temptation

It is a constant marvel that there are relatively few moral failures among missionaries married or single. Bearing in mind the loneliness and isolation, and the sexual permissiveness common today throughout the world, it is remarkable evidence of God's protection. It's not a proof of our outstanding moral character, but a demonstration of God's goodness in providing a 'way of escape' (1 Corinthians 10:13, AV). Have you noted the Scripture which says: 'Therefore, he who rejects this instruction does not reject man but God, who gives you [present continuous, rather than past tense] his Holy Spirit' (1 Thessalonians 4:8)? That is, at the moment of temptation we have to choose between disobeying God (we are not merely rejecting some outmoded human notions of morality) and accepting him. We can either turn away from God in wilful disobedience, or turn to him and receive his Spirit who will make us and keep us holy. It is an extraordinary turn of events and a remarkable blessing that God offers his Spirit's help at the time of sexual temptation.

2. Scripture warmly approves the service of the unmarried

The Lord Jesus, himself an unmarried person, speaks of this (Matthew 19:12) and so does the apostle Paul (1

Corinthians 7:32–35). In this latter passage Paul describes singleness as a *charisma* from God. Some single missionaries can think of it in this way, while others accept that nobody has proposed marriage and still find it hard to believe singleness to be a gift of God. Around fifty per cent of women missionaries are unmarried, and merit great respect for their selfless commitment. Every time I found myself visiting mountain tribes, I marvelled at the energy and endurance of senior women who had toiled those trails for many years. My respect grew every time I saw such women in action. A few have problems because of their singleness, but then others have difficulties because they are married. The unmarried may rejoice that they are free to serve the Lord, unhindered by a husband and children. The unmarried probably bond better with national Christians than expatriate married couples do. Scripture speaks of female prophets (Luke 2:36; Acts 2:17ff; 21:9; 1 Corinthians 11:5); female deacons (1 Timothy 3:11), female teachers (2 Timothy 2:2 is *anthropoi* meaning human persons, and not *androi* meaning males), and most probably a female apostle (Junia in Romans 16:7).

In that chapter of greetings to Christians known to Paul in Rome, there appear to be only three men workers (Aquila, Andronicus and Urbanus) and six or even seven women involved in some kind of ministry – Phoebe, Priscilla, Mary, Tryphena, Tryphosa, Persis and probably Junia. Under the guidance of the Holy Spirit, Paul goes out of his way to commend these women. That proportion has been sustained more or less across the whole range of mission societies in the twentieth century. In general women have had greater freedom to serve churches abroad than they have had in their own home countries.

3. Both marriage and unmarriage are temporary states

In heaven there will be no marriage and we shall all be 'like the angels' (Matthew 22:30). This seems to imply that the exclusive relationship between one man and one woman, which God has blessed on earth, is a temporary condition which will not continue in heaven. Human relationships in heaven will apparently transcend the exclusive marriage relationships appropriate here for the conception and rearing of children. All of us are unmarried for at least the first quarter of our lives, and a high proportion of married women are unmarried again for the closing years of their lives. It seems correct therefore to regard the unmarried state as the norm in eternity, but certainly we are to regard the married state as a temporary arrangement. We have to avoid two extremes of false teaching.

First, the deduction from the Genesis account (especially Genesis 2:18) that the unmarried are incomplete as human beings, because God created 'humankind' as male and female with a view to marriage and childbearing. This view of incompleteness is sometimes expounded in wedding sermons: John and Mary are like strawberries and cream, salt and pepper, and so on. But Scripture itself never says that the single person is incomplete. Indeed it would be heretical to suggest that the Lord Jesus was incomplete, and misguided to suggest that the apostle Paul was incomplete because he was unmarried. With the Lord Jesus this is surely decisive: human perfection is not impaired by singleness. The unmarried do not necessarily feel incomplete, nor ought they to do so.

Secondly, we must avoid the opposite extreme notion that the sexes are totally self-sufficient. Apart from being biological nonsense, the similarities between men and women are much greater than their differences. We must recognise our interdependence and the enrichment of human interchange precisely because we come in two varieties. The contribution of women on boards, councils and committees (including church leadership) is not merely so that they may 'represent the women's point of view', but because they make a distinctive contribution in their own right. The ultimate glorified human life in the new heaven and the new earth apparently transcends the marriage relationship, but we are not told that gender distinctives are blurred or obliterated.

Some specific difficulties of being an unmarried missionary

1. Feelings and longings

Unmarried men missionaries will have normal heterosexual and paternal instincts, and unmarried women missionaries will have normal heterosexual and maternal instincts. Such problems may be exacerbated if people were converted later, after they had already enjoyed active sexual experience. We should never forget that our instincts are God-given, but nonetheless require disciplined control and adjustment. The Lord may remove such longings from some, but more people have to live with them. They are at least partially due to those hormones which make us distinctively male or female. (A few missionary men and women experience homosexual problems, but most missions would not knowingly accept missionaries with a homosexual orientation, not as discrimination, but because loneliness and alienation can be aggravated when living within foreign culture.) There are no easy solutions.

There can be few of us who do not feel lonely when we find ourselves alone on a rainy night on a bus in which everybody else is paired off except ourselves. We can claim the powerful help of the Lord in controlling the instincts (which he has given) in line with commandments (which he has also given).

This is a reason why our clustering together in missionary fellowships is important for more than pragmatic labour-saving reasons: there needs to be a warm, family spirit which helps to meet our social needs and longings for human fellowship. In such a warm, extended family group we should be able to share our specific problems with two or three missionaries of the same gender, and also to experience the unexpressed understanding and sympathetic fellowship of married missionaries. There needs to be great sensitivity. Are there people who are manifestly lonely and need friends? What can others of us do about it?

2. Insensitivity and unkindness on the part of married people

We have already noted the way in which more earthy cultures than our own may embarrass us by not believing that we are unmarried. It is, however, unpardonable if unmarried missionaries suffer because of foolish and insensitive remarks by married people. Let single people make jokes about themselves if they wish, but the rest of us should avoid foolish jocularity, and show sensitive understanding.

3. Unmarried missionaries of the opposite sex

I have heard a mission lady doctor comment on a number of occasions: 'Bachelors are a menace!' Hopefully, none would be consciously so, and most behave like perfect gentlemen (unlike the sixty-year-old who, when asked why he had never married, replied: 'Why delight one and disappoint a thousand!'). They are unwitting, unconscious trouble-makers. Wherever there is a single male missionary (and they are an endangered species) it is common to find several women nourishing hopes in their hearts, often with subjective guidance, and even 'verses from the Lord' to prove it. This may sound mildly amusing, but it is not meant to be, and certainly is not at all funny for those suffering unrequited affection.

Occasionally someone may be so unwise as to encourage rumours about their feelings to reach the object of their affections, or even to propose to the man in question. He usually takes fright and bolts. He wants his own guidance. While such happenings are rare, it underlines how difficult is normal courtship in a small limited subculture. No man can make up his mind intelligently without opportunity to make the acquaintance of visibly eligible ladies. However an invitation to coffee, or an extended conversation at a conference is likely to cause comment by other observant missionaries (who may or may not be competitors) and can inevitably raise the hopes of the lady concerned that she is being seriously considered. Such complications are further increased when the missionary group is international and multiracial, and some have much more conservative backgrounds than others. The enterprising have always overcome these hurdles, and the present generation is less awkward than its predecessors were. But some cultures with their expectations and taboos may make it difficult even for them. Single people need to pray for grace to behave normally and sensibly without embarrassing others.

I have mentioned exceptions only as cautionary tales. We must aim at a level of social and spiritual fellowship, where both men and women can enjoy the benefits of companionship with those of the opposite sex without it being a matter for comment, gossip or a cause of strain in relationship. Humans may, and indeed ought, to enjoy stimulating companionship with one another without there being any interest in permanent relationships. Christians in particular need to enjoy cheerful fellowship. Sometimes people foolishly speak as though all the unmarried are on the lookout for an opportunity to join the ranks of the permanently committed.

Sometimes some people may be, but that needs a wise word from friends, and not public gossip.

4. Loneliness

This is not restricted to the single, but also to widows and widowers especially, as they grow older. The matter was expressed with some poignancy in a book of poems written by Mr Mitsyo and Mrs Ayako Miura. Cycling home late, Mr Miura noticed the shadow behind the frosted glass of the sliding door, as a lady missionary locked herself in for the night. He wonders why this single lady endures such loneliness and recognises that it is 'for the sake of the gospel'.

Dendoo no tame ni	For the sake of evangelism,
Hitori sumu Missu Howardo	Living alone Miss Howard,
Yofuke hikijoo o orosu	Locking the door late at night
Kage.	Her shadow.

Asking a single missionary returned from a period spent in their home country: 'Did you have a good furlough?' I got the reply, 'Do you want me to be honest? I was miserably lonely most of the time, it's a relief to be back here on the field!'

In our later years, our parents may have died, and we may have few immediate relations. We visit old friends, have a good chat, but after three or four hours have exhausted topics of conversation, and we leave them to carry on with their busy lives. While we are pleased to have spent time with them, it can make us feel curiously all the more alone. Unmarried people who stay in their home country will have their own home full of their own possessions, but the missionary, temporarily on home assignment, feels they have nowhere to lay their head, and it can be really lonely. A single lady who had spent most of her life in Thailand was killed in a road accident caused by some joyriding youngsters. I felt distressed for she seemed to have no close relatives to mourn her passing. I found that I had it all wrong. She had been dreading approaching retirement, when she could have become truly lonely at home. But when I heard her fellow missionaries speak of her at a memorial meeting, it became clear that she was much appreciated and cared for, as one of the most caring and loved people in that group of missionaries.

Comparisons with the married

Married couples blissful in their home with their spouse and children can sometimes be most thoughtless and irritating to the unmarried, ignoring the differences in lifestyle. This was rather effectively addressed many years ago by the essayist Charles Lamb (who was a clerk in the offices of the East India Company when Henry Martyn was being appointed chaplain).

As a single man, I have spent a good deal of my time in noting down the infirmities of Married People, to console myself for those superior pleasures, which they tell me I have lost by remaining as I am.

What offends me at the houses of married persons where I visit, is an error of quite a different description; it is that they are too loving. Not too loving neither: that does not explain my meaning. Besides why should that offend me? The very act of separating themselves from the rest of the world, to have the fullest enjoyment of each other's society, implies that they prefer one another to all the world.

But what I complain of is, that they carry this preference so undisguisedly, they perk it up in the faces of us single people so shamelessly, you cannot be in their company a moment without being made to feel, by some indirect hint or open avowal, that *you* are not the object of this preference.

Nothing is to me more distasteful than that entire complacency and satisfaction which beam in the countenances of a new-married couple, in that of the lady particularly: it tells you, that her lot is disposed of in this world: that *you* can have no hopes of her. It is true, I have none; nor wishes either, perhaps; but this is one of those truths, which ought, as I said before, to be taken for granted, not expressed.

But what I have spoken hitherto is nothing to the airs which these creatures give themselves when they come, as they generally do, to have children. When I consider how little of a rarity children are, that every street and blind alley swarms with them, that the poorest people commonly have them in most abundance, that there are few marriages that are not blest with at least one of these bargains, how often they turn out ill, and defeat the fond hopes of their parents, taking to vicious courses, which end in poverty, disgrace, the gallows etc., I cannot for my life tell what cause for pride there can possibly be in having them.[5]

While we may laugh at this eloquent expression of extremely sour grapes, there is surely a warning here to those who are married to avoid such complacency, preening ourselves on our marital bliss and bragging about our kids in front of single people. As missionary children are deprived of grandparents, uncles and aunts when overseas, they much appreciate those honorary unmarried aunts and uncles who may choose to become 'significant adults' in their lives. Many unmarried people enjoy the affection of other people's children, but quite properly resent being taken advantage of as cheap babysitters! Parents need to be careful to allow 'aunts' and 'uncles' to volunteer themselves.

Conclusion

Some unmarried people can accept their unmarried state as a calling from God. Others, while not claiming to be called to singleness, recognise that being overseas may have reduced opportunities to marry. For some this can be as grievous as it was for Hannah when 'the Lord closed her womb' (1 Samuel 1:5–6). Hannah recognised the sovereignty of God himself in withholding children from her until Samuel was born. We have to accept his sovereignty in our lives in respect to our size, proportion and physical features, height, hair colour, whether we are beautiful but not so bright, or bright but not so beautiful, whether we were born with the advantages of an affectionate, stable home or otherwise. We have to face the fact that God is responsible for our sexuality, and our married or unmarried state. Our master commended those who were unmarried for the kingdom of heaven's sake. Many of those who have understood African and Asian cultures best and have identified with them most, are those who have remained unmarried. One day we will all be 'like the angels' (Matthew 22:30) in heaven where there is no marriage. We can look forward to the time when that which is perfect has come.

In the meantime, the family spirit of our missionary fellowships should provide the social, intellectual and emotional needs of their members. If we are considerate, caring and imaginative, then there should be no lonely people in our ranks. People need people. Happiness in its adult form is not two fingers and a blanket (as it was for Linus in the *Peanuts* cartoons). Happiness is people. It always delights me at the start of any conference or gathering of missionaries, to stand back and watch people who have not met for many months greet each other. Warm eyes, hearty handshakes, brotherly hugs and sisterly kisses demonstrate that it's good for people to be linked together with commitment to a team of like-minded Christians.

Notes

1. A.J. Broomhall, *J. Hudson Taylor and China's Open Century*, Vol. 3, *If I had a Thousand Lives* (London: Hodder and Stoughton, 1982), pp.41–42. Or see 2001 new edition under the title *The Shaping of Modern China* (OMF / William Carey Library / Paternoster).
2. Donald Lewis, ed., *Dictionary of Evangelical Biography*, Vol. 2 (Oxford: Blackwells, 1995), p.1157.
3. Pierce Beaver, *All Loves Excelling: American Protestant Women in World Mission* (Grand Rapids: Eerdmans, 1968), p.65.
4. Quoted by Beaver, *Ibid.*, p.66.
5. Charles Lamb, 'A Bachelor's Complaint of the Behaviour of Married People' in *Essays of Elia*.

CHAPTER ELEVEN

MARRIED LAMBS BOND WITH OTHERS

We have observed that the unmarried may learn language faster and bond with indigenous brothers and sisters more quickly. This can be harder for those who are already married when they arrive in their new field of service, especially if they already have children. In the 'old days' when the average age of new missionaries was in the early twenties, almost all arrived on the field unmarried. The regulations forbidding marriage until the completion of two years' language study by both parties were not unreasonable then. However, today when the average age of new workers is often in the late twenties, it is seen as a good thing if they arrive already well settled into the marriage relationship. Indeed, interviewers on selection committees will want to determine that those who go out already married are well bonded and secure in their relationship.

I do not wish to be misunderstood for one moment as suggesting that such couples should become in some way 'unbonded' in order to bond effectively with the new culture. Indeed, the reverse is the case, for if the missionary couple are to model biblical bonding in a good Christian marriage, then continuing communication and strengthening of the bonding between husband and wife is essential. As we shall see, in the time-consuming process of setting up home, learning language and adjusting to the new cultural surroundings, some Christian couples may neglect each other, assuming that simply because they are Christians they will never have marital problems. How naive can one get? But I am rushing ahead too fast.

Married people bonding with others

The husband will bond with men and the wife with women. Cross-gender bonding across cultural divides is almost certain to be misunderstood. When missionaries first arrived in China, the rumour in the market was that the foreign men were after Chinese women (Chinese men commonly accumulated more than one wife as a mark of economic success). For this reason the visiting of women in their compounds had to be done by women. This explains why a hundred years ago most Chinese Christians were men, and why it was 1939 before the numbers of Chinese women believers equalled those of men. Even in Britain in the late nineteenth century young unmarried women attending university lectures had to be accompanied by chaperones.[1] Muslim and Hindu women were even more strictly segregated, and many women's missionary societies were founded explicitly in order to reach the zenanas in India. Even today it is still true that in most of Asia only women can reach women. Even in 'liberated' western cultures, close friendships with those of the opposite sex may be perceived as threatening the marriage relationship. Elaine Storkey takes gracious issue here, but expresses the problems arising even in our own contemporary western culture.[2]

In missionary contexts the husband will seek to relate to local men, both inside and outside the church, and the wife similarly with women. Because women seem to relate better with each other than men do, the missionary wife may have the easier road, especially if she is caring for small children, just as most local mothers are. In some cultures women work together in the fields, while the men sit in coffee houses or watch cock fighting (Philippines). Or the men may commute to offices and be absent from home from dawn till after dusk, while women make their own lives (Japan). Every culture has its own very different (and changing) work patterns, and missionaries have to solve the problem of access. But the missionary mother carrying her baby, walking with toddlers or waiting with other mothers at the school gate enjoys immediate access, and there can be an exchange of ideas about their common domestic and child-rearing responsibilities. The missionary man has to work harder to find common ground, especially if he is an evangelist perceived by non-Christians as paid to proselytise them, or seeking religious merit by so doing. The self-supporting 'tentmaker', the medical or social worker has more immediate ways in which to make contact with men. The victorious tortoise of our first chapter achieved a breakthrough when he agreed to act as coach and referee for the football team at the local school.[3] A pharmacy lecturer teaching at universities in Bangkok made many contacts through refereeing football matches, and that opened the door to forming student Bible-study groups.

Provided it is culturally appropriate, having established friendships independently, the men can then bring their wives together, or the wives bring their husbands together. In the early days of the Japanese Christian Fellowship in Singapore, everything started with the wives. Working in the business community, it was culturally appropriate to have farewell meetings for couples and families returning to Japan after the completion of a contract. These were great opportunities for Japanese wives, already bonded through their own weekday gatherings, to bring their overworked and as yet unbelieving husbands to places where they could meet Christian men and hear the gospel simply and winsomely presented in a less formal setting. There are Japanese men that I first came to know as national colleagues, student leaders or church members; the places where I first became acquainted with them were men's meetings. But today, my wife and I regard the husbands together with their wives as couples who are friends to both of us. In Japanese women's meetings, my wife would have met and built relationships with other wives, normally some months before I ever had a first opportunity to meet the husbands. It takes time to break through the barriers of formality, language and etiquette, but such bonding deepens every time we are able to meet together, either as individuals or as couples.

The married home too is a great place to welcome young people and singles, often curious to know how these strange aliens conduct their domestic lives. People often ask what advantages missionaries have over national Christian workers, who could be supported for much less money. At first sight, it seems obvious that people who have grown up in a culture, understanding how it works and speaking the language(s) fluently, have all the advantages. There are some advantages in coming from outside however, which is why the American Billy Graham or the Argentinean Louis Palau have been effective in Europe and beyond. Foreigners are outside the class system whereas local Christians are part of it: Billy Graham can identify with British people right across the social spectrum, whereas few English people can. Curiosity is another trump card – when language acquisition makes conversation possible, there is much to discover about how foreigners think, talk and act. Missionaries have a certain novelty value! So, married missionary couples can bond with national couples across cultural barriers, just as we can play doubles as well as singles at tennis!

If we have recognised that some problems arise from being a single, unmarried missionary, there are corresponding problems arising because of being married. Scripture says of the married: 'they will face many troubles in this life' (1 Corinthians 7:28), which J.B. Phillips translates as 'Those who take this step are bound to find the marriage state an extra burden in these critical days, and I should like you to be as unencumbered as possible.' Richard Baxter, the great Reformed pastor of Kidderminster, in his *Christian Directory* gives some seventeen reasons for not getting married and added a few more for those in full-time Christian work. When he finally married at forty-five he remarks: 'The King's marriage was not more spoken of than mine!'

When C.S. Lewis was due to speak on *The Four Loves* explaining *agape* and *eros* on radio in the United States, he was warned that he must not mention 'sex'! Lewis roared with laughter – how can one possibly talk about *eros* without mentioning sex? Because some episcopal bishops found Lewis 'too frank for the American people' in 1958, the talks were not given the wide hearing that had been planned.[4] The Bible has no embarrassment in talking about sexual enjoyment in marriage: see passages like Ecclesiastes 4:9–12; 9:9; Proverbs 5:18–19; 1 Peter 3:7 not to mention the Song of Solomon. The wolfish cultures in which missionary lambs are called to work may often be much more frank about sexual matters than the sending cultures. 'There are things I can say in this language that I could never say in English,' reported one missionary. But first for some general observations.

Different personalities face differing problems

Human beings generally provide a spectrum of personality types, and missionary wives are no exception. At the one extreme is the woman who is perfectly satisfied and fulfilled by being domesticated, a 'homemaker' caring for husband and children. Her expectations are of pleasant evenings sitting sewing and knitting in one armchair, while her husband sits companionably opposite. But if she is the only Christian woman in a town of 30,000 people, and is satisfied to live in smug domesticity without becoming actively involved in Christian witness, then she is irresponsible and either needs to be booted into active service or back home where she belongs! Precisely because she feels so fulfilled in the domestic role, she needs to make vigorous efforts to get on with language study and to get out and make friends and seek to win them to Christ. Hudson Taylor was clear about this from the earliest days:

It is most important that married missionaries should be *double missionaries* – not half or a quarter or eight-part missionaries. Might we not with advantage say to our candidates: Our work is a peculiar one. We aim at the interior, where the whole of your society will be Chinese. If you wish for luxury and freedom from care . . . *do not join us.* Unless you intend your wife to be a true missionary, not merely a wife, homemaker and friend, *do not join us.* She must be able to read and be master of at least one gospel in colloquial Chinese before you marry. A person of ordinary ability may accomplish this in six months, but if she needs longer there is the more reason to wait until she has reached this point before you marry. She must be prepared to be happy among the Chinese, when the duties of your calling require, as they often will, your temporary absence from home.[5]

Having said this however, we do not want young wives to feel any conflict between being wives, mothers and missionaries. It all needs careful talking through with understanding husbands who are prepared to carry their share of household tasks, and making appropriate adjustments as the size, needs and ages of our families increase. Above all we need the help of the Holy Spirit at every stage in getting the right balance of activities. The way home and family are managed is part of our total message in modelling Christian discipleship to those for whom it is all so new.

At the opposite end of the spectrum is the wife who before her marriage has already been a schoolteacher, executive in a profession, or Christian worker in a position of significant responsibility. She has an entirely different set of problems. She now discovers to her dismay that marriage involves her in a home-minding, child-tending responsibility which she finds a hindrance to her full involvement alongside her husband in the way that was possible before they started a family. The pastoral advice to this kind of person is the exact opposite of that to the naturally domestic woman. She needs to be reminded that whether she eats, drinks, washes dishes or does the laundry she does all to the glory of God (1 Corinthians 10:29–31). Her husband will need to take his fair share of domestic chores. But she needs to accept that for a few years her main ministry will need to be focused on her children and that she cannot be as actively involved outside the home as she was before she had children. At the same time, her babies and toddlers will open up fresh doors of opportunity in reaching out to local mothers who have children the same age as her own.

When most missionaries began as single workers in their own right, and became used to serving alongside missionary or national colleagues before they married, it was perhaps easier than today. Now when so many arrive already married with no experience of serving there as a single person, it can be more difficult. Arriving older and already married may make it harder to relate and bond with local people whether already Christians or not.

But there is another factor, which could either ameliorate or exacerbate the problems of the married woman's temperament. This is the nature of the husband's work responsibilities. Church planting, for example, often begins in the missionary home, and husband and wife can be jointly involved. This makes it much easier for the wife who has been a 'professional' or was used to being a Christian worker in her own right. However, if the husband's work requires him to be away from home most of the day – for example in student ministry, literature work or some administrative responsibility – this makes it much harder for the wife. The 'domestic' wife can survive easily, but the 'professional' wife finds it extremely frustrating, and needs the sympathetic understanding of her husband, as well as those in leadership. The situation can be made worse if government regulations require that wives be issued with a 'Dependants' Visa' which limits their direct involvement in Christian work. (It can happen the other way around: a retired Anglican bishop was given a visa as 'an unassigned spouse', because his wife had a specific mission task.)

The married missionary woman must be urged to see her thirty or so years of missionary life as a totality. Life must not be divided artificially into the allegedly 'spiritual' and the allegedly 'secular'. God is to be glorified in the whole of working life, whether that takes place outside or inside the home. For some early years, the married woman's opportunities for direct involvement may be influenced by the number of children she may have in a pre-school or primary school bracket at any one time (see later).

The five ages of missionary wifehood

Shakespeare chauvinistically wrote of the 'seven ages of man'. It took Flanders and Swan to remedy this. As the stages of infancy and schooldays have long passed before starting long-term service, we may elaborate on the 'five ages of the married woman missionary'.

1. *Language learning*

I have to emphasise the problems for young mothers embarking on time-consuming language study when they already have small children. It is best to delay starting a family, if aiming at a straightforward run of full-time language study. That makes sense when spoken to the newly married. But if people are already married with children when they first arrive in a new country, they need to give their energies to language acquisition. This may be more difficult for the young mother, but it is not impossible provided her husband takes his share of childminding responsibilities, and she is disciplined. If the man just careers ahead disregarding his wife's needs, then her language will fall behind, and many other sad consequences follow.

A considerate husband is as much concerned for his wife's progress in the language as his own (Philippians 2:4). This means that he should not take over when female visitors appear, but retire and let his wife initiate the conversational gambits. It is essential that the wife has as much opportunity as her husband for comprehending and responding to the language of the wolf-pack. A wife who cannot understand properly or communicate effectively will be unhappy. She will start questioning her own and her husband's call, and may bring the whole family back to their homeland prematurely – all because she was not given, or failed to take, opportunities for thorough language acquisition when she first arrived. My personal observation would be that women learn the everyday language of home and society better than their husbands, who may have more theological vocabulary, but less everyday vocabulary. In some cultures, too, the language of women is different from that of men in levels of courtesy and politeness.

2. The pre-school child's mother

One might think that this is the period of life when all of a mother's time must be given to her children. But that would overlook a major opportunity which occurs only at this stage in a mother's life. Common ground has been established with other local mothers. The missionary wife is no longer a cultural oddity with no apparent home responsibilities, but someone with the same concerns as their own, carrying their babies and lumping their children around the market. Children are wonderful ice-breakers and contact makers. The foreigner travelling alone may not seem approachable, but when travelling with children is almost bound to make contact! Children open doors for us on every side, and we need to be alert to go through them while we have the chance. The young mother has great opportunities at this time in her life. Just when the mother back in the home country might be putting her feet up for a quiet evening, the missionary mother is getting her study books out to improve her ability to share the gospel and teach new believers in their own language. Time must be found to continue studying and to take the increasing opportunities for bonding with other wives and mothers living all around.

3. The playgroup/nursery child's mother

Many openings arise when the missionary mother joins other mothers in taking children to playgroup or nursery, and waits with other mothers for their children to emerge again afterwards. There are opportunities to participate in local community life, in parent-teacher organisations and in beginning friendships that will open the way for the gospel. There is no way that the missionary man can make contact with this significant group of people: only a wife and mother enjoys this opportunity. She may feel her language is inadequate, but it will develop as she spends time with other women, in a way that will not happen if she remains isolated in her home.

4. Primary school children's mothers

With small children now in school for part of the day, or older children away at school, the missionary mother now has more hours in the day to be working with her husband or together with local Christian women. If the mother has neglected her language learning earlier, then at this stage she will begin to feel frustrated at her lack of ability to communicate. During school holidays both parents will be busier with their children than ever, but meeting their friends and their families will open still more doors for friendship evangelism.

5. When the children have fled the nest

When this happens will vary from continent to continent, and country to country. In South America or Europe it is easier for missionary families to identify completely in using local schools. In Africa and Asia, where the ethnic barriers are higher and harder to cross where skin colour is different, there may be special schools for foreigners or Christian secondary schools for missionary children. The emptying of the nest leaves the missionary home very quiet, clean and horribly tidy for a change! There is now the greatest possible freedom for the wife to join her husband in the work, but her effectiveness will depend upon the hard grind of disciplined study in the earlier years. If the children are away in school, then writing letters to them and waiting for their replies become part of life. An interesting by-product of this letter-writing stage is that missionary children often become very good letter writers, because writing letters home has been part of their lives often from quite a young age.

Particular problems

1. Weariness

It is no surprise if young mothers get tired in pregnancy and in looking after toddlers, even in western countries with all the modern conveniences. It is not at all unexpected that mothers caring for their families in remote and materially undeveloped parts of the world should get tired. At home we take running water, electricity, central heating, washing machines and refrigerators for granted. Recent letters from one friend speak of having to fetch water from the well, and another of an average six hours of electricity every seventy-two hours, while others would have none at all. Just everyday living, feeding a family, sterilising food and keeping disease-spreading insects away can be a time-consuming process. Add the welcoming of visitors, the learning of language and writing letters home to church and family and the day becomes even fuller than that of other busy parents at home. Evenings after the children have gone to bed may be taken up with meetings, correspondence, accounts and language study. Retiring thankfully to bed seems to be followed only too soon by the crowing of cocks and the start of yet another busy day and the unremitting round of activity without much opportunity for recreation and getting away from it all.

Husbands need to accept their wives' tiredness as a feature of these busy years of childbearing and looking after small children. They need to bear their share of the workload, and be considerate and mature when their wives are too tired to be responsive. Sulky husbands and resentful wives are both difficult to live with.

One delightful family somehow arranged to have all their babies born in April. The gynaecologically curious wanted to know what happened in July. The answer was simple: their annual holiday, the only time of year when they were really rested from the pressures of being busy in a tropical climate.

2. Too many children too close together

When young couples in many sending countries are planning for zero population growth (ie not more than two children), one wonders if they will go on supporting missionaries who insist on having large families. At one time posters in Singapore explained government policy: 'Two are enough, even if both are girls.' While thoughtful missionaries are increasingly aware of this issue, not all realise how important it can be to plan the spacing between children.

> In planning the spacing of children there are health factors to be borne in mind. Bearing a child is a drain on the mother's strength. Nursing the child is a continuing drain until the child is weaned. The mother's body then needs about six months to replenish her reserves in order that the next pregnancy does not 'overdraw the account'. If pregnancies are too close together it may be not just the mother who suffers. Too many closely spaced children may result in the younger ones being less well endowed in terms of physical health and resistance to infection. Each child must feel loved and wanted by both parents in order that his emotions develop properly . . . too many children, or children too closely spaced, may overtax the parents' resources to meet the needs of each individual child.[6]

One problem with alleged 'family planning' and so-called 'birth control' is that with the best will in the world we cannot always plan or control, and the Lord sometimes overrules the best laid plans of mice and men. There are times when we want children and fail to conceive. Such times can be painful for any couple. There are other occasions when our planning decides that we will not have children, and then we discover that the Lord's timing is always better than ours. So frankly, though it is certainly better to delay starting a family in order to complete language study courses, nonetheless if the baby comes, then for goodness sake, the child's sake and your own sakes, don't feel guilty about it but enjoy the baby with all your hearts.

3. Insecurity

Some psychiatrists have suggested that most women have problems of self-image and feel insecure. Where people marry on the mission field it is not uncommon to find that the wife is insecure. She is unsure she would have been chosen if there had been a larger choice: perhaps she happened to be the best of a rather poor bunch! This is not a problem for those who were already married when they joined a mission society. If the husband was initially keen on someone else, and the wife feels she was second best accepted on the rebound, her feeling of insecurity may be deeper still. Husbands need to be unusually sensitive to give extra love and affirmation to an insecure partner.

An unfortunate side effect of some recent teaching on male 'headship' is the insecure man who uses what he has been persuaded is the 'biblical position' to achieve dominance over his wife. Though the word 'authority' is often bandied about in this context, Bible study soon reveals that Scripture seldom uses the word, and when it does sees 'authority' as mutually exercised between husband and wife (1 Corinthians 7:4). Scripture does not seem to teach the subjection of all women however wise and experienced to all men, however stupid and clueless, but only to one chosen husband, who loves her and is ready to sacrifice for her. In each case the possessive 'their own' husbands makes this clear (1 Peter 3:1; Titus 3:5; Ephesians 5:22).

Moreover this subjection is voluntary. In Scripture, no human ever subjects anyone to himself, for only God can do that. If a husband arrives at the point where he has to say, 'You are supposed to be subject to me!' then he is clearly losing the argument and in danger of forfeiting respect as well. We should expect husbands and wives to make joint decisions. It must be a rare event when the husband's considerate love and wife's submissive love fail to come to a common mind. It is important that mission leaders should consult with husbands and wives together when decisions about their placement affect them both as a couple.

4. Neglect

One of the commonest problems of first and second-term missionaries is that they neglect their marriages. Because they are committed Christian workers giving themselves to the master's service, hurling themselves into diligent language study and industrious church planting, they foolishly imagine they will have no problems in marital relationships. It is unfortunately almost a commonplace for clerical and missionary wives to feel desperately neglected, because their husbands are so busy allegedly 'in the Lord's work'. Some years ago a magazine published on the field asked thirty-five couples from various societies what were the greatest tensions they faced.[7]

The wives listed tensions:

1. With their husbands: not having enough time together, differences in raising children, communication problems.
2. With fellow-missionaries: jealousy, criticism, etc.
3. With children: separation if they were away; not enough to occupy them if they were at home, especially if their fathers were away.

The husbands put their problems in quite a different order of importance:

1. Relationships with their children: not having enough time with them, fear of failure in bringing them up and problems of discipline, etc.
2. Relationships with Japanese fellow-labourers, long frequent meetings and the cultural misunderstandings which can so frequently occur.
3. Relationships with their wives: not enough time together, divided interests.

The questionnaire brought out again the sense of neglect which women feel.

Arnold Lea, then Overseas Director of OMF, was telling me about a cartoon in which a husband and wife were waking up in the morning: the husband's hand was switching off the alarm clock, while his wife was sitting up and saying: 'And as I was saying when you so rudely went off to sleep last night . . .' Imagine the previous night: the husband comes home late, tired and weary. He just wants to put his feet up and read. His wife has been shut up at home all day and wants to tell him all that has been happening with the children at home. He falls asleep.

This mutual neglect is one of the biggest causes of missionary failure, for it may produce insecure and unhappy marriages. While bonding with local people and local Christian friends is important, it must not be at the expense of bonding with your life-partner. When did the busy husband last bring his wife roses or other flowers to show his appreciation and love? When for that matter did he buy her an attractive or frivolous nightdress? (This would not be appropriate in all cultures: in some tribal situations the locals peer through the split bamboo to see whether the missionaries are normal human beings, how they make love, etc., and it is unwise to leave the light on!) The longer one serves among missionaries, the more it becomes clear that good, healthy, happy sexual relationships between husband and wife are given to them by God as a source of rich blessing, strengthening the bonding between them. When marriages are allowed to be unhappy or stale through neglect, then all the other relationships can be negatively affected.

In screening married candidates, assessing the happiness and stability of the couple's relationship is crucial. But problems can still arise later: one couple was refused return to the field until both parties could say that they were enjoying their marital relationship. Unhappy missionary marriages are like unexploded bombs imperilling the work. A very senior missionary husband once responded to my somewhat intimate question of how his marriage was going (missionaries do ask each other these interesting questions!) with a broad smile, saying, 'It's wonderful thank you. I have been much blessed by the woman I married!' In much recent discussion about 'the rector's wife' syndrome, it has emerged that missionary wives enjoy much greater marital satisfaction than those married to clergymen.[8] It may be that facing the cross-cultural adventure together serves to strengthen and deepen the bonding between married couples who provide each other with major emotional resources.

5. Childlessness and adoption

Like any other married couple back at home, missionary couples can find it painful longing for children who are not conceived. Those with children can sometimes be insensitive when bragging about their own children (as we saw in Charles Lamb's 'Complaint' earlier). At the same time, where couples can accept that childlessness may providentially set them free to give more time to church work, they can throw themselves into fruitful ministry with liberated energies. I have been privileged to know some outstanding childless couples, much loved by their friends, and much used by the Lord.

Adoption is usually a possible option. A mission treasurer concerned about the funds available for support, once caustically observed that where clear medical evidence was provided that they could not have children, and permission had been given to adopt, six out of seven adopting couples immediately conceived!

In multi-racial international missionary fellowships, there are usually today no limitations placed on the race of adopted children, because to do so would savour of racial discrimination. However, before children of different race from the parents are adopted, careful thought needs to be given to the possible accumulated stresses and identity crises which may result. All children of long-term missionaries face the pain of separation for education at earlier or later stages in the educational process anyway. It is something of a commonplace that some adopted children also face identity crises later on. If to this double jeopardy, one adds yet a third, the identity crises typically experienced by children of mixed race, it seems common sense that missionary couples are not suitable adoptive parents for such needy children because of their chosen vocation as missionaries.

Before rushing into irrevocable decisions, we need to give thought and prayer to such considerations. All couples who find themselves childless need to ask whether the fact that God has not given them children in the normal way, might mean that he wishes them to remain free from distraction in the work to which they have been called.

6. Continuing physical attractions

Frank discussion among missionaries suggests that it is not uncommon for happily married men nonetheless to go on noticing attractive members of the opposite sex. The problem was somewhat exaggerated in places where a man travelling alone could be mistaken for an American GI assumed to be looking for a woman. In some garrison towns in Thailand, the situation was so bad that missionaries grew beards to make it clear they were not with the military. Non-Christian western-ers often set a bad example, but the problem arises generally from the sinfulness of the human heart (Mark 7:21), and Christians are not immune from sexual temptations.

During a men-only discussion at one field conference, several of the men confessed to occasionally feeling physically attracted to women other than their spouse. One much respected veteran confessed that this had been a problem to him. A silent member of the group came to me afterwards, and said: 'You have no idea what a relief that discussion was to me.' It emerged that he had been deeply disturbed and ashamed, feeling that he was somehow abnormally perverted and wicked. 'When I discover that saintly men like that wrestle with the same temptations, I realise that I am normal!'

Such thoughts may not in themselves be sinful, provided they are promptly rejected. I like the Zen story of the two monks who see a beautiful young woman hesitating before attempting to cross an extremely muddy morass in the road during the wet season. One of them kindly carries the girl across the road. They continue the journey, and an hour later one of them addresses the other: 'I don't think it was right for you as a monk to help that girl!' The man addressed, smiled and said: 'I put her down an hour ago, but it seems you have been carrying her in your head ever since!'

The Christian man needs to remind himself of the stern warnings of Scripture. The unmarried man who finds an unmarried female contemporary attractive cannot be said to be 'committing adultery in his heart' (Matthew 5:28). The very use of the word 'adultery' implies that the man or woman concerned has already entered into a marriage covenant; but while attraction may register, any continuing interest is manifestly illegitimate. The problem needs to be confessed to the Lord and such thoughts rejected.

Alexander Whyte writing about Elijah being a 'man of like passions as we are' said this: 'What were those horses of fire that day but all Elijah's passions all harnessed, in all their heaven bounding strength, to that heavenly chariot?'[9] The bridling may be helped by memorising Bible verses about the inappropriateness of sexual sinning in professing Christians, let alone those set apart as messengers and models of the gospel. In secular professions like medicine and teaching, sexual unfaithfulness involving those with whom we have been professionally entrusted can have serious consequences in being struck off the medical register, or losing a teaching post; the implications for Christian workers are perhaps more serious still.

In all such cases marriages are put under threat, but for Christian workers it means loss of credibility, church discipline and most probably the termination of their ministry. This may be one reason why sexual failures are relatively rare, and while it does not mean that missionaries are unusually saintly, it does mean that God in his grace does watch over and protect his servants. Where there is true repentance, restoration to church fellowship is easier than return to ministry, though even there rehabilitation is possible. The impact on spouse and family can be distressing, and the emotional and spiritual damage may be extreme. The shame and loss of credibility inflicted on the Christian church can be disastrous. A last-minute cry for help may make it possible for those at risk to be whisked away from the place of danger.

Problems arising between married and unmarried people

1. Criticism

In many mission societies the proportion of women to men is two to one; often this means one unmarried woman for every married one. Inevitably bearing babies, nursing them and caring for them can absorb a great deal of the married woman's time, making it difficult for her to be as deeply involved in church work, especially when the children are small. This isolation in itself can create spiritual problems for the married woman. As Jonathan gave encouragement and support to David, going to him to 'strengthen his hand in God' (1 Samuel 23:15–18), so there needs to be such mutual caring and bonding among missionary women, that will deepen the sense of team sharing and involvement. It is possible for there to be criticism of the married woman – too many children, too close together, or possibly too house proud and committed to her home and too little alongside her husband in the work. Instead the overburdened and harassed young mother needs an unmarried 'Jonathan' to come alongside and encourage her (see also 1 Samuel 18:1–4; 19:1–7; 20:1–42). Here then is a bonding between adopted sisters that will provide strength to all concerned.

2. Working relationships

As in other walks of life, married and unmarried missionaries are often working together closely in field situations. Wives and mothers will be tied to their homes, and husbands and fathers may have to work with unmarried lady missionaries. Back in the 1960s, Dr John Laird of Scripture Union used to warn his staff about relationships with their secretaries. He was refreshingly realistic and helpful. He suggested that women secretaries frequently become emotionally attached to the men whom they assist. This makes it essential that the man never crosses the boundary of a gentlemanly Christian relationship. He must be scrupulously careful not to be careless or thoughtless. From the single woman's viewpoint there is some corresponding helpful advice from Audrey Lee Sands:

> One of the most carefully drawn lines in your mind should be concerning discussions of a personal nature – spiritual or otherwise – when you are working alone together. Your personal affairs are none of his business, nor are his your business. This is a common pitfall. If you work together constantly, it is a very big temptation . . . It is altogether possible for a man to begin to feel that you understand him better than his wife does. And you may feel the same way. Perhaps you do understand him better . . .[10]

However, it is not merely in office situations that married men may be working with unmarried women. When small teams are working together in tribal situations, there may only be three or four people working together using a particular language. It is important that the team should bond together as a team, but without imperilling the exclusive marriage relationship. Mutual respect, friendship and proper Christian affection are essential and result in a genuine family spirit. However, great care and wisdom is needed to keep such relationships within proper bounds. There may sometimes be mutual attraction, and, in a small team, leaders cannot merely move the parties to a greater distance away from each other. It is essential that all concerned keep the barriers in place in respecting the marriage covenant so that no other deep relationship is possible. In the days when people used the language of Mr, Mrs and Miss that very formality helped, but in these more egalitarian and informal days when all are on first-name terms, it is much easier for misunderstandings to occur. This is especially dangerous when kindly sympathy and realisation of another person's problems make an individual feel sorry for someone, wanting to help them. In other words, there are degrees of bonding depending on degrees of intimacy, and secondary relationships must not be allowed to interfere with primary commitments.

3. Unwise confessions

When we have sinned against another person, we need to confess our failure and apologise when they are aware of what we have said or done. However, we should not do this when the sin is in thought rather than word or deed, and we should never confess that we have been sexually attracted to somebody who is not our committed life-partner. In one small tribal team under the influence of teaching about openness and confession, a married man confessed to an unmarried woman that he had been attracted to her and apologised. Then the fool went home and told his wife about his confession. You may well imagine that this fouled up relationships all round! The unmarried person was thrown into emotional turmoil, embarrassed by the man and feeling guilty towards the wife. The wife was, understandably, mad with both of them, and the man was in the doghouse with everyone.

The wife could understand confessing this to her as implying that she was not enough for him and that he wanted something more. Unwise confession may hide a need to get rid of a sense of guilt. The individual transfers his problem to his partner. Such confessions are not mature and loving acts. This man had no right to attempt to shift the guilt on to either of the other two parties.

Sexual attraction and unrealised fantasies about another person ought never to be confessed either to the person who aroused them or to one's own committed partner. If the need to confess is irresistible then it needs to be to some disinterested person of the same sex, who is a trusted counsellor who will keep their mouth shut. If some lady's skirt is too short, then it's not wise to tell her that this is a problem for you! Let somebody else mention it to her tactfully.

If some of this chapter seems too direct, please remember that we should not be ignorant of the enemy's devices, and that even in missionary flesh there is no good thing. It is important to be frank so that we can learn from other people's mistakes and not repeat them. Problems tend to reoccur and we need to know how to deal with them in our own lives, and to be able to counsel others meeting similar problems.

Notes

1. Rita Tullberg, *Women at Cambridge* (Cambridge: University Press, 1998), p.57.
2. Elaine Storkey, *The Search for Intimacy* (London: Hodder and Stoughton, 1995), pp.145–147.
3. Patrick McElligott, *op.cit.*, pp.231–235.
4. Green and Hooper, *C.S. Lewis: A Biography* (New York: Jovanovich, 1974), pp.231–232.
5. Mrs Howard Taylor, *Hudson Taylor and the China Inland Mission* (London: CIM, 1918), Vol. 2, pp.155–156 in a letter to Mr Berger.

6. *OMF Bulletin*, January 1975, a paediatrician's letter quoted in the General Director's letter on 'Family Planning'.
7. *Japan Harvest*, Vol. 29, No. 2 1979, 'Men who are blameless'.
8. *Faith Today*, magazine of Evangelical Fellowship of Canada. Missionary couples gave each other A+, but ministers gave their wives A– and the wives gave their husbands B-. However the sample seems inadequate.
9. Alexander Whyte, *Bible Characters* (Edinburgh: Oliphants, 1952), pp.363–367.
10. Audrey Lee Sands, *Single and Satisfied* (Wheaton: Tyndale House, 1971), p.122 and whole chapter.

CHAPTER TWELVE

QUALITY OF LIFE FOR ISOLATED LAMBS

The time will come when all the initial life-change and cultural shock becomes a thing of the past. We are beginning to feel at home in the new culture, and are less likely to be puzzled or surprised by it. However, the everyday business of living continues to present many problems not always appreciated by those with high expectations.

Chores

Wherever we live, the daily routines of life can take up a great deal of time. Even in the western world with all its modern labour-saving devices, we know that keeping houses and children clean, and family fed, can be a full-time occupation. When the former naval officer Henry Williams' wife, Marianne, arrived in New Zealand she came with the expectation of taking an active part. And in spite of raising no fewer than eleven children, that she did, together with her sister-in-law Jane, wife of William Williams who joined them in 1826. Both of them had a better than average education before they reached New Zealand. They ran a daily school for Maori women and girls, and a larger Sunday class. They also ran a school for five European girls, destined to become in turn teachers in Maori schools.[1] These two were a role model for others in sharing in teaching. Thus in Kerikeri there were four missionary wives sharing in running the school, along with functioning as mother, nurse, cook, counsellor, seamstress, laundress and hostess. Sharing the responsibility was practical, because it allowed for those times when a woman might need to absent herself from teaching because of family pressures like having yet another baby. This approach became a paradigm for all those who arrived later: the missionary wives established a tradition of involvement for wives who arrived later. But it was a far from easy task as Marianne explains:

> The missionary's wife must for the sake of cleanliness and preservation from multitudes of fleas[2] wash and dress her children, make her own bed and her children's and her visitors'. She must be housemaid and chambermaid and nursemaid, and must superintend everything with regard to cooking. The best of the Native Girls, if not well watched, would strain the milk with the duster, wash the tea things with the knife cloth, or wipe the tables with the flannel for scouring the floor. The very best of them will, on a hot day, take herself off (just when you may be wishing for someone to relieve you) and swim; afterwards she will go to sleep for two or three hours. . . . The moment a boat arrives, away run all the Native Servants – men, boys and girls – to the beach. If there is anything to be seen or anything extraordinary occurs, in New Zealand, the Mistress must do the work while the servants gaze abroad.[3]

Marianne Williams speaks frankly of how a busy missionary mother's involvement in home and mission affects her devotional life: 'Since we have been here we have greatly missed the congregation ... here a solitary two or three retiring to a shed or to one of the rooms with seven little children to attend to, deadens that spirituality, at which a Christian aims.[4]

The continuing discipline of language study requires that time must be made for that in the missionary's day. There are meetings and classes to prepare for, along with a stream of expected and unexpected visitors. All other duties have to be dropped to make the visitors welcome and then resumed afterwards, before yet more visitors arrive. The perfectionist who likes to organise their day's schedule ahead is likely to find such constant interruptions very irksome.

In more primitive situations, the need to fetch water from the nearest supply, or in cold climates to dig snow off paths and roofs, can be time consuming. Just finding and arranging to keep supplies of basic foodstuffs can also take much time. A retired Indian lady missionary confided the other day that they never went to the bazaar to shop themselves, but employed a man who would go and do the shopping for them. The days when missionaries could afford servants or it was acceptable to employ them have disappeared for ever in many countries. This means that a great deal of time has to be spent just living and staying alive. This is not necessarily negative, for that is the nature of life for all our neighbours who live around us. Shopping in the market or escorting children to nursery provide many opportunities to meet with other people. Often they are watching us to see how we live and whether our faith in Christ really does help us to cope with the normal everyday strains and stresses of living. The extra trip to the nearest store to pick up some item we have forgotten may give an opportunity for us to bump into some acquaintance in immediate need, or enable us to encounter some other needy person for the first time. If we go on foot or on a bicycle we are more likely to meet people than if we roar past in an expensive vehicle like a rich westerner.

Recreation

There was a young single American woman in our town on a
short-term (three-year) appointment to help in schools work
teaching English. What she found so difficult, and nobody
seemed to have warned her and helped her to anticipate this
problem, was that the social life to which she had been accus-
tomed at home had totally disappeared. No more dates and
very few invitations to come out to do this or that. Worse still,
no car to drive out and about in. Because she had minimal language, she could not bond with local Christians, and so
became extremely lonely. In the end she just gave up, packed
it in and went home. Better preparation and orientation
beforehand might have prevented all this. Ensuring that there
would be some compatible colleagues with whom she might
spend her free time would have helped. There is a sense, and
some parents might feel this to be ironical, in which having
children provides recreation as well as constant employment!

It might seem idyllic to live surrounded by beautiful green
paddy fields – apart from the constant croaking of frogs and
the myriads of mosquitoes that breed in the water essential to
the growing of rice. But what might we do on a day off? In
more sophisticated cities, there might be tennis courts, thea-
tres and concert halls. By the sea, we can find a beach, swim,
snorkel among the coral (if pollution hasn't wrecked it all),
but the cultural dress codes will have to be followed, and that
may mean not bathing in public at all. New ways of relaxing
and entertaining oneself will have to be found – keeping tropical fish (without any need to heat the water!); bird watching;
butterfly catching; insect watching; orchid collecting and
growing; fishing; and relaxing in the way that local people do.
The riches of the natural world lie all around us in rural and
more isolated parts of the world. There are local arts and skills

to study and learn to enjoy. There are new forms of music and new instruments on which to play them. And all these things need not be solitary pursuits but give opportunity to meet more people and make more friends. For some, cooking and going out to eat can be a relaxing and bonding activity in congenial company.

Family holidays in some delightful out-of-the-way place give parents freedom just to be with and enjoy their children free from interruptions. For the unmarried, finding other people to go on holiday with takes some organising, and is especially difficult for unattached men. There are not always many of them, and they may be eccentric loners who find friendship difficult.

The arrival of television almost everywhere in the two-thirds world has opened a door to understanding national culture for the missionary community. Before it was in general use even in Japan, I can remember trudging back with my senior colleague through slushy snow and joining a crowd of Japanese men clustered around a shop window watching the final bouts of a *sumoo* (Japanese wrestling by overweight giants) tournament. The locals clearly knew all these large fat men by name, and knew their current form, and the technical niceties of throws and thrusting attacks. It was part of their life and interest. I bought a book on it and it provided me with some good indigenous sermon illustrations! Missionaries initially resisted television as an encouragement to worldliness (which it was and still is), but when the Japanese started throwing away their black-and-white sets and changing to colour, most of us succumbed because we could pick up a black and white set for virtually nothing. Then I too could keep up with what was happening in a Japanese national sport. It provided both recreation and the opportunity to hear good secular language being spoken!

It may seem odd in a book about missionary work even to mention the possibility of recreation, but missionaries themselves need to pray about how they use their little free time (and home churches need to think and pray about it also). I once asked a very gifted and committed bachelor, whom I greatly respect for his significant missionary contribution, exactly when he last took a day off. 'I tried it once,' he said. I went on to ask when he last took a holiday, as mission regulations require. 'Well, I stayed back at the holiday home by the sea once after a conference, but by lunchtime I was so bored I took a bus back to Bangkok!' I had to laugh. He scored full marks for dedication, but I could not help wondering to myself if he would have been a better human being, and a better missionary, if he had wider dimensions in skills and interests to enliven his preaching and help him relate to others.

Voluntary poverty

Quality of life does not depend upon having a great deal of money to spend, but eating out and taking up some hobby or interest does require some spending money. Different groups of missionaries tend to expect different standards of living. Some denominational missions from Germany, Scandinavia and America often seemed to live 'high on the hog' as they themselves might put it. Other groups were known for living on a shoestring, and surviving a hand-to-mouth existence. One mission was running their own mission aeroplane when there was hardly any food on their tables. Missionaries who have been living comfortably on the support reaching them can be propelled into poverty overnight – as when the South African rand was devalued. Or a mission with a long and honourable history, which has managed well for many years, finds that the economic success of their target country means that it is harder and harder for their workers to make ends meet – as happened with the Japan Evangelistic Band, for example. Missions working in a wide spread of countries have fewer problems if they pool resources, because countries where living costs are lower subsidise those in countries where prices are higher.

When we ourselves started out as missionaries, the general theory was that we would try to live at the level of secondary school teachers. In poor post-war Japan that was not at all difficult, but gradually we became increasingly aware that our living standards were falling further and further behind the local people. Living in poorer developing countries, or in disadvantaged communities anywhere, the missionary must adopt a simpler lifestyle. Someone living among mountain tribes in the Philippines once told me they felt ashamed to have a second dress to change into! A couple working in a South Thailand group of villages had their bathroom water running out through a channel on the living room floor and the children were playing in huge mud puddles outside (what fun!), and most of us would have called the house a hovel. But from the point of view of the local peasant people they were perceived as among the richest families in the village. That quarter their food allowance was ten per cent down and their more general living allowance cut to fifty per cent because of shortage of funds.

They themselves were feeling the pinch and very short of money, but it did not seem that way to the people they were living among. It is not easy to live when every penny has to be counted. When looking for necessities, we always buy the cheapest thing on offer. When thinking of luxuries, we usually have to deny ourselves. While this doesn't matter because we have determined that sacrifice is part of our Christian commitment, nonetheless we often have to pray

about having the right attitude towards the cost of identifying and bonding with fellow human beings who enjoy (or
perhaps suffer) a very different standard of living from that
of our home countries.

In our first term of four years, my wife and I went out for
an evening together only a couple of times. That was partly
because of the pressures of bringing up children, and the total
commitment to language study night after night when we did
not have meetings, or meetings to prepare for. But it was also
because we did not have money spare to be able to afford to
eat out very often. We never owned a car until our last year in
Japan, when we bought one for £50 from a Japanese pastor
in Tokyo. (It was sold a year later for scrap.) Now we could
take our kids out and visit places we had never been to before.
Our lack of personal transport did not matter then, because
the Japanese themselves, still recovering in the aftermath of
the war, did not yet own personal vehicles, or not in the cities
we lived in up north. Today, of course, it's different and missionaries live like poor relations often overwhelmed by the
kindness and generosity of local Christians.

Many peoples rich and poor alike live in generous, hospitable cultures, and nothing is too much trouble for the honoured guest. When the community is economically
disadvantaged, this can be embarrassing, and one has to find
culturally acceptable ways of returning kindness with kindness. When we feel like poor relations because of the huge
disparity between the levels of church support from home,
and the people among whom we are living, our own pride
needs to be humbled to accept graciously and with genuine
appreciation the kindness of others. Most of the pictures on
our walls, and treasured carvings in wood or stone, are
appreciated gifts that remind us of good friends in other
cultures.

Monotony

I was shocked once to hear a respected senior missionary couple speaking about returning to the small coastal logging town where they worked as 'that dump'. To the newly arrived young missionary it sounded most unspiritual. But the drab, unpainted wooden houses partly hidden under dust-polluted snow, a long train journey from the nearest city, could not unfairly be described as 'a dump'! It did look better in the spring. The fact remained that they worked there, and gave themselves to the people there. It was not an attractive looking community outwardly, but a living congregation of God's beautiful people was coming into existence. Most human beings live monotonous lives, whether it's hard physical farm work in the fields day after day, and year after year, or commuting daily to an office on the 7.42 am train five days a week. 'The daily round, the common task, should furnish all we need to ask' as the hymnwriter put it. We ought not to be surprised therefore if monotony enters the lives even of some Christian workers some of the time.

Frustration (disappointment)

Christian workers are even more influenced by frustration and disappointment in their work than other people are. The feeling of being ineffective, unappreciated or in the wrong niche can be difficult for anybody. But when one is a missionary, saving souls, baptising bodies and planting churches is the whole purpose of being where one is. What is the point of living as a not always welcome alien in a foreign culture, making sacrifices for oneself, one's spouse and one's children, if all of that is apparently yielding nothing? I may begin to feel that I am wasting my time, and want to pack it all in. A recent letter from a missionary working in Austria, a notoriously difficult field, underlines all this.

> Please pray for the following in 1999: conversions, new leaders, conversions, wisdom for us elders, conversions . . . we have seen no other fruit. I thank God for invisible fruit, but please, please pray for conversions! I am struggling with disappointment . . . I see very little fruit. Please pray! Frustrated. I don't feel we're making much progress, either in the church or in student work. Conversions sometimes feel like a thing of the past. Of course, there is always invisible fruit, but I long to see changed lives.

Reading these letters certainly stirs the readers up to pray, but we can see how the sense of failure to see conversions troubles the whole of life. Yet so often it is only when we become really desperate and see that nothing will happen unless God himself acts, that out of the ashes of our sense of failure, God is to bring blessing.

Working in Muslim lands can be harder still. The BBC book *Missionaries,*[5] which is anything but sympathetic to its subject, gives a realistic picture of the problems of Christian mission hospitals in Pakistan:

> Apostasy is a life and death issue, and the apostate must expect to face it alone. The hospital staff are neither permitted, nor do they have time to follow up the evangelistic work done on the wards. When a patient leaves the hospital all contact with the missionaries abruptly ends. If that patient was converted while at the hospital, he or she plunges straight back into Muslim society, isolated and vulnerable. At best he could be expected to be ostracised by his friends and family, at worst he might be killed. Yet even against that background, the hospital staff continue to attempt such evangelism.

We know of only one or two people converted through Henry Martyn. One of them, Sheikh Salih, heard Martyn explaining the Ten Commandments, and got himself engaged as a copyist of the Urdu translation. He was baptised by Chaplain David Brown (after Martyn had left India for Persia) on Whit Sunday 1811, and took the name Abdul Masih. He was the first person salaried by the Church Missionary Society to work in India (which was still closed to missionaries). Just over a year after Martyn's death, in December 1813 Abdul Masih baptised forty-one adults and fourteen children in Agra, the first of many converts.

I have introduced this story because it underlines the fact that we always need a long-term view. The agonies of feeling that the work is too slow and that little is happening is the problem of being so close to the everyday work of evangelism and church planting. When I first visited Nepal in 1968 I think the whole church would have numbered fewer than 1,000. On my second visit in 1980 it had increased from 2,500 the previous year to almost 5,000. On my most recent visit figures in excess of 100,000 were being quoted. When we are living daily and working close to the action it can seem slow. But those like a Cambridge contemporary of mine who went to Nepal not long after qualifying in medicine and made serving Nepali people his life's work, could see how God blessed and prospered the church in that land in spite of persecution and opposition.

The biblical spur and motivation

Does this idea of embracing a lower quality of life than we might enjoy at home suggest the cost is too great? What is it that inspires a succession of young men and women in each generation to embrace voluntary poverty and a simple lifestyle to identify with and bond with fellow Christians of other races and nationalities? It has to be the example of the one who, though he was rich, for our sakes became poor, so that we through his poverty might be made rich (2 Corinthians 8:9). The example of the apostle Paul also reminds us that this self-sacrificing attitude to mission life has been blessed and used by God from the beginning. In his letter to the Philippians, Paul outlines five costs of commitment.

1. *Cultural privilege and status*

In Philippians 3:4–10 Paul uses the language of price. He says that all his seeming assets and gains that he once took pride in had become loss for the sake of Christ. A teaching post in Jerusalem or the University of Tarsus would have enabled him to hang on to all he had gained earlier. To the Gentiles to whom he went, his Jewish pedigree and rabbinic education at the feet of Gamaliel meant nothing at all. In our own country we may have been a somebody by virtue of our family background, educational honours or professional attainment. When we go abroad we lose all that and become nobodies, stupid ignorant aliens who cannot express ourselves at all clearly. All existing status is wiped out and we have to start all over again to establish relationship and win respect. Jesus can ask this price because he did this in the most extreme way possible, leaving the courts of heaven and the worship of the angelic hosts to become a human baby laid in a feeding trough, and then a refugee fleeing into Egypt with his parents. Are we willing for Jesus' sake to become a nobody, falling into the ground and dying in order to bear fruit?

2. *Standard of living*

Paul writes again that

> I have learned to be content whatever the circumstances. I know what it is to be in need, and I know what it is to have plenty. I

have learned the secret of being content in any and every situation, whether well fed or hungry, whether living in plenty or in want. I can do everything through him who gives me strength (Philippians 4:11–13).

Notice that in these latter words he is not bragging about supernatural powers, but the 'everything' that he can do is to sacrifice comfort and a full stomach for the sake of the gospel. He writes elsewhere that they are 'poor yet making many rich; having nothing, yet possessing everything' (2 Corinthians 6:10). To be an authentic follower of Jesus Christ requires the willingness to sacrifice the standard of living which we have known since childhood in order to identify with the poor and outcast. Jesus is entitled to ask this price because he himself did just this in entering our human world.

3. Security and health

Paul writes his letter from a prison, and it was not a modern deluxe establishment (Philippians 1:13–14). He had been in prison many times in the course of his career as a missionary. He had learned that God is not interested primarily in our safety and security, but in blessing us and blessing other people through us. He says of Epaphroditus (Philippians 2:30) that he had gambled or risked his life for the sake of Christ. Jesus chose to spend his incarnate life in one of the deepest troughs on the land surface of our globe, Galilee and Jericho, by the Dead Sea. Infant mortality was high, and under the Romans life was cheap and often short, as he discovered himself. He can ask us to pay this price because he did this himself. He taught on more than one occasion that those who try to save their lives will lose them, and those willing to lose their lives for his sake will find them.

4. Family and friends

Paul said that he suffered the loss of all things (Philippians 3:8). He left his sister and nephew behind in Jerusalem (Acts 23:16). Timothy left his mother and grandmother behind in Lystra. Would they ever meet each other again? Jesus said that if anyone did not 'hate his father and mother, wife and children, his brothers and sisters – yes, even his own life – he cannot be my disciple' (Luke 14:26). (Note that 'hate' is relative to our love for the Lord, for Paul tells the Christian man to love his wife as Christ loved the church and gave himself for it.) Yet a few chapters later the Lord adds that 'no-one who has left home or wife or brothers or parents or children for the sake of the kingdom of God, will fail to receive many times as much in this age and, in the age to come, eternal life' (Luke 18:29–30).

Much of the physical costs of being a missionary faced by nineteenth-century missionaries are gone today. The early missionaries in the Arctic got their mail once a year. Missionaries like Thomas Valpy-French left his wife and children behind for considerable periods in order to serve in India, and poured out his love for her and them in his letters home. David Livingstone sent his beloved Mary and the children back to Scotland, as he set off on yet another exploratory trip into Central Africa. Sure, we hate separations from beloved parents and deeply loved children, but we may sometimes have to leave them behind for the sake of our work and their education. It costs. It hurts. But Jesus can ask it because he left his glorious heavenly home. His earthly brothers could not understand why he took such risks. His friends all forsook him and ran away. Dying on the cross, he handed his mother over to his cousin John. Certainly there are the compensations, the hundred times as many, but there is also a cost and he has the right to ask it of us if we claim to be his followers.

5. Life itself

Paul expects to pour out his life as a drink offering (Philippians 2:17). He wants Christ to be exalted in his body, whether by living or by dying. He wants 'to depart and be with Christ' (Philippians 1:20–23). He has the model of Christ himself who gave his life a ransom for many, and would lay down his life for his sheep. In the early nineteenth century the vast majority of missionaries were short term, because they died of disease before they had built up any resistance. They never became long term. Nowadays missionary deaths do happen, but they are far, far less common than they once were. Today they suffer fewer casualties than other expatriates travelling abroad, and probably little more than those dying in accidents or of disease in their home countries. But we must not allow fear of losing our lives prematurely to keep us from the task of spreading the light of the gospel.

Many of us who never leave our homelands can waste years being scared of dying before we finish our education, or before we marry, or before we have children, or before those children grow up. Fear of death is something we are supposed to be delivered from in the gospel (Hebrews 2:14–15). We cannot allow such normal fears to stop us obeying the commission to make disciples of all nations, no matter how difficult their living conditions or dangerous their political scene. The Christian faith is about living (and dying) with great purpose. Jesus gave his life for us. Stephen and the apostle James are both martyred in Jerusalem. Paul and Peter both have their lives taken from them in Rome, after long lives of usefulness.

Conclusion

I am sure I have said enough to show that we must be willing to sacrifice quality of life for the sake of the gospel. Actually, though this may sound mildly heroic, all of us who have gone abroad for the sake of the gospel, would want to confess that although we fussed and agonised about the possibility of sacrifice before we left home, afterwards we recognise that our lives have been immeasurably enriched by the privilege of serving as Christ's messengers wherever we have been.

Notes

1. Robert Glen, ed., *Mission and Moko: The CMS in New Zealand 1814–1882* (Christchurch, NZ: Latimer Fellowship, 1992), p.64.
2. This relates to the origin of the word *pakeha* still used by Maoris to describe 'whites' who when they first landed from ships were often verminous. The word means 'fortress of fleas'!
3. *Ibid.*, p.69, quoting M. Williams *Missionary Register*, Vol.14 (1826), p.616.
4. Davidson and Lineham, *Transplanted Christianity, Documents illustrating aspects of NZ Church History*, (Auckland: College Communications, 1987), p.38.
5. Pettifer and Bradley, *Missionaries* (London: BBC Books, 1990), p.204. Reading this book made me wonder when the media will stop this kind of sniping at Christian missions, and allow journalists with an understanding, sympathetic approach to tackle an enthralling subject.

CHAPTER THIRTEEN

LAMBS BOND WITH THEIR SHEPHERD

Having stressed the cardinal importance of 'bonding' all the way through this book, it would seem appropriate finally to emphasise that nothing is more indispensable to the effective Christian worker than 'bonding' with the Lord Jesus Christ himself. Of course, bonding with fellow Christians in emerging churches is essential, but the whole harvesting operation is being organised by the chief harvester so that constant, close communication with him as our work leader is fundamental. The chief difficulty here is that in the pressures of daily living, language study and, above all, demanding work, we ourselves may neglect our devotional life, and our relationship with our teacher and lord. Such is his sovereignty that he takes constant initiatives to relate with us, and such is his mercy and humility that he is always near and close to us and ready to respond to our call. As Moses expressed it: 'What other nation is so great as to have their gods near them the way the Lord our God is near us whenever we pray to him?' (Deuteronomy 4:7).

I was very impressed when I read about Chris Maddox's discipline in his own devotional life. As a heavily pressured hospital superintendent in Thailand:

Chris developed the routine which he subsequently followed throughout his career, of spending up to an hour before breakfast in Bible reading, meditation and prayer, with a separate period of intercessory prayer later in the day, and a few minutes for further prayer and Bible reading last thing at night. It is a demanding programme, especially when regarded as an adjunct to a full and exhausting routine of clinical and administrative work.[1]

If we have become less disciplined, what a blessing it is to know that the Lord, whose fellowship we have neglected, has never ignored or neglected us, and is patiently ready to welcome us back into a closer than ever bonding relationship. Perhaps a rapid review of the biblical foundations for such friendship with God, in all three persons, may be helpful.

The Old Testament

In the Old Testament, the relationship of God to both Abraham and Moses is expressed in terms of the intimacy of human friendship. In those early days Abraham's bonding with the Lord was such that he was known as 'God's friend' (2 Chronicles 20:7; Isaiah 41:8; James 2:23). Abraham's intercession for Sodom and Gomorrah indicates that the Lord wants him to understand what he is doing and why (Genesis 18:17). After the Israelites left Egypt, the Lord's presence with his people was signified by the pillar of cloud by day and the pillar of fire at night. Moses was an effective spiritual leader, because the Lord spoke with him in the tent of meeting 'face to face as a man speaks with his friend' (Exodus 33:11).

The Psalms of David demonstrate how in every crisis, in every trial of suffering David sought the Lord, whom he calls 'my rock, in whom I take refuge' (Psalm 18:2). He expresses great yearnings for close intimacy with the Lord: 'One thing I ask of the Lord, this is what I seek: that I may dwell in the house of the Lord all the days of my life, to gaze upon the beauty of the Lord and to seek him in his temple' (Psalm 27:4). Again we find it in the well-known verse: 'As the deer pants for streams of water, so my soul pants for you, O God' (Psalm 42:1). The desire for bonding is certainly there in the Psalms.

The prophets also reveal the Lord meeting with and reasoning with his servants at times of crisis and failure in their lives. He asks Elijah in a gentle whisper 'What are you doing here?' (1 Kings 19:9, 13) and reasons with Jonah when he is so angry (Jonah 4:4, 9). The Lord encourages fearful Jeremiah with promises of strengthening him like a fortified city, a bronze wall and iron pillar, and vows 'I am with you and will rescue you' (Jeremiah 1:8, 18–19). Even in the distress of his deteriorating marriage relationship, Hosea is enabled to understand and to express the love of the Lord for his unfaithful people (Hosea 2:19–20; 11:3–4).

The New Testament

The teaching of Christ to his closest disciples, surely bonded with him after three years eating at the same table, sleeping in the same rooms and in the open, travelling together in a close-knit group, is that 'apart from me you can do nothing' (John:15:5). The words he uses in that chapter is what evangelical Christians soaked in the Authorised Version used to call 'abiding in Christ'. The horticultural metaphor of the dependence of vine branches on their vital supply of life-giving water and nutrients from the rootstock is a further expression of what we mean by 'bonding'. Fruitfulness can come only from being grafted into Christ, drawing our life from him and being filled with his vitality. So this is the metaphor of botanical 'bonding' if you like. However, we Christians sometimes speak as though this kind of close relationship with Christ was a feature of the apostles' relationship during the period of the incarnation that came to an end with Christ's death, resurrection and ascension. Now he has gone away into heaven, sending his Holy Spirit to make him real in present-day Christian experience. Do we Christians then believe in 'the real absence' of Jesus?

Evangelical reductionism: the great commission

The famous closing words of Matthew's Gospel are often spoken of as the 'great commission'. Inadvertently we often concentrate upon verse 19, the command to Christ's apostles – and to us – to 'go and make disciples' to the virtual exclusion of verses 18 and 20, both of which contain great statements about the Lord Jesus. These verses focus much more on him than on us! Some of us, preaching on the great commission, may be likened to naughty children who eat the filling out of a sandwich and then leave aside the two significant slices of nourishing bread on each side of it! It is noteworthy that not one of the so-called 'parallels' to the great commission in Luke, John and Acts are presented in the form of commands, but all three are statements focusing on the Lord Jesus himself. Luke 24:46–48 is a statement about Christ: 'The Christ will suffer and rise from the dead on the third day, and repentance and forgiveness of sins will be preached in his name to all nations. . . . You are witnesses of these things.'

John 20:21 is another statement about what Jesus continues to do as the Father's 'sent one', and is followed by a further promise of the Holy Spirit. 'As the Father has sent me, I am sending you. . . . Receive the Holy Spirit.'

Acts 1:8 is yet another statement, focusing upon Christ's action rather than human response: 'But you will receive power when the Holy Spirit comes on you; and you will be my witnesses in Jerusalem, and in all Judea and Samaria, and to the ends of the earth.'

This gives us a helpful clue to a proper understanding of Matthew 28:18–20. It follows that the great commission also must be seen as primarily two great statements about Jesus himself: 'All authority in heaven and earth has been *given to me*', (v.18) and 'surely *I am* with you always, to the very end of the age' (v.20) (my italics). We must shift our thinking from stressing human obligation in verse 19 to the two great Christological statements in verses 18 and 20. Let's look at the whole passage afresh.

> All authority in heaven and on earth has been given to me. Therefore go and make disciples of all nations, baptising them in the name of the Father and of the Son and of the Holy Spirit, and teaching them to obey everything that I have commanded you. And surely I am with you always, to the very end of the age.

Verse 18 carries more punch when we recognise, as the apostles would have done, the allusion to Daniel 7:13–14 which portrays the son of man having authority over all peoples and nations.

> In my vision at night I looked, and there before me was one like a son of man, coming with the clouds of heaven. He approached the Ancient of Days and was led into his presence. He was given authority, glory and sovereign power; all peoples, nations and men of every language worshipped him. His dominion is an everlasting dominion that will not pass away, and his kingdom is one that will never be destroyed.

Jesus was telling his followers that Daniel's words are now being fulfilled. We know these words were on his mind because he had alluded to them a few days earlier when the high priest charged him under oath, 'Tell us if you are the Christ, the Son of God.' Then Jesus had replied, 'In the future you will see the Son of Man sitting at the right hand of the Mighty One and coming on the clouds of heaven' (Matthew 26:63–64). By applying Daniel's words to himself he infuriated the Jews and was sentenced to death for blasphemy. Now he uses that same passage to explain both the apostles' future activity and his own continuing ministry.

It is no accident that the Gospel concludes with these words, for they serve to sum up many of its main themes. Now Jesus is risen and glorified his power and authority is even more apparent. This conclusion illuminates many earlier passages of the Gospel. The early promise of 'God with us' (Immanuel) (Matthew 1:23) is now understood to be a permanent rather than a temporary blessing. The temptation in Matthew 4:1–11 offered a wrong way of winning the world; now we are shown the right way through progressive evangelisation of all nations. Throughout the Gospel, mountains have provided the backdrop for events of great significance (4:8; 5:1; 14:23; 28:16). This mountain in Galilee is the most impressive of all. The great commission, as we choose to call it, may be compared to a suspension bridge where the command to us is suspended between two great theological pillars, each of them a great statement about the person and work of the Lord Jesus, and without which the commission lacks both authorisation for its mandate and power for its fulfilment.

1. *All authority is given to him (v.18)*

Mathew's Gospel progressively reveals the authority of Jesus: in calling disciples (4:19); in teaching (7:29); in healing (8:9); over the elements (8:27); in forgiving sin (9:6); over death (9:25); over demons (8:32; 12:28). He is finally asked, 'By what authority are you doing these things?' (21:23). Now the truth is finally revealed that 'all authority in heaven and on earth' has been given to him, as Daniel 7:14 had prophesied. The significance of this for Christian belief in the supremacy of Christ cannot be over emphasised. All power in heaven and earth is his. Do we really believe that? Jesus is not just one more among the world's significant prophets and teachers like Siddartha Gautama, Guru Nanak or Mahomet, but the one to whom all authority in heaven and on earth has already been given.

This is the only authority we have to say that Christian belief is true in a way that other religious traditions are not. Some would accuse us of arrogance in presuming to make disciples of 'all nations' many of whom have been born into Hindu, Buddhist, Muslim or Sikh traditions. The only possible justification for our doing so is because of the identity of the Lord Jesus as the image of the invisible God (Colossians 1:15; Hebrews 1:3). How could we possibly dare to go and make disciples of these adherents of the world's 'great religions'? Only Jesus himself has the authority to command us to do so, and Jesus himself is with us as we go out to do it. Waldron Scott, writing on Karl Barth's *Theology of Mission,* explains: '(Jesus Christ) is the true missionary. The church merely accompanies him in mission, assisting as it can. Barth illustrates this by reference to acolytes who assist the priest in the performance of his duties'.[2] Mission is not merely some human task of propagating one among many possible religions by a process of proselytisation, but the mission of God himself.

2. He promises to be with us always (v.20b)

Traditionally we have seen the great commission as a command for us to obey. We challenge young men and women: 'Will you obey Christ's command to make disciples of all nations?' This seems far too anthropocentric: the theological basis for mission is much stronger than this. It seems doubtful whether the apostles took the good news to the world merely because someone told them to do it. Everything hangs on the identity and authority of the person who commands us to 'go do it'. These Jewish apostles had been instructed earlier not to go to Samaritans or Gentiles (Matthew 10:5–6). What, now that Jesus has died, risen and ascended, was motivating them to go to the Gentile 'all nations'? 'Go and make disciples' is properly the logical outcome of realising who Jesus is and what he has done. Thus Roland Allen wrote:

> Had the Lord not given any such command, had the Scriptures never contained such a form of words . . . the obligation to preach the Gospel to all nations would not have been diminished by a single iota. For the obligation depends not upon the letter, but upon the Spirit of Christ; not upon what He orders, but upon what He is, and the Spirit of Christ is the Spirit of Divine Love and compassion and desire for souls astray from God.[3]

The principal commanded activity of making disciples by the methods of baptising and teaching is a logical consequence of understanding exactly who Jesus really is. We obey simply because he is the one Lord, 'image of the invisible God, who has made him known' (Hebrews 1:3; Colossians 1:15; John 1:18). The structure of the 'great commission', then, is *first* a statement about Jesus' authority (based upon Daniel 7); *second* the missionary consequence, the commission to go and make disciples of all nations; and *third* the promise that Jesus would be permanently with them as chief harvester throughout the whole operation. It is perhaps for this reason, because

Jesus will always be with them, that Matthew includes no account of the ascension, nor of the outpouring of the Spirit, or even mention of his anticipated return in glory at this point. For his disciples, Jesus never leaves them.[4]

This discussion depends upon our place in time: from God's timeless perspective it is obvious and self-evident that he is always with us and will never, never forsake us. While we are to understand the ascension as pointing to the fact that 'God has highly exalted him' (Philippians 2:9) and that he is now enthroned in heaven at the right hand of the majesty on high, interceding for us, we are not to understand this to mean that he is now in some way 'absent' from the world which he created and away from humankind whom he longs to bring to himself.

Notice, by the way, that while our English translation seems to stress the word 'go' this is just a common grammatical construction which Matthew uses repeatedly. 'Go' is an auxiliary verb, strengthening the imperative of another main verb. For example, 2:8 – 'Go and worship'; 9:13 – 'Go and learn what this means'; 11:4 – 'Go back and report to John'; 17:27 – 'Go and throw out your line'; 28:7 – 'Go quickly and tell his disciples'. In each case the word 'go' can be omitted without any loss of meaning. It does not imply travelling from one place to another, but underlines the verb that follows: thus it is not first 'Go!' and then 'Make disciples', so much as 'Go make disciples'. The first verb serves to reinforce the action of the main verb and adds a note of urgency to it.[5] Because of our English translation we have tended to stress the action of going more than what the going was for, and in consequence have stressed the geographical act of going 'abroad', more than the significant action to be performed, in this case 'making disciples'.

Matthew only once uses the word 'apostle' (10:2) in the significant context of 9:38 – 'Ask the Lord of the harvest,

therefore, *to send out* workers into his harvest field', and 10:5
– 'these twelve Jesus *sent out*' (my italics). Mission is seen to
be the task of the chief harvester who involves others with him
in fulfilling his mission.

3. These verses are not a farewell speech handing over responsibility

These verses are sometimes used to suggest that Jesus at the
moment of departure delegated all future responsibility to
eleven fallible men, who had very recently shown general
unreliability and cowardice!

We may know the totally unbiblical and theologically
unsound story about what Jesus is supposed to have replied to
a hypothetical question from theologically uninformed angels:
'What plans do you have if these eleven unreliable human
beings fail in this task of making disciples?' Jesus then supposedly replies: 'I have no other plans.' This is frankly an absurd
Arminian overstatement. It misses the whole point. Jesus has
not now abandoned his mission following his death and resurrection, and passed it on to ineffective deputies. He has ministered for three short years in the tiny province of Palestine to
people who have been blessed and enlightened by God's revelation through the Law and the prophets. It would be grossly
unfair to desert his apostles now and leave them all alone to
tackle the vast and more difficult task of taking the gospel to
all the other nations over many centuries.

The Gentile nations lack revelation through Law and
prophets that might help them to understand. This mission to
the ends of the earth continues to be his, and he now invites
frail human beings to join him in it. Father, Son and Holy
Spirit form the oldest missionary society in the world. Its three
experienced directors (in whose name we are all to be baptised) were formerly assisted by several legions of angelic

helpers. They are now taking on eleven human helpers, who are immediately charged to recruit yet others, 'teaching them to obey all that I have commanded you'. Incidentally, if I may say this in the politest and most courteous way, the notion of the Pope as the vicar of Christ on earth, representing an absent Christ, is also sadly mistaken. Jesus Christ doesn't need a vicar on earth because he is still here in person himself. The whole concept of his needing an earthly representative is an example of the same serious theological error where Christ is supposed to have abandoned earth. In any case, as the farewell speech of a departing Lord, this is quite an extraordinary paradox. 'Goodbye now, I will never leave you' is a contradiction in terms. There can be little doubt that Matthew himself understood the last verses of chapter 28 to be the key to his entire Gospel.[6]

4. Motivation for us today – realise who Jesus is and where Jesus is

Response to this Gospel is not limited to those called as cross-cultural missionaries. Every man or woman who becomes a disciple is to be baptised in the name of the three directors, and is to be taught to obey all the commands of Jesus – including this one. If you are a disciple, baptised in the name of the three directors, then you are already part of God's great missionary operation: and he is with us in it. Our motivation, explained by Matthew, is twofold: First, to realise who Jesus is: the crucified and risen Lord, given all power and authority. Second, to realise where Jesus is: with us always to the end of the world. If we are gripped by these two great biblical truths – the two key nourishing elements of this theological sandwich, the two great statements expressing truths about the Lord – then the great commission makes much more compelling sense than it does when looked at without the two great

Christological truths of verses 18 and 20, which support it!

So we are not called to bond with some mystical, absentee Lord, but with a risen, glorified Christ who is here on earth with us himself, and utterly committed to making disciples of all nations. The very nature of a disciple is defined in Mark 3:14 – 'that they might be with him and that he might send them out'. The disciple sits at his teacher's feet and learns, letting not a single word fall to the ground. His promise of being with us always means that he is with us and we are with him. This indeed is a bonding relationship.

The apostle Paul

The apostle Paul demonstrates the centrality of his relationship with Christ throughout his ministry. Luke gives us his extraordinary account of the days of constant stress, battered by wind and waves, out of sight of land, sun and stars, and expecting imminent death for fourteen days. The cargo of grain, swelling as it got damp, could split the hull, thus the ropes cast round to hold them together. The passage with all its stark nautical details is one of brutal life and death realism. Then suddenly the Lord sends his angel messenger, zooming down through the overcast sky, to reassure his servant. Paul says: 'Last night, an angel of the God *whose I am and whom I serve* stood beside me and said, "Do not be afraid, Paul"' (Acts 27:23–24, my italics).

It is this sense of belonging to the Lord, that I am his and he is mine, that is so basic. The expression 'bond-slave' used in some translations does express the loyal commitment of the slave or retainer to a beloved master, and is itself a proper expression of Christian devotion, but is not quite what we mean by 'bonding' here. Let us examine some passages to see what Paul himself says at various times in his ministry. Unfortunately, though some of the prophets dated their prophecies, Paul never seems to have dated his letters so their actual sequence is inevitably conjectural. Much of the time Paul is concerned with the crises and confusions within local churches that made it necessary to write each of his letters, but from time to time he reveals much about his own relationship with the Lord Jesus. So both when he explains his own personal experience, and when speaking to Christians of their relationship with Christ, this sense of 'bonding' emerges.

Lessons from Galatians

This is acknowledged to be Paul's earliest letter. Paul sees himself as commissioned as an apostle sent by Jesus Christ (1:1), whose servant he is (1:10), and from whom he had received his revealed gospel (1:12). Here is the famous statement that expresses both the theological significance and the thoroughgoing nature of that bonding: 'I have been crucified with Christ and I no longer live, but Christ lives in me. The life I live in the body, I live by faith in the Son of God who loved me and gave himself for me' (2:20). He speaks of that bonding between Christians which is ours because we are bonded with Christ: 'all of you who were baptised into Christ have clothed yourselves with Christ. There is neither Jew nor Greek, slave nor free, male nor female, for you are all one in Christ Jesus' (3:27–28). It is because of our primary bonding with Christ that we may be bonded together with all who belong to Christ.

Lessons from 1 Corinthians

It was while Paul was in Corinth that he was much encouraged by the Lord Jesus' revelation of his presence with an involvement in mission (Acts 18:9–10). 'One night the Lord spoke to Paul in a vision: "Do not be afraid; keep on speaking, do not be silent. For I am with you, and no-one is going to attack and harm you, because I have many people in this city."' The Lord gives not only the assurance of his immediate presence alongside Paul, but promises that he himself is active in mission in Corinth. Paul was able to continue on in that city in a way that never seems to have been possible up to that point, because in almost every city persecution, riots and threats had driven him out. The mission to Corinth was a highly successful one, even if subsequently problems arose which necessitated Paul writing three or four times.

In the first letter Paul says he was sent by Christ, not to baptise, but to preach the gospel (1 Corinthians 1:17) and determines to know nothing 'except Jesus Christ and him crucified' (2:2). They are not to form factions supporting Apollos or Paul, because both are 'only servants' to whom 'the Lord has assigned to each his task' (3:5). Using the language of agricultural project (3:9 'field' is an inadequate translation), it is God who makes it grow, and using the language of the building project, Jesus Christ is the only foundation. The servants who sow seed and water it, or who lay upper courses upon the foundation are utterly dependent upon the one who is both the creator of the project, and the one who makes its completion possible.

Paul is giving reasons for Christian sexual purity when he expresses the concept of bonding most clearly. It is a key passage here. 'But he who unites himself with the Lord is one with him in spirit' (6:17). The word he uses for 'unite' is the same as that used by the Lord Jesus about the union of husband and wife, quoting Genesis 2:24, when speaking of divorce (Matthew 19:5). The explanations of the meaning of the word in the Lexicon are illuminating: 'bind closely, unite someone with or to someone, cling to, join oneself to, enter into a close relation with.[7] It is evident that we are not stretching the concept from human 'bonding' beyond biblical thinking when we urge that for the cross-cultural missionary 'bonding' with the Lord Jesus must be regarded as the outstanding secret of effective work. When Paul is speaking of his working harder than everybody else, he attributes this to 'the grace of God that was with me' (15:10).

The second letter, as we call it, has much more in it concerning Paul's own personal struggle, sufferings and walk of faith. We realise that we are not trying to bond ourselves to a distant, disinterested redeemer, but that he has first chosen to bond us to himself: 'he anointed us, set his seal of ownership on us, and put his Spirit in our hearts as a deposit (downpayment) guaranteeing what is to come' (1:22). The initiative in bonding has come from him in the first place. Moses' relationship with God was, as we have seen, far beyond his own contemporaries, as being like a man talking with his friend. Yet Paul speaks of our unveiled fellowship reflecting Christ's transforming glory as much greater than anything Moses knew in the Old Covenant (3:18). In the passage about not being 'unequally yoked' with unbelievers his whole point is that if we are bonded with Christ, we cannot have fellowship with darkness and wickedness (6:14–16).

Paul knows, as every missionary needs to know, his own frailty. Those key words: 'My grace is sufficient for you, for my power is made perfect in weakness' (12:9) express the daily practical outworking of the crucial bonding experience of the suffering emissary of Christ.

Lessons from Philippians

In a famous passage where Paul speaks of his own pursuit of closeness to Christ we catch that sense of his desire for close bonding with Christ: 'the surpassing greatness of knowing

Christ Jesus my Lord. . . . that I may gain Christ and be found in him. . . . I want to know Christ and the power of his resurrection and the fellowship of sharing in his sufferings, becoming like him in his death' (3:8–10). We understand that for Paul bonding with Christ lies at the centre of his Christian experience and forms the essential basis of his missionary ministry.

Lessons from Colossians

Paul's injunction to people in danger of being carried away by speculations about angels and legalistic asceticism is to remind them that 'in [Christ] are hidden all the treasures of wisdom and knowledge' (2:3). He urges them therefore to 'continue to live in him, rooted and built up in him, strengthened in the faith as you were taught' (2:7), which we may read as an instruction to bond with Christ. In contrast to the system of rules, regulations and speculations in which they had become enmeshed, and which failed to deal with the real issues (2:23), the actual solution to the holiness, which they seek, is being bonded to Christ. 'Set your hearts on things above, where Christ is seated at the right hand of God. Set your minds on things above, not on earthly things. For you died, and your life is now hidden with Christ in God' (3:1–3). The secret of holiness is not ascetic practices, but focusing upon Christ with whose death and resurrection we have been bonded through baptism.

Lessons from 2 Timothy

This final epistle seems to have been written shortly before Paul's martyrdom during Nero's persecution of the church. Paul states that at his first court trial everyone deserted him and nobody was there to support him. After all, nobody wants to be too obviously identified with a man about to be sentenced to death. In that lonely and frightening situation, facing a death penalty, Paul can confess: 'But the Lord stood at my side and gave me strength, so that through me the message might be fully proclaimed. . . . The Lord will rescue me from every evil attack and will bring me safely to his heavenly kingdom' (4:17–18). His experience had been that in all the persecutions and sufferings he had endured, 'Yet the Lord rescued me from all of them'(3:11). In the past, in the present and in the future, the one to whom Paul belongs will go on delivering him. The Lord is not a distant figure far away in heaven, but one who stood at his side even in a Roman court sentencing him to death.

Fellowship means partnership

The word 'fellowship' is sometimes seen only as Christian jargon, but the Greek word it translates derives from the word for a business partner. For example, it is used early in Luke to explain that Peter and Andrew, James and John were business partners (Luke 5:10). In this modern world, it might be better to translate it as 'partnership' in order to convey something of its financial flavour, as when Paul thanks the Philippians for 'your partnership in the gospel from the first day until now' (Philippians 1:5) when he is thanking them for monetary support. Fishermen surviving storms or poor catches together would certainly bond together as partners. In the innumerable television films about policemen and women risking their lives together, the relationship of partners is inevitably pressed upon us. Policemen are expected to bond with each other. John writes, 'We proclaim what we have seen and heard, so that you also may have fellowship with us. And our fellowship is with the Father and with his Son, Jesus Christ' (1 John 1:3). It seems extraordinary, even comical, to illustrate from something quite so mundane, but I believe there is some mileage in recognising that we are called into partnership with the Lord Jesus, and that consequently we are to bond with him. Paul is speaking of himself and Apollos when he says: 'we are God's fellow workers' (1 Corinthians 3:9).

The need for bonding with the Lord Jesus

It is stating the obvious, then, that for every Christian, abiding in Christ and being bonded with him provides a simple contemporary definition of what it means to be a Christian. Speaking of having been born again tends to look backwards to conversion, though the new birth is the essential first step to a lifelong walk with Christ. Abraham was commanded by the Lord: 'Walk before me and be blameless' (Genesis 17:1) and if we can learn always to be conscious that we are walking with the Lord then we are constantly kept from sinning because of his near presence. So defining every consistent Christian as somebody who is bonded with the Lord Jesus Christ provides a neat definition of present and ongoing experience.

This emphasis or way of expressing Christian experience can become all the more meaningful for the cross-cultural missionary wanting to relate and belong to a new culture and to bond in genuine human friendship with people within it. But there are formidable barriers: the need to learn language, not in a few months, but over years; those fears that come so easily because we know we are foreign and alien and looked at with suspicion; above all the fear that we shall be ineffective and unfruitful. In all this, for us to know that we are bonded with and accompanied by a holy person who understands all languages and can communicate directly with the human heart can make a wonderful difference. Human language teachers and interpreters can be so helpful, but the presence of this ever-present teacher and enabler must mean so very much more. Archibald Fleming speaks of his problems in recruiting workers for the rigours of working up in the Arctic in months of darkness amid snow and ice:

> The most difficult part of it, then as now, was to secure workers sufficiently dedicated to the call of Christ. The missionary task, in whatever land, is a high challenge, with its dangers and austerities, its isolation and temptations. I have frequently been asked how it is possible for a person to be happy in the face of the privations involved. I would answer that the realisation of the need of the people for that which the Christian message alone can bring inspires the hours of each day. Only men and women with the glowing love of their Saviour and a pastoral heart stand up adequately against the hardship and loneliness . . . One of our most pressing needs is to impregnate the theological colleges with evangelistic fervour. Let the men be fired with spiritual enthusiasm for their Lord and Master.[8]

Today the sense of human beings in physical need prompts many people to work with both secular and Christian aid organisations. Kindly humanists may be moved to sacrifice much in order to go to places that are both deprived and dangerous. Our Christian sense of people's deep spiritual need and hunger is also a worthy motive. But when things get tough and difficult, commitment to human need alone may not provide sufficiently strong motivation. It is the certainty that we belong to the Lord Jesus and are bonded with him, sharing his heart of compassion and committed to his cause, which is essential to effective mission.

Lessons from Acts

Paul's Corinthian vision in Acts 18:9–10 reminds us that we are never to be so foolishly mistaken as to think that we are all alone, engaged in some solitary suicide mission. Every Christian needs to apply the truth of these words expressed first in Corinth: 'Do not be afraid; keep on speaking, do not be silent, for I am with you.' Paul knows for himself that the promise of Matthew 28:20 is true for him as opposition builds against him following the conversion of Crispus, ruler of the synagogue and 'many of the Corinthians'. It is equally true for every believer in his or her office or other place of work that we are not alone as solitary witnesses to the truth surrounded by disinterested postmodern pagans. We should not be afraid because our Lord Jesus is alongside us every hour of every day.

'No one is going to attack and harm you, *because I have many people in this city.*' It could not be made plainer that mission is his work, and that Jesus sees these people, for whom he has paid such a ransom to redeem them, are the focus of his ongoing concern.

Once we have been alerted to this truth of the Lord Jesus continuing his evangelistic mission in his world, we begin to see that it lies behind mission all the way through Acts. Why was the initial apostolic harvesting mission to Jerusalem so successful, we may wonder? '*The Lord* added to their number daily those who were being saved' (Acts 2:47).

Who was it that harvested a proud, insolent persecutor of the church, humbling and then transforming him into a remarkable self-supporting, church planting missionary? 'Who are you, *Lord*?' 'I am Jesus, who you are persecuting' (Acts 9:5).

How was it that this gospel made such an impact in the third largest city of the Roman Empire? '*The Lord's hand* was with them and a great number of people believed and turned to the Lord' (Acts 11:21). The Lord's hand scarred by the nails held the sickle that harvested these Gentiles.

How was it that the first convert was made in what we now

think of as part of Europe? '*The Lord* opened her [Lydia's] heart to respond to Paul's message (Acts 16:14) (my italics).

We need to appropriate this truth and make it part of our practical everyday theology. Namely, the Lord Jesus is present and active in mission. He loves all human beings more perfectly and is more committed to the conversion of men, women and children than we ever could be. He is the chief harvester, not seated far away in some heavenly head office, but with his sleeves rolled up, labouring alongside us. And if I am truly bonded to him, then I care what he cares about and can put first things first. I need to see people the way he did: when he saw the widow taking her only son to burial, 'His heart went out to her.' He could look into the eyes of the rich young ruler and read there what his real problems were.

Being bonded to Christ

Bonded to Christ and in communion with him, as his junior partners as it were, we may be led into a sensitivity in relationships that is not naturally ours at all, but arises because we share in 'the mind of Christ'. We may be anxious about making cultural gaffes because our understanding, even after several years of living in a foreign country, is still so partial and incomplete. And although cultures shape all who belong to them, no two individuals are exactly alike. We need to be conscious of his presence so that we may share his sensitive and penetrating understanding of men and women.

There will be times in pioneer mission when very little may seem to be happening, and we wonder whether an indigenous local church will ever come into being. At such times, reminding ourselves that we are bonded to the only one who has the power and authority to turn men and women from darkness to light and liberate them from the power of Satan will enable us to wait patiently for his moment and his opportunity. At such times we realise afresh and with wonder that conversion of sinners and planting of new congregations is his work. The one who calls us is faithful and will do it (1 Thessalonians 5:24).

The remarkable Jenny E. de Mayer, called to Muslim work at Keswick in 1908 through Samuel Zwemer, was a Russian colporteur in Central Asia in the early 1900s. She travelled on ships taking pilgrims to Mecca and ran a small clinic in Jeddah for them two years in succession. She wrote:

> I invite you to come with me to far-away places – to East Siberia, to the vast steppe lands of Central Asia, to the prisons in Soviet Russia and to Arabia, then almost a closed land. I invite you to share with me the ever present, tender Companionship in my unique wanderings. . . . May we be conscious of the Lord's presence as we move with Him and for Him amongst those of our fellow men who sit in darkness and in the shadow of death.[9]

This book has been all about ways of thinking and acting as we move into a strange and new cultural situation in order to work for the chief harvester. Practical suggestions and advice from many sources has been offered, but the key truth is surely this: 'Without me, you can do nothing' Jesus says, and therefore 'so then, just as you received Christ Jesus as Lord, continue to live in him, rooted and built up in him' that is, 'bonded' with him.

Notes

1. Stephen Hayes, *Turbulence and Toeholds: The Life and Work of Dr Christopher Maddox OBE* (Bangkok: Kanok Bannasan (OMF Publishers, 1991), p.207.

2. Waldron Scott, *Karl Barth's Theology of Mission* WEF (Downer's Grove, Illinois: IVP, 1978), p.12.

3. Roland Allen, *Missionary Principles* (London: Lutterworth, 1968), p.31.

4. David Bosch, *Transforming Mission: Paradigm Shifts in Theology of Mission* (New York:Orbis, 1991), p.80.

5. David Bosch, 'The Structure of Mission: An Exposition of Matthew 28:16–20 in Wilbert Schenk, ed., *Exploring Church Growth* (Grand Rapids: Eerdmans, 1983), p.229. A most helpful article.

6. David Bosch in Shenk, *Ibid.*, p.223.

7. Arndt and Gingrich, *A Greek-English Lexicon of the New Testament* (Cambridge: University Press, 1952), p.442.

8. Fleming, *op.cit.*, p.212.

9. Jenny E. de Mayer, *Adventures with God* (Toronto and New York: Evangelical Publishers, 1942), p.6.

HOW INTERNATIONAL DO YOU THINK YOU ARE?

Answers to the Quiz on other Countries

1. Main Languages

It is important to know that even if people speak English they may have a different heart language.

Canada – English, French, Inuktituk, Indian languages & Cantonese!

Great Britain – English, Welsh, Gaelic

Philippines – Tagalog, Cebuano, English & other tribal languages

South Africa – Afrikaans, English, Zulu, Xhosa etc.

Switzerland – German, French, Italian, Romanch

2. National Dishes

Birchermuesli – Swiss dish mixing oats and fruit

Biltong – South Africa, dried meat chewed dry

Hagelschlach – Holland, grains of chocolate eaten on bread

Yuudoofu – Japan, beancurd hot from boiling water, flavoured with fish

Pine sauce – Australia, 'strine' for pie and sauce

Hushpuppies – Southern US baked potatoes
Pulgogi – Korean meat stewed in its own juice, 'Genghis Khan'

3. National Days

Anzac Day – Australia, NZ, 'Armistice day'
Day of the Covenant – South Africa (Afrikaaner)
Merdeka – Indonesia, Malaysia Independence Day
Orangeman's Day – Northern Ireland Protestant Independence
Guy Fawkes Day – UK Celebrating frustration of Popish plot

4. National Sports (most characteristic national sport)

Brazil – Football
Canada – Ice-hockey
Ireland – Shinty (Shinney)
Japan – Judo or Sumoo wrestling
New Zealand – Rugby
Scotland – Curling or Golf
Switzerland – Skiing
United States – Baseball or American football

5. National Characteristics

Anybody who attached such to any nations is reckoned to have failed the test! Our popular stereotypes and caricatures of other nations are a hindrance to fellowship and working with Christians of other national backgrounds!!

6. Unusual Words (meaning and national origin)

Ningnong – Australian for idiot, nit etc.
Nosh – English slang for food as in 'a nosh up'.

Verkrampte – South African word for narrow nationalism (from Afrikaans)

Galah – Australian for idiot, fool etc.

Grits – American (Southern US) for porridge-like cereal

Robots – South African for traffic-lights

Split nair dyke – medical condition in Australia (splitting headache!)

Greeting – Scottish word for weeping

Drongo – Australian for idiot, fool, with suggestion of idleness

Balut – Filipino delicacy – chick eaten in the shell, feathers and all

7. Geography

This question designed not only to remind us of our ignorance of other countries, but also to pick out the wild guesses of bluffers – Auckland is not in Australia at all; nor Colombo, Kathmandu and Karachi in India; nor Toronto in the United States. Check the atlas.

INDEX

375

ENGLISH-SPEAKING OMF CENTRES

AUSTRALIA: P.O. Box 849, Epping, NSW 2121
Freecall 1800 227 154   email: omf-australia@omf.net
www.omf.org

CANADA: 5759 Coopers Avenue, Mississauga ON, L4Z 1R9
Toll free 1-888-657-8010   email: omfcanada@omf.ca
www.omf.ca

HONG KONG: P.O. Box 70505, Kowloon Central Post Office, Hong Kong
email: hk@omf.net   *www.omf.org*

MALAYSIA: 3A Jalan Nipah, off Jalan Ampang, 55000, Kuala Lumpur
email: my@omf.net   *www.omf.org*

NEW ZEALAND: P.O. Box 10-159, Auckland
Tel 09-630 5778   email: omfnz@compuserve.com
www.omf.org

PHILIPPINES: 900 Commonwealth Avenue, Diliman, 1101 Quezon City
email: ph-hc@omf.net   *www.omf.org*

SINGAPORE: 2 Cluny Road, Singapore 259570
email: sno@omf.net   *www.omf.org*

SOUTHERN AFRICA: P.O. Box 3080, Pinegowrie, 2123
email: za@omf.net   *www.omf.org*

UK: Station Approach, Borough Green, Sevenoaks, Kent, TN15 8BG
Tel 01732 887299   email: omf@omf.org.uk
www.omf.org.uk

USA: 10 West Dry Creek Circle, Littleton, CO 80120-4413
Toll Free 1-800-422-5330   email: omf@omf.org
www.us.omf.org

OMF International Headquarters:
2 Cluny Road, Singapore 259570